Ria Mooney

RIA MOONEY

The Life and Times of the Artistic
Director of the Abbey Theatre,
1948–1963

by James P. McGlone

McFarland & Company, Inc., Publishers
Jefferson, North Carolina, and London

Frontispiece: The Abbey Theatre as it appeared in 1948, the year Ria Mooney began her tenure as artistic director. (Courtesy Mrs. G. A. Duncan.)

Library of Congress Cataloguing-in-Publication Data

McGlone, James P., 1932–
 Ria Mooney / the life and times of the artistic director of the Abbey Theatre, 1948–1963 / by James P. McGlone.
  p.   cm.
 Includes bibliographical references and index.
  ISBN 0-7864-1251-8 (softcover : 50# alkaline paper) ∞
  1. Mooney, Ria, 1903–1973.   2. Theatrical producers and directors— Ireland — Biography.   3. Abbey Theatre.   I. Title.
 PN2601.M63M34   2002
 792'.028'092 — dc21   2001007162

British Library cataloguing data are available

Cover photograph: A scene from *Long Day's Journey into Night:* Philip O'Flynn (top) as James Tyrone, Ria Mooney as Mrs. Tyrone, and Vincent Dowling as their son Edmund *(G. A. Duncan)*

Manufactured in the United States of America

McFarland & Company, Inc., Publishers
 Box 611, Jefferson, North Carolina 28640
  www.mcfarlandpub.com

To my wife, Virginia

Acknowledgments

Many people have had an influence upon this work, and among the most important are the members of the Celtic Theatre Company, who, for the last 24 years, have spent under my direction countless hours rehearsing and performing many of the plays that appear in this study for our faithful audiences at the Theatre-in-the-Round at Seton Hall University, South Orange, NJ.

I owe a great debt to Charles Ginnane of Cork, Ireland, for his enthusiastic interest in Ria Mooney, when many questioned the value of her contribution to the Abbey Theatre. His willingness to help me seek out pictures of all the principals, and his careful reading of the text helped me both professionally and personally.

To those busy yet cordial actors and actresses who worked with Ria Mooney, who gave me their time and candidly answered my inquiries— Kathleen Barrington, Derry Powers, Vincent Dowling, Aideen O'Kelley, Val Mulkerns Kennedy, Ronnie Masterson, and Mary Manning Adams— I offer my heartfelt thanks for their cooperation. Of course, it goes without saying, that any opinion or interpretation found in the book represents my judgments and does not reflect upon these generous Irish performers.

I am indebted to Seton Hall University for two travel grants to Ireland, and to the Dean of the College of Arts and Sciences, Dr. James Van Oosting, and Communication Department Chairman, Dr. Donald McKenna, for advice and support. Thanks, also, to Dr. Dermot Quinn and Dr. Tracy Gottlieb, as well as my friends, talented author Jane Waterhouse and Dr. Bernard J. Ransil of Harvard Medical School, for carefully and critically proofreading and editing the text. I also wish to thank Michael Twomey of Cork for his interest and encouragement and reading of the manuscript. My thanks, also, to Jerry McCrea for his expert photographic work on the pictures, and Catherine McGlone for administrative support.

Finally, I appreciate the patience of my children, Virginia, Joseph, Pegeen, and Anne Marie, for listening to me talk on and on about my findings, while retaining a look of interest and even enthusiasm for the subject. Last but first in all things, my wife, Virginia, who has accompanied me on this journey with unstinting support.

Contents

Preface

This book has three principal purposes. First, it provides a theatrical biography of Ria Mooney, one of the most important of Ireland's 20th century theatrical artists, and one who has been completely neglected in the writings about the Dublin stage. Second, I hope to give an impression of how she assembled and nurtured her acting company, and her method of dealing with playwrights whose works she mounted on the stages of the Abbey and the Queen's playhouses. Finally, I want to create a picture of the swiftly changing theatrical, cultural, political, and social climate of Dublin during the period in which she served as the artistic director of the National Theatre (the term used in the Irish theatre for artistic director was, at that time, resident producer). I have tried to show that an artistic director must work within the limitations of the theatrical and social world around her.

My treatment limits itself to Mooney's theatrical career, except as her private life impinges upon her professional life. In these times, sensitive as we are to cultural history's neglect of the achievement of professional women, it is hard to understand why Ria Mooney has been ignored in Abbey Theatre histories. She was the first woman to run the Irish National Theatre, worked with all the celebrated names of Irish theatre, distinguished herself as an actress and director of the most important playwrights and performers of her time, and received excellent contemporary reviews for her life's work. Since her departure from the Abbey scene, she has disappeared from the theatrical annals of that time. I have tried to remedy that oversight by demonstrating her importance to any story of Irish theatre in the 20th century.

It would give me great pleasure should the readers of this story decide to read and produce some of the 75 new Irish plays produced by the Abbey

1

Theatre during Mooney's years as artistic director. There is a treasure of stageworthy scripts awaiting adventurous directors and audiences, scripts that first saw light on the Abbey stage between 1948 and 1963. Ria Mooney was in the company of some of Ireland's most gifted actors and playwrights, and her efforts then can find a valuable voice now on the stages of playhouses willing to restage the plays she mounted for the Dublin audiences of her day.

— PART ONE —

The Actress

CHAPTER ONE

"A Little Glowing Light"

On Saturday 7 November 1947, a bit player and Abbey regular with the appropriate name of Valentin Iremonger stood at his seat in the stalls just before the curtain was to rise on the final act of the latest Abbey revival of Sean O'Casey's revered play *The Plough and the Stars*, and indignantly harangued the Dublin gathering.[1]

"Ladies and gentlemen," he began, "just before the show proceeds, I would like to say a few words."

Why Mr. Iremonger thought he had a right to address that audience has not been recorded for us.

"When the poet Yeats died, he left behind him to the Irish nation as a legacy his beloved Abbey Theatre, then the first theatre in the world in acting, in production and in the poetic impulse of its tradition."

That there was anything to dispute in his not entirely objective evaluation of the Abbey does not seem to have occurred to the speaker. His ire increasing, he was determined to deliver his condemnation, for which his nod to the sacred memory of William Butler Yeats was but prologue.

"Today, eight years after, under utter incompetence of the present directorate's artistic policy, there's nothing left of that fine glory," Iremonger lamented. "Having seen what they did to O'Casey's masterpiece tonight, in acting and production, I, for one, am leaving this theatre as a gesture of protest against the management's policy."

With that, Valentin Iremonger made his final exit of the evening. We can only hope that it was taken with the right mixture of righteous indignation and sublime hauteur.

A mass exodus of the Abbey on that night was not reported in the morning press, but the daily newspapers did throw oil upon the fire by printing letters from George Bernard Shaw and Paul Vincent Carroll,

From this perch, Valentin Iremonger looked down on the Abbey stage and auditorium. (G. A. Duncan.)

demanding the resignations of the theatre's directorate. The defendants thus arraigned were Lennox Robinson, Ernest Blythe, Dick Hayes and Roilbeard O'Farachain.

The most theatrically distinguished of the culprits was Lennox Robinson, who had his first play staged at the Abbey in 1908, and who had been a fixture there as playwright, producer, director, and sometime actor for the preceding forty years.[2] A tall stooped figure whose expression and walk seemed shrouded in Irish Mist, Robinson was near the end of his career and haunted the playhouse like the ghost of one of the big Irish mansions he wrote about.

Roilbeard O'Farachain — born Robert Farren in Dublin in 1909 — was cofounder with Austin Clarke of the Irish Lyric Theatre in 1944. Many considered Yeats's mantle had been bestowed upon Clarke and association with him lent credibility to anyone's pretensions. Farren, a young poet who had already had two plays performed at the Abbey, could hardly be considered artistically inept.

Since Dick Hayes seems to have been a silent partner in the quartet,

Iremonger's spleen was commonly believed to have been aimed directly at Ernest Blythe.

Small, bald, taciturn and imperturbable, Blythe had been one of Ireland's freedom fighters and retained the reputation of a man of ruthless efficiency.[3] As Minister for Finance in the twenties, he engineered the first direct government grant to the Abbey Theatre. Later, he managed to secure for the Abbey an additional government subsidy to perform plays in Irish.

The Irish language seems to have been his defining passion. It was said of him that, as a young man of the north, he took a winter's job on a Gaeltacht farm for a pittance in order to learn Irish. The hearsay evidence against Ernest Blythe was summed up best by one of his trusted associates, Tomás MacAnna: "Even before I joined the Abbey, I had been told so many things about him — that he was utterly ruthless, a fanatic for the Irish language, with little or no artistic judgment, and certainly the decisive influence that had brought the once-famous theatre to its ever-present lamentable stage."[4]

Of course, if Blythe had deigned to reply, he could have reminded the irate young man that all the talk about the decline of the Irish theatre had been said and written before many times.[5] The same cry had gone up in 1903 when Dudley Digges, Maire Quinn and P. J. Kelly left for America. In 1908 Willie and Frank Fay resigned from the theatre many thought they had created. Then, the sisters Sarah Allgood and Maire O'Neill went, and Arthur Sinclair and Fred O'Donovan joined the exodus. Finally, Arthur Shields and his brother, Barry Fitzgerald, sailed for Hollywood.

Now that World War II — remembered in neutral Ireland as "the emergency"— was over and travel was once again possible, Irish actors were taking movie offers at salaries no theatre, subsidized or otherwise, could hope to match. Siobhan McKenna and her husband Denis O'Dea were making fabulous sums of money in England and America, and, though neither officially left the Abbey, they were unavailable for Abbey productions. McKenna was paid just 12 pounds a week for her performance in Dublin of Shaw's *St. Joan*, while a contract for one movie netted her 12,000 pounds.[6]

Some actors took time off to make the big bucks with every intention of coming back to their native stages. Then, Ireland's most adored and, perhaps, the Abbey's greatest actor, F. J. McCormack, died at the top of his form in 1947. Blythe could hardly be blamed for the loss of so many fine performers.

If there wasn't much he could do about the flight of so many Irish acting notables, Blythe knew he could blunt the criticism by changing play directors. Sean O'Faolain, the stylish and witty writer and editor of his

Ernest Blythe on the right greets President Sean T. O'Kelley at the Abbey Theatre, ca. 1950. They fought on the same side in the war of independence, but on opposite sides after the split over the Free State Treaty. (G. A. Duncan.)

own magazine, the *Bell*, had already badgered Blythe about all the plays being directed by Frank Dermody. What O'Faolain demanded was "a change-round of preacher." Why not give Dermody a rest and time to freshen up his theatrical ideas?

Whether because of Valentin Iremonger's intemperate display and the subsequent newspaper flap, or because Frank Dermody was about to leave for London, Ernest Blythe announced in December 1947, the appointment of Ria Mooney as the new resident producer at the Abbey Theatre.

The Dublin theatrical world was more than familiar with the name Ria Mooney. Since her notorious appearance as the prostitute Rosey Redmond in Sean O'Casey's *The Plough and the Stars* in 1926, she had been prominent in all the city's major playhouses. Nor did anyone seem surprised that the position went to a woman, instead of to an old Abbey stalwart like M. J. Dolan. The shocking thing was that she had no Irish. Wasn't Blythe's principal interest in theatre as a media for the spreading of the Irish language? Hadn't he required his players to travel to the west of Ireland for months at a time to improve their academic Irish?

Furthermore, it was rumoured that Blythe didn't particularly like Mooney as an actress. Why appoint her the chief theatrical officer in the one area in which he had almost no experience or expertise?

Did anyone know Ria Mooney well enough to answer those questions? Who was this woman that Blythe had unaccountably chosen to run his theatre?

"She was," wrote Micheál MacLiammóir, "a very little girl with hair as black as the hair of an Indian or a Japanese doll. She had long, slow glancing green eyes and an oval face with an expression of curious sweetness—curious, because she always looked as though she were apologizing about something, even when she was doing nothing of the kind — so it was really no wonder that whenever she came into a room or made an entrance on stage everybody was glad to see her."[7]

Ria Mooney's tentative glance came, perhaps, from her quick understanding of the pitfalls of self-revelation in the circumscribed world of theatrical Dublin. It may also have reflected the seriousness of a child of lower-class origins, trying to learn the ropes of a sophisticated society into which she wished not only to enter but to dominate.

She was born on April 30, 1903. Later she was fond of relating the Irish country tale of fairies coming to steal the souls of newly born babies from their cradles on that May Eve.[8] She remained, she thought, much like the rest of her family in appearance, but like the changeling's fairy-tale life, hers had been "a little glowing light moving with unexpected achievement across a luminous stage decor of clouds and stars."

Born in Ranelagh, a working class district of Dublin, her earliest recollections were strolls amidst the shops along the streets that led from
Coombe through Meath to Thomas Street, and thence to Winetavern
Street alongside Christ Church Cathedral and down the hill to the quays.
It was there her parents liked to walk on Saturday afternoons. Later, as a
greenroom regular, she enjoyed reciting a sensual list of the smells of open
sacks of potatoes and kippers and pig's cheeks and trotters in barrels of
brine, as well as the scents of tallow candles and paraffin oil for house
lamps, and candy of pale coffee-colored toffee, "covered with shredded
coconut and sugar." There was never a doubt in the listener's mind that
Ria Mooney had been born and bred, and remained for life, a Dubliner
in heart and bone.

The family eventually settled in Lower Baggot Street beside the place
where her father, William Mooney, had been born in 1873. The sensitive
child remembered her grandmother's story of marriage to a young groom
with blue eyes and wavy fair hair. Since grandmother Jane was the ward
of Dr. and Mrs. Waller, and a Protestant by birth, her union with a coach-
man and Catholic was socially unacceptable. Ria always remembered that
the Wallers never acknowledged the Mooneys.

Her mother, born Margaret Connolly, was an amateur actress who
played Moya in Dion Boucicault's play, *The Shaughran*, with the old York
Street Club Amateurs. William Mooney, by now a chef by trade, was a
walk-on confined to crowd scenes, but his enthusiasm for the talents of
the leading lady led to their eventual marriage.

At about the same time, her mother's sister Lizzie married her father's
close friend Tommy Hayes. The two elder Hayes boys had young friends
named Frank and Willie Fay who sometimes rehearsed their plays in her
uncle's home. It was from this Ormond Dramatic Society that the Irish
National Theatre Company was eventually formed. Already hers was developing into a theatrical family tree.

At age eight, Ria remembered, she pressed her moonlike face against
the window of her father's shop in Baggot Street, watching the odd-looking people passing by. Her father told her they were from the Abbey Theatre and were on their way to the Arts Club in Upper Fitzwilliam Street.
The aristocratic man who walked with head held high and hands at his
back was William Butler Yeats. His usual companion was a slender man
who walked with his gaze on the ground and had the strange name
"A.E."(George Russell). There was a small fellow with a big hat and dramatic ankle-length cloak whose name was James Stephens. He wrote books
about fairies and leprechauns and looked to her childish eyes like a gnome
from one of his own stories.

Ria arrived at the idea that anyone who was odd-looking must work in the theatre. She found that something in her prompted a sneaking desire to be considered different from the average person.

The opportunity came sooner than she thought. She had already been taking dancing lessons at Madame Rock's Dancing Academy. Someone who had seen her perform with the school suggested she might be suitable for a part in a new play at the Abbey by Yeats entitled *The Land of Heart's Desire.*

Her father took her to the theatre on Marlborough Street which he told her was "the old Mechanics." To her youthful eyes, the Abbey Theatre seemed drab and colorless. She never forgot her audition for the part of the Fairy Child in Yeats' play. The man who listened to her reading mysteriously advised her to go to the mountains and "listen to the wind sighing through the trees," and come back to him in a few days. She thought he was mad and had no desire to go back. She needn't have worried. Her mother read the play and had no intention of letting her darling take a part in so pagan a production.

So she continued Madame Rock's weekly classes and rehearsals with performances at the Gaiety or Theatre Royal twice a year, where everything seemed crimson and gold, rather than the drab of the Abbey's black, brown and cream. She found the gypsy colored skirt and bright head scarf, and the tambourine with gay ribbons glamorous and exciting. She loved the bouquets of flowers and boxes of chocolates she received after each evening's performance. It was a logical next step, as she grew and matured, to join the Rathmines and Rathgar Musical Society and continue the romantic evenings of music and dance.

Mixed in with these youthful impressions were two incidents quite unconnected with theatre.

On the premises of her father's shop, across the passage in the backyard, was a bakehouse with a large oven door that glowed brightly in the dimly lit interior. Two flights above this structure was a sleeping room for the apprentices. Ria recalled as a child going back to the bakehouse with a young shop girl named Murphy. While filling a pail of water, she heard a voice singing overhead, and, looking up, saw a boy laughing at her from a square opening. He had red cropped hair with a fringe, she thought, and she asked the shop girl who the boy was. Her description of the singer elicited a scream from Miss Murphy, who dropped her pail and ran from the yard. Some time later she was told that she had described a child in the clothes of the 18th century, who, it was reported, had been murdered up in the dormitory.

The second tale was set at a summer place the family went to each year at Brittas Bay called "Thonelagee." It was an isolated spot with only a few scattered cottages and farms and one lonely stone house rumored to be haunted. The local legend had it that the owner, a handsome middle-aged man with a splendid beard, had made it ready for the girl he was going to marry. When she died before the wedding, he closed up the house just as it was, and went to live with his sister. Later, Ria was given a tour of the place by a woman said to be that sister, and she was gripped by a strange foreboding when she saw the dusty mahogany furniture and caught sight of tiny grey ants moving in the silent room. She thought she had once seen a faint flickering light behind one of the windows, and it seemed to her someone was wandering about in the empty mansion.

Ria Mooney always maintained that she had "been cursed with an extra sense." She did not read cards or have them read for her, nor did she seek out fortune tellers. Nevertheless, she believed she possessed "this extra sense, which tells me of forthcoming change."

She became aware of this gift at about age 11, when she found herself haunted by a powerful premonition of a change in her life around her 14th birthday. Instinct instructed her to confide this feeling to everyone in the family except her mother. Six months before her 14th birthday, her mother began consulting a doctor, and seven days after Ria's birthday her mother died. Her father's hair turned white overnight, and, although she never saw him shed a tear, he never remarried. She remembered thinking that now she was free to do as she pleased. While her father treated her as though he trusted her, she wondered if he might simply have ceased to care.

Her prophetic sense did not extend, however, to the national tragedy taking place around her. The rebellion of Easter, 1916, seemed merely an annoying interruption of her holidays at the village of Dundrum just outside Dublin. She was whisked back to Ranelagh to stay with her aunt and uncle, from which vantage point she could see the sky reddening over the city. She was full of sympathy for the poor "Tommies" who seemed bewildered to find themselves in Dublin fighting a handful of Irish, especially since they had so many Irish friends in the British Army.

Her family circle was affected by the loss of one of her father's employees, a young man accidentally shot while waving to a friend on St. Stephen's Green. Her father also told her of a young volunteer who shot an old man's horse as the man was passing through the volunteer's lines to get to his home. Her memories of the succeeding years appear to have come from other stories her father told her of Black and Tans and Michael Collins. But the most vivid memories of those years concentrated on the loss of her mother.

In 1920, the 17-year-old Ria Mooney and a friend joined the Rathmines and Rathgar Musical Society. How they managed to negotiate the city at the height of the civil disturbance is never mentioned in her memoirs. What did impress her was the opportunity to play the young lead in *The Duchess of Danzig* with Frank Fay, one of the founders of the Abbey Theatre and a guest artist in the company. Intrigued by her diction, Fay asked her if she'd like to study with him. She declined the offer because she hadn't the slightest interest in becoming an actress.

Her dancing began to reap monetary rewards, taking her as far afield as County Galway, where she performed a Spanish dance at a musical evening. Next she was asked by a family friend in Dublin, at the time a manager of the Queen's Theatre, to play in a film. When that experience failed to attract her interest, she decided to enroll with Madame Rock's daughter, Lily, in the Dublin Metropolitan School of Art. She had no particular gift for fine arts, but she liked the idea of the camaraderie of her girl friends, and the rigor of the training appealed to her determined disposition.

Then, quite casually, she joined a drama group called the United Arts Club and was cast in her first legitimate play. Typically, she never could remember the title, but she did recall the young man playing the leading role. His name was William Shields, but he took the stage name Barry Fitzgerald because he had a steady civil service job and outside employment was forbidden. She must have impressed the casting director, because she was later chosen to replace Shelah Richards, who was unable to repeat her performance in Chekhov's one-act play *The Proposal.*

Yeats described Shelah Richards "as the girl with the head like a lion."[9] She was a rising star in Dublin theatre circles. He immediately gave her roles in his plays that he had never permitted anyone save Maire O'Neill to play. Ria Mooney must have been pleased to be bracketed in her profession with so popular and well-placed a young woman, for Shelah Richards' family were bridge-playing, golfing, society people. Her father was a successful lawyer, and a branch of the family could be traced all the way back to St. Thomas More. She had been sent to study at Alexandra College in Dublin and a convent in Paris. Shelah, and her school friend Mary Manning, who later had her first play produced by the stylish Gate duo of MacLiammoir and Edwards, took acting lessons from the celebrated Abbey actress, Sarah Allgood. Her early career was helped by Lady Glenavy and Lennox Robinson. This amateur theatrical connection became Ria Mooney's introduction to class-conscious Dublin's high society.

In 1922, Ria and three girl friends, Molly Nolan, Sally Byrne, and Evelyn Egan, along with two older male students decided to open a craft studio on Anne Street. She continued to play for the United Arts Club, until she was asked to take a part in Pirandello's *Henry IV*, with Lennox Robinson playing the king, Arthur Shields directing, and sponsored by the Dublin Drama League for performance at the Abbey Theatre.

This production, given on Sunday night, April 27, 1924, elicited from Joseph Holloway, Dublin's famous first-nighter, the remark that Robinson's "acting of this part surprised everyone in the theatre, and made many call him a great actor."[10] Ria played a young woman who takes the place of a portrait of herself (painted for the production by Lady Glenavy), stepping from the frame like an apparition and solemnly approaching the king. Stiff with opening-night stage fright in such exalted company and in so celebrated a place, Ria knew her wooden performance was unconvincing. Suddenly, Robinson, who had always seemed remote in rehearsals of the sequence, changed his thin piping treble voice which he used in everyday life to a commanding and more authoritative tone in keeping with the character of Henry IV. Ria was startled out of her self-consciousness and feigned hysteria so effectively that the reviews the next day spoke of the promise she showed in her last scene.

A short time after that production, Shelah Richards turned up at the shop on Anne Street, saying she had been sent by Lennox Robinson to ask Ria Mooney if she would like to play for the National Theatre. She was 21 years old.

The young actress made her entrance upon the Irish National stage at a moment when conflicting cultural forces met at the theatrical crossroads. The Easter Rebellion had created a climate of patriotism that interpreted all public actions in its light. Dublin society, in an effort to be more sophisticated, and reacting against the charge of parochialism, became at once more sensitive to intellectual criticism of its Catholic convictions, and more open to fashionable trends in international art and ideas. Finally, Dublin society was too small in number to support a theatre with its own resources. So, for the time being, the artistic elite seemed unable to control the program at the National Theatre. The Abbey budget was small, relying on its actors to work for little or no money, with scenery considered inferior to that available to continental producers, and playwrights who received royalties that would have discouraged a less hearty race of writers. Even with these painful economic strictures, the playhouse needed box-office receipts to survive.

The fight for control of the National Theatre was among intense battling elements. There were those who wished to make it a political organ of the state or of the religious community. An artistic elite needed an outlet for their poetic plays. Still others sought control to make the theatre a medium to disseminate the voices of native playwrights and actors, while the ordinary playgoer simply sought an evening's entertainment. These aspirations were not mutually exclusive, and the years were to see many strange combinations. Ria Mooney's career mirrored this struggle within the soul of her profession.

Most of these conflicting influences found a confluence in the startling plays of Sean O'Casey. Their relation to the political and religious climate of the capital city, their vibrant theatricality, their verbal ebullience, and their scandalous language and portrait of Irish womanhood, guaranteed that O'Casey's plays would be the dominant topic of every conversation. What was Ireland, and particularly Dublin, to make of it all?

Joseph Holloway kept a diary of his reactions to Dublin and Abbey productions, and has left a treasure of comment and fact about the leading personalities of that time. He is indispensable to any study of the first 40 years of the Irish theatre. (Julien O'Sullivan and the National Gallery of Ireland.)

Gentle and tolerant first-nighter, Joseph Holloway, recorded the following in his Journal of August 23, 1922. "News reached Dublin that General Michael Collins, Commander-in-Chief of the King's own Irish army, was shot dead in an ambush near Bandon, Co. Cork, R.I.P. He served his English masters only too well. Nightmarish Civil War stalks the land."[11]

Michael Collins, the Irish Republican Army specter, known affectionately as the "Big Fella," had been generally credited with bringing the

English Lion to the bargaining table. Sent to Britain as chief treaty nego-
tiator, Collins signed the best deal he thought it possible to extract from
his English adversaries. One condition of that treaty separated six northern counties from the Irish Free State and another required Irish government ministers to swear loyalty to the British king. Die-hard opposition
to the treaty sounded Mark Antony's theatrical alarum: "Cry 'Havoc!' and
let slip the dogs of war." Not since the Parnell–Kitty O'Shea scandal had
Ireland been so divided over the action and reputation of an Irish leader.

The following March, 1923, Holloway attended the funeral of one of
the Abbey's earliest and most popular playwrights, William Boyle, whose
play, *Family Failing*, had recently been successfully revived. Holloway sadly
noted in his journal that "unfortunately he held a different opinion from
mine over the War and the Rising, and, as he couldn't brook opposition
or silence on matters that moved him strongly, he grew cold to me and
never replied to any greetings or good wishes I afterwards continued to
send him. It takes two to make a quarrel, and I had none with him. May
the Lord have mercy on his soul, amen."

Just one month later, Holloway went to his seat in the stalls at the
Abbey for the premier of an unheralded new play called *The Shadow of a
Gunman*.[12]

Set in a Dublin tenement, the plot concerns two men sharing a room
that is raided by the notorious Black and Tans, English hired guns employed
in terrorizing the Irish countryside in an effort to defeat the IRA. The
script is a succession of character studies of a braggart, a pompous neighbor, an intellectual, a woman who could talk the hind legs off an ass, and
a suspender salesman. Playwright Sean O'Casey had deftly created an
affectionate if unsparing portrait of Dublin's poor, little people. The dramatic second-act raid centers on a deposited parcel containing incrimi-
nating explosives, and the irony rests in the detached and disdainful
intellectual allowing himself to be taken for an IRA hero to impress pretty
Minnie Powell.

The topical and biting dialogue, the gunfire echoing throughout the
theatre as the gunfire had rattled down Irish streets, and the sight of ordinary citizens caught in the crossfire of warring parties touched a core in
the Irish soul. The National Theatre was, without warning, confronted
with an overwhelming demand for tickets.

In all of this, the contradictions abound.[13] O'Casey was a Protestant,
and a Mason, who had been drummed out of his lodge for joining the
annual Parnell Procession to Glasnevin cemetery. He told them all they
might go to hell and joined the Gaelic League, learned Irish, and became
a Nationalist. He turned Communist in a Catholic country, loved Ireland

so much he took up permanent residence in England, and, after admitting that his original draft of *The Shadow of a Gunman* was improved by the criticism of Yeats and Robinson, left the Abbey in a huff when his fourth play was similarly treated.

That play, *The Silver Tassie*, departed radically from the realistic style of O'Casey's first three plays. It employed a European *avant-garde* method known as *expressionism*. Yeats turned the script down for, he said, artistic reasons, even though O'Casey's plays had been acclaimed as great art and had garnered helpful box-office receipts for the always financially strapped playhouse.[14] Nonetheless, Yeats' own plays experimented with exotic theatrical styles such as Japanese Noh drama. Although they placed a great strain on the Abbey budget, they were deemed artistic successes. On what grounds, other than the obvious one that the new play would hardly be as popular as the other O'Casey plays, did Yeats dare refuse to give *The Silver Tassie* a hearing? Could O'Casey be blamed for thinking that Yeats was jealous that his realistic plays were artistic as well as commercial successes. Hadn't they demonstrated into the bargain that there need not be any contradiction between the two?

Juno and the Paycock arrived on the Abbey stage March 3, 1924, and was immediately acclaimed a masterpiece. The now familiar tenement setting has entrapped the titled character, Juno Boyle, in squalor, while Die-hard and Free State enemies help destroy her already disintegrating family. Her drunken husband, Captain Jack Boyle, and his barroom buddy, Joxer, are working men who never go to work. Maimed son Johnny is haunted by the specter of betrayal, and his sister Mary is left pregnant by a smooth talking young cad. The devastating irony of the drunken conclusion changes humor to disbelief in the passage of a theatrical minute.

One of O'Casey's declared playwriting models was the popular 19th century melodramatist Dion Boucicault. Yeats and Lady Gregory always maintained that the Abbey was created to displace the "stage Irishman" figure created by Boucicault. However, Seamus Shields and Captain Jack and his friend Joxer were great liars, drunks, irresponsible braggarts, and charming and funny characters of eloquence and imagination; in other words, "Stage Irishmen" were now being hailed as great artistic creations. Furthermore, O'Casey's plot makes use of the old melodramatic technique of the unexpected windfall of a relative's last will and testament.

The play that succeeded *Juno and the Paycock* upon the Abbey stage was George Shiels' comedy, *The Retrievers*. Just as Shelah Richards and Ria Mooney were theatrical contemporaries, so, too, were playwrights George Shiels and Sean O'Casey. However, whereas O'Casey was hailed as an artistic genius, Shiels was patronizingly referred to as a mere entertainer. F. J.

McCormack, one of the company's rising stars at the time, played the raffish characters of both creators to great critical acclaim, but Shiels somehow never got any credit for his part of the creation. It was prophetic that Ria Mooney's first company appearance was in a Shiels play, while her Abbey reputation was established by her performance as the prostitute in O'Casey's third play in the Dublin trilogy, *The Plough and the Stars.*

"There was electricity in the air before and behind the curtain at the Abbey tonight," wrote Joseph Holloway, Monday, February 8, 1926, "when Sean O'Casey's play *The Plough and the Stars* was first produced."[15] The theatre was thronged with distinguished Dubliners, and not a quarter of the people trying for general seats in the pit were able to gain entrance.

The time is the Easter Week Rebellion of 1916. Newlywed Jack Clitheroe leaves his protesting and pregnant wife to fight for Irish freedom and is killed in the street. After Nora hears of her husband's fate, her baby is born dead and she loses her mind. Crammed into O'Casey's familiar tenement are gossipy, kind-hearted Mrs. Gogan, drunken old Peter, and the eloquent, slightly inebriated, and always ebullient Fluther Good. There is harsh irony in the accidental shooting of Bessie Burgess, who curses the rebels for the murder of her son and is felled protecting Nora from the gunfire in the streets.

Added to this mix is the character of Rosie Redmond, who is a sharp-tongued version of the melodramatic "whore with the heart of gold." Ria was cast in the part by the playwright himself.

For Ria, the events of the past nine months had been a delightful roller-coaster ride. Her first Abbey appearance had been in *The Retrievers,* by George Shiels, a fairly new and an unusually popular playwright with general audiences. Ria was cast as a young Irish-American girl returning to Ireland in search of her roots. The play had done so well at the box office that, after the June holidays, it reopened the Abbey for the summer season. After that, Ria found her name appearing in cast lists and assumed she was a member of the company. For the part of the American girl, she borrowed a leopard skin coat as part of her costume from a Mrs. Reddin, an Abbey regular and wife of a distinguished Dublin lawyer. Ria was making the acquaintance of the people that mattered in the city's cultural life. She even made an effort to learn Irish because it was considered patriotic, but she admitted having no flair for languages and never acquired a respectable acquaintance with the Irish tongue. She did have a flair for the stage, though, and, under the tutelage of M. J. Dolan, and with the chance to play every week in a different role at the Abbey, she gained in confidence and technique. Eileen Crowe had decided to tour with an English Company at that time, and Ria was asked to play her parts.

Sean O'Casey signed this photograph of himself and Ria on the set of *The Plough and the Stars*—"Be clever maid, and let who will be good." (University of Delaware Library Special Collections.)

In November 1925, she was cast as the cross old nun, Sister Feliciana, in Gregorio Martinez Sierra's *The Kingdom of God*.[16] One night as she crossed the stage after a performance, she was stopped by Sean O'Casey. He thought she was "bloody good as th' oul nun" and said he had instructed Robinson to cast her as the prostitute in his new play. Ria often wondered in which part she'd been type cast.

Some of the women in the company tried to scare her away from the part, because they felt it reflected badly on their profession for one of their company to play such a role. She was advised to consult her confessor, but, as she had none, she asked a friend, "a very intelligent priest," if she should play the role. He roared with laughter and said, "Of course."

Abbey actors supplied their own costumes in contemporary plays, so Ria had to know what a Dublin prostitute looked like. She was referred to the lane at the back of the Abbey after the evening's performance: she was sure to come across some of these girls. There she saw "very young girls, their faces daubed with white powder, and circles of red paint on their cheeks," talking with feverish intensity to soldiers. Without knowing why, she "felt deeply sorry for them." Here it is best left to Ria Mooney to tell her tale.

"Quite honestly (and you may find this hard to believe) I had reached twenty-three years of age without knowing precisely what was meant by a 'prostitute.' I had certainly learned what prostitutes looked like and how they dressed ... but that was as far as my knowledge went. Without knowing exactly why, however, I felt very sorry for these young girls I had seen in the lane. So when the Covey sneers at Rosie, and says he is not 'goin'' to take any repremandin' from a prostitute,' I was so hurt that real tears came as I rushed at him, crying 'yer no man! I'm a woman anyway, an' I have me feelin's....'"[17]

O'Casey sought her out after the opening and, gazing at her out of his better eye, thanked her "for saving my play." She stared at him in disbelief, but he insisted, "I mean that," and walked away.

Ria believed she had learned a great deal about acting from this incident. In later years, she gave the exact same technical performance of the part, but it never again felt right, because her total sympathy with the character had gone. "Technique," she said, "without feeling and concentration, is like Faith without Good Works: it is dead." In other words, when she first played Rosie Redmond, Ria really believed in "the whore with the heart of gold." O'Casey knew that, interpreted any other way, Dublin might be offended by his portrait of a prostitute, especially if the character were played realistically.

Leaving the theatre that night, Holloway noticed a policeman in Abbey Street stalking four "Rosie Redmonds" who retreated before him. He thought it ironic that "the fight between the two women in the pub scene was longly applauded, yet who is not disgusted with such an exhibition when one chances on it in real life?"[18]

Then all hell broke loose!

O'Casey tells a stirring version of that week in his autobiography, *Inishfallen, Fare Thee Well*; Holloway gives a day-by-day account in his journal; and Ria rendered her own idiosyncratic version in her autobiography. Tuesday night's audience seemed to relish the Rosie Redmond fight, but Chief Justice Kennedy openly stated "he thought it abominable," while Dr. Oliver Gogarty was glad it would "give the smug-minded something to think about." Obviously trouble was brewing and the whole town wanted to be there when the ferment exploded.

On Wednesday evening, a moaning or whispering sound greeted Rosie's entrance, and by Thursday night the act was played in what amounted to pantomime. Ria noticed lumps of coal being thrown in her direction and pennies fell noisily around her on the stage. When members of the audience shouted for her to get off, it only "made me more determined to stay on." They had tried to intimidate the wrong lady. She was convinced that she passed from the amateur to the professional players' ranks on that evening.

A young woman tried to set fire to the curtain and Seaghan Barlow, the wizened carpenter-*cum*-designer rudely dumped her into the pit. The curtain was opened on an empty stage where the melee began anew. Someone saw Barry Fitzgerald in a stand-up fight with a man on the stage — the actor succeeded in knocking him over into the stalls. The players led by McCormick lined up on stage and asked for a hearing. When things quieted down a bit, McCormick said his audience should treat the actors as distinct from the play, and his plea was met by general applause. O'Casey never forgave him for what he considered an act of desertion.

Friday saw the playhouse lined with policemen, and O'Casey, surrounded by admiring ladies, declared to all who could hear, "I want to make money!" which Holloway thought summed up his attitude toward art. In fact, Holloway was saddened by the whole affair. "Alas," he wrote to his journal, "tonight's protest has made a second *Playboy* of *The Plough and the Stars*, and Yeats was in his element at last...."[19]

As the week drew to a close, the fight was taken up in the press, where Mrs. Sheehy-Skeffington's protest appeared in the *Irish Independent*.[20] "The demonstration was not directed against the individual actor, nor was it directed to the moral aspect of the play," wrote Mrs. Sheehy-Skeffington. Ria might breathe a sigh of relief to discover she was not to be the target of public fury. "It was on national grounds solely," declared the dignified lady, "voicing a passionate indignation against the outrage of a drama staged in a supposedly national theatre, which held up to derision and obloquy the men and women of Easter Week."

O'Casey unloaded his reply in the *Irish Times*. Dripping with contempt, the playwright mocked Mrs. Sheehy-Skeffington for a sentimentality that ignored human nature, the conditions in Ireland, and the political sham of military rhetoric. It all made him sick, he said, and, in a parting shot, he ridiculed the story going around that there was ever a question of a refusal to play the part of "Rosie Redmond," which he deemed "splendidly acted by Miss Mooney." Ria had stumbled into a notoriety no one had seen coming, and she had come out of the fracas without a drop of mud on her character or a scratch on her person.

In one short year, Ria Mooney had played in two popular plays by two playwrights who were to dominate the Irish stage for the next two decades.

In the first play, George Shiels' *The Retrievers*, she had enjoyed a relatively long run to full houses in a pleasant comedy that general audiences took to at once, in spite of what the critical establishment said. In the second, Sean O'Casey's *The Plough and the Stars*, she had been at the center of one of those Irish artistic squalls that add the delight of scandal to an otherwise tame and dull theatrical season. She was famous as the young girl who had dared to play a prostitute on the Irish stage and face the storm that followed. The fact that the censorship came from the political and not the religious sensibilities of the Irish did not seem to affect the daring of her feat.

The contrast between the plays by O'Casey and Shiels reveals the fissures in Irish artistic opinion that endured throughout Mooney's entire theatrical career. The three plays upon which O'Casey's reputation is founded were realistic in construction and set in tenement houses in working-class Dublin. Shiels' plays are realistic, rural, good natured satires reflecting a kindly disposition that seemed to seek good in all humanity.

O'Casey's plays, though realistic and even melodramatic in structure, caused a sensation and a scandal because they employed strong language, introduced characters upon his stage that offended local sensibilities, and might be construed as preaching antiwar themes. Shiels' plots, often referred to derogatorily as kitchen comedies, developed into complicated stories with strong characters in primitive situations. Shiels remained popular with Irish audiences for three decades, and his technique in such plays as *The Rugged Path*, *The Passing Day*, and *The New Gossoon* developed into more subtle explorations of human motive as he grew older.

What was the young Ria Mooney to make of all this? She was ambitious, had a taste for society, and a desire to excel in her profession. She came from the tradesman's class which enjoyed popular entertainment. She soon discovered, though, that critical Dublin opinion was capable of inconsistency and outright contradiction. Yeats saw his theatre as a haven for people of taste, not an entertainment factory for the multitude. Yet he defended the hugely popular *The Plough and the Stars* as art, while rejecting *The Silver Tassie* because of what he considered its flawed craftsmanship.

Ria wanted to be liked by Dublin's elite as well as by the general public, and Yeats was the acknowledged trendsetter followed by that elite. Her performer's desire to please and be liked was in conflict with her social need to be accepted. As if to complicate matters even further, Ria shared Yeats' sympathy for supernatural visitations on and off the stage. Some referred to it as a poetic disposition. Even if Yeats was right about *The Silver Tassie*, why not let the audience decide the issue? O'Casey had demonstrated, beyond doubt, that he was a fine playwright. There was an audience interested in his work, and his new play, even if it turned out to be a failure, would attract the attention of the artistic community.

The confusion was compounded by the Abbey's straitened financial condition. If a play didn't do well at the box office, who was to pay for the production, including actors' salaries?

When in August 1925 the Abbey Theatre received its first subsidy from the Irish Free State government, a solution seemed to be at hand. In a speech addressed to the House, Yeats acknowledged the government's generous grant, but he reminded those present that the Abbey had always been endowed since its inception by actors and dramatists who received almost nothing for their services.[21]

Was there an implication in his statement that, under no circumstances, should popularity with audiences be sought? Was the opinion of audiences, expressed by their willingness to attend and pay for their entertainment, to have any say in the evaluation of the work done at the National Theatre? Was there a contradiction between artistic merit and popular appeal?

Furthermore, if the actors were to be paid for their services without having to seek audience approval, whose approval should they court? Did the fact that actors were being paid mean they were automatically talented? Was an actor's salary to designate their ability?

Was George Shiels a lesser talent because he was popular with Irish audiences, and, if the Abbey was Yeats' theatre, what did that say about O'Casey's plays? Yeats defended the popular plays as art. Did his rejection of the expressionistic Tassie signify that it was not art? The international art world seemed to praise Sean O'Casey's expressionistic work as art precisely because it was experimental and daring. So was O'Casey an artist because, in spite of his popular successes, he turned to writing unpopular plays that pleased literary critics?

Finally, where did that leave the actors? Should they care about playing to empty houses as long as the critics extolled their work? Who were they to play for, Yeats's small coterie of cognoscenti, or the paying public?

For the moment, those questions were held in abeyance. Before too long, though, Ria Mooney would have to resolve those contradictions in her own theatrical life.

CHAPTER TWO

"A Fairy City
Resting on a Cloud"

The euphoria of February and March 1926 was quickly dispelled by the return to playhouse routine. Gone were the stink bombs and the scuffles in the auditorium and onstage. Slowly the controversy between patriots and playwright faded from the editorial pages, as the business of getting up the next play took precedence. If discussions of Ria's celebrity still invoked scandalous comments, the troupe hardly had time to countenance them.

For much of 1925, Ria had been gaining experience and stature playing Eileen Crowe's parts, while the young actress toured England with the Irish players. When on December 4, 1925, Crowe became the wife of the Abbey's most highly prized character actor, F. J. McCormick, Mooney's position seemed relegated to the company's second rank.[1] Since she was paid ten shillings a week unless cast in a featured part, and only received one pound a week when playing a lead, she was finding it increasingly difficult to make ends meet on her salary.[2]

Furthermore, she had been given the part of Rosie Redmond by O'Casey himself, probably against the wishes of Lennox Robinson. Nonetheless, though she had made the most of that opportunity, it wasn't likely that many had competed seriously for the role of the Dublin prostitute.

In an attempt to exploit her newfound celebrity, Ria approached Robinson about a contract as a permanent player. He turned her down. She was already angered by the unequal distribution of salaries among the performers, and the expense and annoyance of outfitting herself for modern plays. Unlike many of her contemporaries, Ria had no private income or family support. Her wardrobe was obviously limited and that made her social standing embarrassingly evident. Though she was traveling in higher circles and might borrow clothes from her friends, the condescension that went with the loan of a costume must have been wormwood to her.

Her last appearance of the season on the Abbey stage was on April 12, 1926, in Brinsley MacNamara's *Look at the Heffernans*, a comedy about bachelors bitten by the matrimonial bug and featuring the popular husband and wife team of Eileen Crowe and F. J. McCormick. Ria's Alice wasn't much of a part and her performance failed to attract favorable attention.[3]

In one month, her career on the Dublin stage had gone from exhilaration to frustration. In just two seasons, she had gone from an unknown bit player to a featured performer, jumping ahead of other bit players who had studied at the Abbey theatre school. In addition, she had been singled out for attention not by the theatre directors, but by the controversial Sean O'Casey. She had shown her courage and pride during the tumult that surrounded her convincing portrayal of a Dublin prostitute. In that moment, Ria Mooney had served notice that she would not be easily intimidated. So, with almost no options open to her, she took the road so many other Irish actors had taken in the previous quarter century. She decided on the emigrant's journey.

When Ria Mooney arrived in London in the summer of 1926, she knew only two people, Sean O'Casey and Sara Allgood. Fresh from her triumph as Rosie Redmond, she came in search of a life upon London's wicked stage. It was a confusing and dispiriting experience.

After a week of wandering in the Underground and standing in agency waiting rooms, she was ready to return to Dublin, defeated but wiser. During that first depressing week, Ria called upon Sean O'Casey who invited her to see the London production of his play *The Shadow of a Gunman*. O'Casey understood Ria's retreat from the Irish theatrical scene. "It takes both courage and patience to live in Ireland," he said. "I like London, and London likes me. That's more than I can say of Ireland."[4] His bitterness was not without cause. Holloway had heard Dubliner John Burke remark that "last year it was all Sean O'Casey; now it is all shun O'Casey."[5]

Always prudent, Ria had paid for her lodging in advance and had purchased a return ticket to Dublin. With her money almost gone, and ready to take the next boat back to Ireland, she called on O'Casey in his Chelsea flat to say farewell. He asked her when she intended going home, and when she told him she was leaving the following morning, he thrust a five-pound note into her hand and told her to stay another week.

"Another week may change the whole course of your life," he said. She tried to explain to him that she already owed a friend's father ten pounds, but he became angry. "This is not a loan," he said. "Take it and don't be a fool."[6] She took it.

Once again, her conviction that she possessed a "second sight" commanded her movements. She roamed London with the vague feeling something predetermined would soon turn up. Passing the office of Barry O'Brien, an agent who had resisted her earlier attempts to gain a hearing, she hesitated for a moment, then turned back and went in. There she was confronted by a long line of girls on the winding stairs that led to the big man's offices. She had been in the queue only a few minutes when she recognized the only other person she knew in London, Sara Allgood.

As she passed by, Sara, obviously surprised to see her, informed her that J. B. Fagan, an important London producer, was searching everywhere for her. Apparently, Fagan had decided to book the Irish Players for a short tour of England and Scotland with *Juno and the Paycock*, and O'Casey had recommended Ria for the part of Mary Boyle. Nobody had any idea where she was staying and none of the agents' offices seemed to have ever heard of her.

At Fagan's office, she was ushered into the presence of the great man himself. She gave him a letter of introduction from Lennox Robinson. He glanced over the paper and, laughingly, handed it to her to read.

"This is to introduce Ria Mooney," it said. "I hope you won't like her, as she is much too valuable to the Abbey Theatre."[7]

Ria returned to Dublin delighted with the promise of a contract to tour England and Scotland with the Irish Players and the back-handed compliment of Lennox Robinson humming in her ears. When word got around of her impending tour, she received a summons from Robinson to talk the matter over. She thought he was astonished by her good fortune, but he quickly regained his composure and offered her a contract with the Abbey, explaining that he had talked the matter over with Yeats and they had agreed upon the terms. Ria admired the director-playwright as a man, but she never believed that he had ever had a conversation about hiring her with the poet.

Though she knew she must refuse the offer, she nonetheless hesitated for a moment before doing so. If only they had accepted her first proposal, she never would have sought work outside her own country, never would have borrowed money to do so, or accepted Sean O'Casey's generous gift of five pounds. It seemed once again that her "second sight" was prompting her to go, and she did. Later in life, she supposed that she would have married and settled down, "like so many other members of the Company, as it was the Abbey's policy to keep their players together for as long as they would stay."[8] Was there a certain wistful longing for a more comfortable old age in a normal household?

Back in London for rehearsals, Ria was introduced to the company headed by Arthur Sinclair and Maire O'Neill. Because the traveling would be rigorous, Fagan decided she should have an understudy, so Ria recommended Mary Manning as someone who would be capable, hardworking, and prepared to enjoy the experience. To her delight, Manning accepted and became not only her understudy but her roommate.

The tour opened in Leeds, where the two young novices got their first barnstorming lesson.[9] Ria's salary was six pounds a week, out of which she had to pay

Lennox Robinson had his first play staged at the Abbey in 1908, and he remained a fixture at the playhouse for over 40 years. (G. A. Duncan.)

for her food and lodging. No one warned her to book rooms in each city before departing on the tour, so, when they arrived in Leeds, she and Mary Manning took a taxi that drove them to slum quarters, the driver collecting his fare and fleeing the scene as quickly as he could. The lodging was a tall house with grimy windows in a red brick square protected by dilapidated gates.

Once inside, they were ushered by an old woman into a bare room with a round table set for high tea. Ria thought the plate of cold mutton looked like dead human flesh. Suddenly, as in popular melodrama, the silence of the house was shattered by a vigorous knock at the front door. It was stage manager Tony Quinn, an ex–Abbey player. He had learned of their address from the theatre staff and decided to come to their rescue. He told them to collect their belongings; he was trading rooms with them. Then he put them into his waiting cab, which sped them to his cheerful digs in a more respectable part of the city.

In Manchester, their landlady was guarded by a ferocious Alsatian dog securely locked behind a wooden gate. The house had an undertaker on one side and a manufacturer of tombstones on the other, with a small cemetery at the back. Mary remembered that Ria got sick in Manchester and she had to go on for her several times. Ria was having stomach problems. "She went to this doctor," Mary said. "She said he was appalling. She was terrified of him."[10] Ria told her roommate that he had attacked her and she would not hear of going to another doctor after that experience.

Mary came down with a cold in the same city. One night, after the understudy had decided to recuperate for the evening, Ria returned to find her sitting up in bed giving a drunken reading of *The Countess Cathleen* by Yeats. Mary had gone out and bought herself some rum and returned to the room to drink and entertain herself till Ria came back. When she saw the amazed look on Ria's face, she burst into laughter and both girls dissolved into hysterics.

On a Saturday night in Glasgow, Ria found her dresser insensible on the floor, so drunk that she couldn't be roused. The two girls found a couple of stage hands who were able to remove the offending lady, and they giggled over the adventure for the rest of the evening.[11]

Mary had an introduction to the poet John Masefield in Oxford, and he kindly invited them to tea. Ria recalled that her friend always carried a copy of Matthew Arnold's *The Scholar Gypsy* with her when they went out walking, and Masefield pointed out "the signal elm" of the Arnold poem to them.

In Edinburgh, they found the men handsome and the women dowdy, and Ria spent some of her cash on the "gorgeous confectionery, bread, buns and pastry." They exulted over hearing men going to work in Bolton in their traditional wooden shoes, and in Yorkshire they wandered on the Brontë moors.

Mary Manning remembered that her friend was "very nice to travel with," though she "was always hard up." She got on well with the company, but she "never had little kissing sessions and little pokes" backstage. "She wasn't very humorous. She was very earnest and ambitious," but they enjoyed each other's company and remained friends when the tour was over.[12]

The winter tour lasted for nearly three months, and, when they returned to London, they heard that an American producer, George Tyler, was taking them to New York. She was proposed for Nora in *The Plough and the Stars* and Mary Boyle in *Juno and the Paycock*. Her "second sight" had sent her to London and told her to refuse an Abbey contract. Now she was about to play a leading role in O'Casey's latest hit in New York City!

Sean O'Casey had other ideas. He had seen her Mary Boyle and called it "bloody awful." Director and leading player Arthur Sinclair had insisted she give the part a more obvious interpretation. Ria liked playing it in that strong and theatrical way, but the playwright had the last word and her trip was off.

George Tyler was an old Broadway denizen cut from the same cloth as the paternal George M. Cohan. He saw her bitter disappointment and suggested that, since she wanted to see America, she could go as understudy. It was her first experience of being told to take a back seat, and her temper nearly got the better of her. Just in time she remembered her "second sight," and, though she felt humiliated, she accepted the offer.

The troupe sailed on a new ship, the S.S. *Laurentic*, in October 1927, and Ria was violently seasick. She overcame her discomfort by drinking a glass of champagne and taking a chair on deck. Forty years later, she remembered her first view of New York City as it appeared before her on a late October afternoon.

"There was a heavy mist lying on the sea, and from it the cluster of giant ski-scrapers [*sic*] rose like a fairy city resting on a cloud."[13]

Rehearsals began immediately for the projected opening night at the Hudson Theatre on November 28, 1927, of *The Plough and the Stars*. Ria's part of Rosie Redmond was given to the better-known and more experienced Cathleen Drago, while she understudied her friend Shelagh Richards as Nora Clitheroe. Soon she began to respond to the rhythm of the city. The pace took pounds off her, and the well-cut American clothes gave her, she thought, a much more presentable figure. This was the *chic world* of Cole Porter, and, with that fashionable bard of Manhattan, she found that she too "happened to like New York." At her first party, she was struck by the beauty and elegance of American women, who all "seemed to be tall, slim, and exquisitely gowned." She made a couple of youthful gaffes and embarrassed her theatrical colleagues in the process. She told Jacob Epstein that he looked like Sean O'Casey, and, in spite of Maire O'Neill's wagging head, reiterated how alike the two men were. When the artist moved away, Maire moaned sotto voce, "you bloody eejut! We were just discussing the plainness of Sean O'Casey before you came in."

She and Shelagh took an apartment in the theatre district and, when a drunk stumbled into their apartment looking for "Jack," and only departed after much coaxing, they retreated to an expensive luxury apartment where they felt relaxed and more secure. Naive as ever, Ria observed that the women visiting in the opposite apartment came swathed in mink and sables, sparkling with diamonds, while their escorts used a distinctive knock before gaining entry.

Eventually, they found a reasonably priced, comfortable place in the center of the city, where they could entertain their newfound theatrical friends. One invitee was Paul Robeson, who was appearing in the smash hit *Show Boat*. He asked the Irish Players if they would like to hear the songs of his people. She remembered "him standing by one of the windows, looking down at the street below as he sang."

Their first production opened at the Hudson Theatre and was a success. Critic Burns Mantle noted that playwright O'Casey had "his most talented countrymen's gift of a sure dramatic sense touched with poetic imagery."[14] *The Plough and the Stars*, however, failed to attract financial support and was replaced after 32 performances by *Juno and the Paycock* with Ria once more in the role of Mary Boyle. Arthur Sinclair wanted it that way, and the playwright was too far away to have any influence in the matter.

Juno opened at the Gallo Theatre on December 19, 1927, and played there for 40 performances. The New York engagement in all played for nine weeks and a total of 72 times. One critic noted that, though "neither engagement proved successful in the popular sense, yet both the O'Casey dramas were generously praised as being forthright and honest in their interpretations of Irish character and were credited with presenting illuminating pictures of Irish tenement life." They also were accepted as evidence that "a new literary figure of promise had arisen in Ireland."[15]

The New York run nearly over, Ria decided to take the advice of a Dublin friend, who knew the city's theatrical climate, and audition for Eva Le Gallienne's Civic Repertory Company. She was told she might have a better chance there than in the commercial theatre, because the troupe's production methods resembled those of the Abbey. Helen Lohman, Le Gallienne's manager, had seen her Mary Boyle, and the director offered Ria a position with the company on her recommendation.

With the promise of employment for the New York theatre season of 1928-29, Ria left New York for Philadelphia, Boston and Chicago in high spirits. Shortly after the company's departure, she read in the local press that a gangster had been murdered in a New York hotel. When she looked closely at the accompanying photograph, she saw that it was the very suite opposite her own rooms in the luxury hotel where she had felt so safe. Charmed by the glamour of the city, she had been curiously unaware of its seamier side.

Michael Scott, later one of Dublin's foremost architects, was a member of the Irish Players, and he and Ria visited the great Wrigley Building in Chicago together to see an exhibition of French paintings. There she came upon the work of the sculptor Brancusi and felt that she immediately knew its secret. There would be secrets to discover in the Eva Le

Gallienne company as well, but it is impossible to discover from her memoirs if she ever had a better understanding of them than she did of Rosie Redmond or the New York underworld on her doorstep.

In Detroit, she finally got to play Nora Clitheroe, for Shelagh Richards had been called back to Dublin. The tour had fulfilled all her theatrical expectations. She was returning to Dublin more sophisticated and thoroughly spoiled by the entertainment provided by her American hosts. Her "second sight" should have warned her to take singer Al Jolson's proud boast, "You ain't heard nothing yet," as a promise addressed personally to her.

Back in Dublin for the summer, Ria was recruited by the Abbey to repeat her original role of Rosie Redmond. While she was taking her place on stage for her last performance before returning to America, a smiling Lennox Robinson approached her with the news that the famous Alla Nazimova was joining the Le Gallienne Company for the coming season. "Again," she said, "I had that queer sensation of knowing this already, but I said nothing."

Nazimova was a silent film star with theatrical credentials that were the envy of the New York artistic elite.[16] She had received her training in Moscow, and in 1904 was the leading lady of a St. Petersburg theatre. She taught herself English in six months and remained in America after an initial tour with a Russian Company in 1906. This vibrant and passionate personality made her reputation in the plays of Ibsen, Chekhov, Turgenev, and O'Neill.

People told Ria that she resembled Nazimova, "so I fluffed out my black hair, or parted it down the centre, and twitched my nostrils to make myself look more like her. Nazimova was my goddess and I wished to resemble her."[17] She had dreamed of playing the star's daughter or sister, selected for the role because she looked like her. She was sure that dream was about to come true.

She sailed for New York from Southampton on a small cargo vessel that had room for only 12 passengers. It deposited her in Montreal. She thoroughly enjoyed the crossing though the journey took a week longer than the cabin cruisers of that day. Once in New York, she presented herself at the old Fourteenth Street Theatre and was introduced to the company. Burgess Meredith, veteran of 50 years of theatrical activity, remembered the playhouse as it must have looked at that time to any excited newcomer.

Eva Le Gallienne "was high priestess in a temple flung about with elevated trains and continuous Communist parades lurching past the gates. Her 14th Street edifice did not have a radiator but which sang like a tree toad, nor was there a board in the floor so young, nor a chair so secure, that did not groan rheumatically when you touched it."[18]

The playhouse had been built in 1866 and in recent years had been home to burlesque. Paint peeled from the pillared Greek facade, the aisles were lined with well-worn linoleum, the auditorium sagged and buckled, and many seats were broken. Le Gallienne promised to give nine-tenths of her earnings to the project, while badgering Otto H. Kahn, an important Broadway commercial producer, and his rich friends into donating the funds to bring the building up to code. Her aim was to recreate the theatrical world.[19]

"One of America's greatest needs is to build up the theatre," she stated in a speech delivered at Yale University in December 1925.[20] "The theatre is yet far away from its loftiest possibilities. To restore or to attain these the actor must take his vow to God as does the priest.... Of the stage and its condition today we might use the words of Christ of the ancient temple: 'This was a house of prayer and ye have made it a den of thieves.'"

Le Gallienne's feisty, boyish beauty was matched by a flamboyant disregard for social custom.[21] She had made her mark in the fall of 1925 playing the young and romantic Hilda Wangel in Ibsen's *The Master Builder*. Her scandalous costume included corduroy breeches, high mountain boots, open-necked shirt, a knapsack with straps, a wooden hiking stick and a pair of jeweled earrings. Around her slender waist was a belt of violet colored silk, a clear symbol to those in the know of lesbian love. The provocative lady was expressing Hilda's defiance of the rules of convention. "She even smoked cigarettes and snapped her fingers impatiently at the Master Builder."[22]

The Civic Repertory Company's professional staff was composed entirely of women, two of whom were whispered to have "relationships" with the director. Rumors abounded that the troupe was "a den of lesbianism." *American Mercury* critic, George Jean Nathan, called the group "the Le Gallienne sorority." The company was composed of dedicated journeymen performers. Before Nazimova joined, its only undisputed star was the notorious Eva herself.

Ria lived for a time in the same boarding house as her one-handed artist friend Patrick Tuohy, who had once tried to teach her drawing at her Dublin art school. In those first and lonely days in the big city, he came to her room in the evening and read Turgenev to her, and she took up the melancholy strains of the Russian's prose with her own mournful tale of separated lovers. Before leaving Ireland, she had fallen in love, but with whom (although there are hints in her memoirs), we do not know.

The excitement of her new home must have assuaged her sadness, for she remembered fondly those early theatrical days. She and Phyllis Flanagan, an old Dublin friend, found an apartment on 13th street around the corner from the theatre. Their cheap furniture was given panache by a struggling assistant scenic designer at the Civic, Irene Schariff. She recommended they cover the couch with royal blue sateen and the cushions with red, yellow, green and black. "We stained the floor black, and with rugs of felt, the apartment was warm and attractive." Greenwich Village fashion was complemented by memorable evenings discussing the art world with new and talented friends like Burgess Meredith, Robert Lewis, Robert Ross, Irene Schariff, and Arnold Moss. Fedya Zarkeyvich, the Russian leader of the Civic's orchestra, played his seven-string gypsy guitar, and Walter Starkie brought his violin. Between the two of them, they gave the company folk songs of Europe until the small hours of the morning. Sometimes they adjourned to Harlem for breakfast at dawn. Between work at the Civic, and society in the Village, there wasn't much time for homesickness.

The season began with Molière's *The Would-be Gentleman* on October 1, 1928.[23] Ria was cast as the daughter, Lucille, and, at the first cast reading of the play, Nazimova sat and listened but took no part in the work. She was to play Madame Renesvsky in Chekhov's *The Cherry Orchard*.

Three plays were rehearsed at the same time, with the indefatigable Le Gallienne staging and starring in a French play entitled *L'Invitation au Voyage*, as well as directing and taking a leading role in *The Cherry Orchard*.

The Civic had a reputation as serious and intellectual, and Eva hoped the Molière would soften that impression, but the production was so amateurish that it failed to persuade anyone that the company had a talent for comedy.[24] The French play, even with Le Gallienne wearing two hats, failed to attract any attention. Ria was the only other woman in *L'Invitation au Voyage* and had a large role. Her work went unnoticed in the failure of the play and the breathless expectation created by the heralded Civic debut of Alla Nazimova.

The Civic Repertory Theatre hit its stride with Anton Chekov's *The Cherry Orchard*, on October 15, 1928, but Ria was not in the cast. She felt fortunate to be able to watch the month-long rehearsals as Nazimova, who had been an understudy for the first Moscow Art Theatre production, recreated the atmosphere of that original performance. The legendary Ouspenskaya, who had been the first Governess, came to many rehearsals, insuring that the production would be as close to the original as Eva could make it. Reviewers remarked on Le Gallienne's ability to

Ria as Jacqueline (seated) framed by director and star, Eva Le Gallienne as Marie Louise, and Donald Cameron as Oliver in Jean-Jacque Bernard's *L'Invitation au Voyage*. (Museum of the City of New York, Le Gallienne Collection.)

blend the company into an ensemble. The demand for tickets insured that *The Cherry Orchard* would run longer than any previous Civic offering.

Six weeks later, Le Gallienne appeared as a mercurial Peter Pan in tight blue leotards, blue suede sandals, and a daring violet colored hat.[25] Once again, Ria got to watch the proceedings from the wings.

The final production of the 1928-29 season was another Russian play by Leonid Andreyev, *Katerina*. Ria's heart must have skipped a beat when she learned she was not in the cast list, but Nazimova intervened and insisted that she play her sister, Liza, who was described as the mirror image of Katerina.

This light-hearted frolic, which featured marital infidelity, voyeurism, and attempted murder, had no more success with the critics than the first two plays of the repertory.[26] Nevertheless, Ria had experienced a heady immersion into sophisticated international theatre. The Civic's prices were far below those of the commercial theatre, and the house was big enough to accommodate large audiences. Nazimova as the star attraction had packed the playhouse for 63 performances, and *Peter Pan* had run another 123 times. The other productions (*L'Invitation* and *Katerina*) reflected the intellectual interests of serious theatre aficionados, insuring extended press coverage and respect from the academic community.

The repertory operation was not designed to make money. Its staggered production schedule, large company of actors (many acted in only half the productions), and the low price of tickets meant that, even with 90 percent of the house filled over the season, a subsidy was still needed to pay the bills. Ria might have looked upon it as a personal grant. It was supplying the provincial Dublin girl with an education in the ways of the modern metropolitan world.

At the end of her first season with Le Gallienne, Ria went back to Ireland for summer vacation. Her mind was a jumble of theatrical experiences and opinions garnered in the presence of some of the most famous trendsetters of that day. She felt that as an actress she was beginning to develop an inferiority complex, an inhibition with a decidedly New York flavor. Journeying from Cobh to Dublin on the train, tears kept filling her eyes. The hectic metropolitan life seemed to seep out of her, and, in its place, she felt a sudden, overwhelming affection for her country.

Her almost infallible "second sense" had brought her back to Dublin theatre at a celebrated and historical moment. On July 3, 1929, the fledgling Gate Theatre Company, headed by its founders Micheál MacLiammóir and Hilton Edwards, opened Denis Johnston's expressionistic play, *The Old Lady Says "No!"* This defining event contained many of the controversies that Ria Mooney was to face in her lifetime in Dublin theatre.

The script was an Abbey reject.[27] Scribbled on the returned manuscript by an unknown hand were the words that became the defiantly ironic title of the play. This not-so-veiled insult to the doyen of the Abbey, Lady Gregory, became the battle cry of the isolated and threatened Anglo-Irish community. Ireland's partition had marginalized an already small Anglophile cultural elite. The emphasis on the Irish language imposed by the new Free State government further exacerbated the Protestant minority's feeling that they were now foreigners in their own country.[28] It was all the more ironic that Lady Gregory, who was quintessentially Anglo-Irish, should be one of the victims of this artistic revolt.

The playwright, Denis Johnston, was an old friend of Ria Mooney's.[29] She had directed him in a play during her early days in Dublin's amateur theatre. Born William Denis Johnston in Dublin in 1901, son of the Hon. William Johnston, Judge of the Supreme Court, educated at St. Andrew's, Dublin, Merchiston, Edinburgh, Christ's College, Cambridge, President of Union, Pugsley Scholar, Harvard, and called to both the English and Northern Irish bars in 1925-26, he was of impressive Presbyterian stock. His play recounted the hallucinatory experience of an actor playing Robert Emmet, who recovers from a British soldier's blow on the head. As a result he makes a hallucinatory muddle of events from Ireland's past and present, in which "Cathleen ni Houlihan" is a foul-mouthed street beggar, and patriotism is derided and ridiculed in the most fashionable theatrical style of the day.

Johnston himself described reading his script as the equivalent of reading a railway timetable.[30] "It wasn't written," he said, "with any idea other than that a director would want to see what would happen if he attempted certain techniques on the stage."[31] The production featured a maze of lighting effects, choral speaking, crowd groupings, literary quotations, and caricatures of Dublin's most famous and notorious citizens. This calculated spit in the eye of the Free State government was exactly what the Gate Theatre's founders wanted. The Gate Theatre's production was mounted in the Abbey's tiny space upstairs from the main auditorium. The Gate itself was a theatrical extension of the personalities and talents of its creators, MacLiammóir and Edwards.

Micheál MacLiammóir was tall, dark and strikingly handsome, while Hilton Edwards was short and chubby with a prominent nose and small, dark eyes. Edwards' theatrical instincts pointed toward European experimental production rather than toward the traditional methods of the English playhouse. He wanted to rely for effect upon sound, music, massed movement and electric lighting, instead of painted sets and eloquent language.

MacLiammóir's life was itself a theatrical event. He was never offstage, and he fretted over his physical appearance to the point of wearing make-up in public. His voice is captured in this short speech written for him by Mary Manning in her play *Youth's the Season...?*

> DESMOND: Now let's gossip. Let's be vilely libelous. Let's be salacious and treacherous. Let's stab our best friends in the back. Let's betray our relations; let's wash our dirty linen in the drawing-room. In other words— let's be *Dublin*.[32]

This might have passed for backstage conversation at the Gate. There the play was never the thing. The Boys, as they came to be known, were always center stage. Flamboyant, gifted prevaricators, improvident with money, and extravagantly homosexual, neither seemed to care a whit for public opinion. Dublin society not only tolerated such behavior but seemed even to admire them for being daring enough to challenge the social conventions of Catholic Ireland.

Ria had been told that the play was very amusing, "with biting satires on certain literary 'At Homes' held in Dublin, and that I would recognize a good many people in the 'drawing room scenes.'" The first night audience at the Peacock climbed a steep staircase into a tiny auditorium with a minute stage. Everyone who was anyone was there, and they laughed as Ria had been told they would at what she felt was a melancholy piece. The year she had spent in a foreign country had changed her. She felt like the "returned Yankee," Rose Sneider, in Shiels' *The Retrievers*.

At the first interval, making her way towards the outside stairs with Mary Manning to smoke a cigarette, she encountered the familiar figure of Joseph Holloway.[33] When asked her opinion of the play, she replied: "I am immensely intrigued by the piece and almost wept at times." He thought that "was appreciation run riot." Did she think that after a year in America she knew more about Ireland and its plays than the people at home? She thought, now, that perhaps she did.

After the performance, Ria was invited to Johnston's home in Lansdowne Road, where everyone praised the play's satire. She found Denis alone for a moment, and told him of her reaction.

"Everyone seems to think your play very diverting, but I found it difficult to keep the tears back. You seem to feel as I do about *Cathleen Ni Houlihan*. I know what you feel, but I can't express it. What's wrong with me?" He put his hands on her shoulders and said, "Thank God someone understood!"[34]

The next day, David Sears, the critic of the *Irish Independent* wrote:

"I dislike it intensely and admire it enormously. Certainly, it is new, stimulating, and sincere.... The Gate Theatre is to be congratulated on a remarkably effective production of this extremely difficult if brilliantly clever play."[35]

In the two years since she had left the Abbey and Dublin, Ria Mooney had traveled England and Scotland and much of the United States. She had been hired by cosmopolitan Eva Le Gallienne, and had witnessed European theatrical practice in its most advanced form. Homesickness and a hint of romantic ennui coupled with an introduction to fashionable society had trimmed her figure and improved her wardrobe. New York had introduced her to racial prejudice, as well as to an upward mobility that had small regard for family background or educational status. Once she landed at Cobh, she was confronted by just how far she had strayed from her native land, and the ensuing sentimental melancholy surprised her.

The irreverence of *The Old Lady Says "No!"* must have seemed tame compared with the scenes she had witnessed at the Civic Repertory Company. What was evident was the cleverness of the production and the brazen sophistication of "the Boys" in the midst of provincial Dublin. Had she gone all the way to New York to find what was there on her own doorstep?

Finally, was she right — was the author's intent smothered by the fashionable frenzy for sophistication? Was Johnston's attack on Irish patriotism a cry from the heart of a marginalized Anglo Irishman? Was he shouting out his protest against all who said he and his kind weren't Irish at all? Was Ireland pushing him and his social set into exile as the Abbey had forced Ria out the door? She spoke no Irish and, though a Catholic, she admired the literary and artistic skill of the legion of Anglo-Irish writers, painters and players. The English language was her language, and she hoped to make her place in English-speaking theatre. Was she to be exiled for that preference?

Joseph Holloway managed to remain a provincial Dubliner, feeling perfectly at home in Catholic, English-speaking, inclusive Ireland, but he had been born into an educated and comfortably situated family. Ria had to make her way into that world on her own. She had to be careful how she expressed her ideas about theatrical matters. Witness her use of the noncommittal word "intriguing" to describe her friend's play. Like the critic Sears, who was able to at once "admire it enormously" while disliking "it intensely," she had acquired the trick of equivocation. Ria wanted to be a part of that upper-class, educated, social elite. She could not afford to be insulted by their moral rejection of her religious background.

On the other hand, Ria Mooney was an actress, and, even if subsidy, however acquired, could pay her salary, what was the point of playing to half-empty houses? Le Gallienne's audiences were rated at about 90 percent of capacity, but she was almost giving tickets away in a big city with a large potential audience. Yet, she still needed a huge subsidy to continue to operate. The Gate Theatre was using the Abbey's Peacock theater and received a small grant to produce Johnston's play. The fashionable first night audience filled the auditorium, but, once society had put its imprimatur upon this artistic triumph, there wasn't much demand for tickets from the general public. They were Catholic and had no taste for an attack on their patriotism or their faith. Furthermore, this play had literary and historical allusions beyond a general audience. The esoteric nature of the material doomed the play to small houses.

It was evident after their first year at the Peacock that—the artistic community's praise notwithstanding—MacLiammóir and Edwards could not produce plays from box-office receipts alone.

Still, the Boys were genuinely talented, energetic and at home in Dublin. Ria never registered any public shock or disapprobation at the backstage behavior at the Civic, nor did she criticize the morality of its play selection. She remained sphinxlike in the face of the Gate's similar profile. Nonetheless, the trick was easier in a big city like New York. Dublin was altogether different. If she remained there, she would be under intense pressure to choose a side.

The trip from Cobh and her reaction to Johnston's play showed her just how much she had missed her native land and city. The Gate had not only rebelled against the narrowness of Catholic Ireland, but it had also created employment for performers as well. When she left the Abbey, there had been no other place in Ireland open to her. Would there now be a place in the Dublin theatrical world for Ria Mooney?

CHAPTER THREE

"The Le Gallienne Sorority"

When Ria Mooney returned to New York in September 1929 to rejoin the Civic Repertory company, the Great White Way was about to be illuminated by the most famous of Broadway stars. There to light up the sky with their glamour were Ruby Keeler, the madcap Marx Brothers, Jimmy Durante and his pals Clayton and Jackson, Will Rogers, Al Jolson, Alfred Lunt and Lynn Fontanne, and George Michael Cohan. Once again, Florenz Ziegfeld was preparing to "glorify the American Girl"; and Earl Carroll returned with further proof, if more was needed, that the city possessed the vanity of "Vanities." The previous season had seen 225 productions, and the 1929 crop promised to be just as bountiful.

The Civic Repertory Company opened its season on September 16, 1929, with Chekhov's *The Sea Gull*. Ria was not in the cast.[1] The following week they revived *The Cherry Orchard* and she was given the role of Dunyasha. The cast list for Tolstoy's *The Living Corpse* had her name beside that of "a drunken woman." Even before she had the opportunity to create so fascinating a character, though, Wall Street, as the show business paper *Variety* proclaimed, had laid an egg. The stock market crash of 1929 signaled the end of "the roaring twenties." With the "Talkies" already luring money away to Hollywood, the theatre was entering hard times. Austerity, like the proverbial wolf, was at the theatrical door, preparing to make an entrance, and Eva Le Gallienne had little experience with such an animal.

"We had rich and authentic furnishings" at the Civic, Ria said. "If the action of the play demanded a meal on stage, we always ate the correct food for the country and period! I remember my amazement at being served with Chianti, actually warmed, when I was playing with Josephine Hutchinson in Goldoni's *La Locandiera.*"[2]

Josie, as the young actress was called by her friends, was the wife of Robert Bell, a theatre director and grandson of Alexander Graham Bell. Her mother was also a member of the Civic troupe. It was awkward, to say the least, that Eva and she had become more than friends. Backstage gossip attributed Josie's rising star to a talent not particularly theatrical in nature. The depression backstage at the Fourteenth Street Theater began to match the business atmosphere on Wall Street.

At her age, Ria should have been in contention for the roles assigned to Josephine Hutchinson, but, with a love affair clouding the director's vision, it seemed unlikely she would ever be cast as a leading young woman. Furthermore, fashion-conscious New York had taught her to regard her physique as a casting hazard. She was told by the Theatre Guild's Theresa Helburn that she had "a tall personality and a small body." Self-conscious about her "broad beam and short legs," she began to think she had always looked middle-aged.

Le Gallienne chose that moment to make a vital decision for Ria's career. She asked her to select a play to be performed by her apprentices. They were to give private performances free from critical scrutiny, using all the equipment and facilities of the Civic. Ria suggested Synge's *The Playboy of the Western World*, which was well known to American students of the drama, and Eva, without any previous sign of her intentions, told her she was in charge. Who better to stage an Irish classic than a former member of the Abbey Players?

One of the young students approached her and asked if he might read for a part. There was one role that had not been cast, Shawn Keogh, and Burgess Meredith's audition impressed her so much that she gave him his first important acting opportunity.

"In the apprentice section Ria directed me in *Playboy of the Western World*," said Meredith, "and after that play good things started to happen."[3]

Good things eventually happened to almost all the 11 assigned to her care, who included John Garfield, Howard da Silva, Robert Lewis, Arnold Moss, Paula Millar, and Irene Schariff. "We acted in small apprentice shows," remembered Meredith, "and we were coached and directed by a remarkable lady from Dublin—Ria Mooney. Ria had been an actress in that fair city before she came to join Le Gallienne. She later returned to Ireland and was appointed director-in-chief of the famous Abbey Theatre...."

As she worked with her young charges, she noticed that, every so often, Eva appeared in the balcony during rehearsals. Whether Ria's *Playboy* was a success has not been recorded for us, but Le Gallienne obviously approved of her methods, because in January, 1930, she appointed her assistant director. Her first assignment was to direct all of the crowd scenes and small-part players in the forthcoming *Romeo and Juliet*.

In retrospect, it is curious that Eva Le Gallienne never played Rostand's *L'Aiglon*, because she had something Napoleonic about her: the confidence to take on a massive organization, make all the central leadership appointments, play a central role on as well as offstage.[4] She raised funds to supply her forces, chose her vehicles to suit her purpose and style, and appeared before the public as the company lightning rod. If she succeeded, she would take the credit. If she failed, she would have the blame. This delicately framed lady had the energy and courage to follow where ambition led her, but she also had keen theatrical judgment and the confidence to give her chosen assistants their head.

Le Gallienne offered the role of Juliet to Josie, and, when she turned it down, was forced to take the part herself, as there was no one else in the company who could play it. As a result, Ria couldn't look for much guidance in her new job, because Eva would be too preoccupied preparing to play Juliet to give much thought to her directorial duties.

She quickly became absorbed in her new assignment. All of her artistic instincts were brought into play to accomplish the task. She turned to the Florentine school of painters for inspiration, discovering that, through the play of light on the color of clothing, and with the placement of bodies, one in relation to another, she could focus the viewers' eyes on the center of the action. She went to the wardrobe mistress to discover the color of the costumes most likely to appear in each crowd scene, and she tried to group her actors not only by size and sex, but also by coordinated color. Having set the mark in each scene where her performers must stand at crucial moments, she experimented by letting them relate to each other as they felt the action, so long as they hit their mark on cue. In that way, she kept the movement fluid, while assuring the principals of their playing space. It was orderly without appearing contrived.

Ria found she liked the challenge of manipulating the players and of pacing each scene. In the process, she discovered she had the gift of command. Although the young apprentices in the cast already had experienced and accepted her use of authority, the rest of the company might not accept it with the same grace. In her presence, Le Gallienne wisely instructed the company that she expected them to regard Miss Mooney as they would herself. This conferral of complete authority flattered Ria and restored some of the self-esteem damaged in the casting.

As the rehearsals proceeded, Ria acquired directorial insights that she might have overlooked before having such responsibility thrust upon her. Eva told the cast the play was the work of a young man, "and it isn't the Bible." Aline Bernstein designed a unit setting which, with furniture or drapes cleverly placed, quickly became a variety of locales. The most fascinating aspect of the production, however, was the interplay between the leading lady's reputation and the story of a teenage passion. With great audacity, or, as they were fond of saying on the lower east side, with *chutzpah*, Eva played Juliet as a young girl "well acquainted with the facts of life and the persuasions of love." The critics remarked that her Juliet was "obviously … no model maiden."[5] It was reported that her performance was so convincing that her leading man, Richard Waring, fell in love with his leading lady and proposed marriage to her. The sensation created by the production closed out a successful season and insured that the Civic Repertory would be watched carefully in the coming year.

Once the Fourteenth Street playhouse closed its doors for the 1929-30 season, Ria joined a group of students from Yale University's Drama School in Arden, Pennsylvania, for summer stock. While there she was asked to arrange a broadcast of Lady Gregory's one-act play, *The Workhouse Ward*. Burgess Meredith was one of the old codgers in the ward, who argues away each day with his neighbor, only to refuse his sister's offer of a home if his crony can't come along. Ria took the part of the sister and coached her colleagues in an Irish accent. The Philadelphia critics liked the broadcast, but thought it a pity the producer couldn't find an actress with a better Irish accent to complement the convincing speech of the men.

In her memoirs, Ria is purposely vague about her social life after the summer stock season. She paints a picture of Connecticut society around the eccentric figure of Robert Chanler, thought by some to have been the model for Scott Fitzgerald's "Great Gatsby." What makes this description so tantalizing is that she met this playboy-cum-screen painter in Rita Romelli's apartment soon after joining the Civic Repertory. The name of this mystery lady appears in the cast list for *The Living Corpse* performed in December 1929 at the Civic.[6] In Ria's memoirs, Romelli is mentioned twice, with the first mention accompanied by a footnote suggesting that she became Mrs. Eleanor (Kick) Erlanger, to whom the book is dedicated. No further explanation of the importance of this "beautiful girl" in her life is offered to the reader. However, it is possible that she was the other part of the "we" in the following account which seems to indicate that Ria's education in America was not confined to the playhouse.

"We walked through the dark woods, guided by the sound of voices, until suddenly we came to the river. I had never before beheld such a scene, not even in a Bacchanalian ballet. A number of people were seated on the ground beside the river, finishing a picnic meal by the flickering light of a huge log fire. They sat in twos, making love between sips, or in groups, having loud and fierce arguments while they drank and nibbled food — and each other. From a large flat rock overhanging the river, naked figures were seen for a moment as they shot through the light in dives that engulfed them in the black waters. Everywhere were the sounds of laughter, arguments, corks popping, bodies splashing into the water, mingling with nature's medley of night sounds. The flames lit up the entire scene and intensified the darkness of the shadows. From this scene of revelry we did not arrive home until the early hours of the morning. I was told that Chanler had been in bed asleep all the time, and never came to these parties."[7]

This scene might have been extracted from popular novels of the period like Dorothy L. Sayers' *Murder Must Advertise* or Evelyn Waugh's *Decline and Fall*. It is out of character in the life of Ria Mooney. Her description seems to distance her from the scene, but she tells us "*we* [my italics] did not arrive home until the early hours of the morning." Who was she with at this bacchanalia, and was she there as a voyeur or a participant? It is curious that she remembers this event so vividly, and completely ignores in her memoirs a scandal on her own doorstep that occurred at about the same time, and with consequences far more important for her theatrical future.

At 3:40 P.M. on July 7, 1930, District Judge Frank S. Dunn ruled in open court that the marriage of Josephine Hutchinson and Robert Bell was dissolved absolutely and forever.[8] Both had disclaimed any interest in the estate of the other. While Eva Le Gallienne is never mentioned in these legal documents, the press accounts sensationalized the event, proclaiming that it was the first recorded instance of a lesbian correspondent in a divorce. The scandal that followed so devastated Eva that she had to admit herself into New York's Doctor's Hospital at the beginning of August, suffering from exhaustion. Told by her doctors that she must rest in the country until September, she was forced to announce a delay in the opening of her season at the Civic.

"The Civic closed down," Ria said, "after America's financial crash had forced its once wealthy patrons to withdraw their help." That is certainly true. But the end was precipitated by Le Gallienne's love affair with Josie, and the health problems attendant upon its public exposure. "Her abnormal perversion," wrote one critic, "was now more publicized than her theater."[9]

Romeo and Juliet resumed its run on October 6, 1930, and Ria had the satisfaction of reassessing her first directorial efforts. The new repertoire was launched on October 20, and the current Parisian sensation, Jean Giraudoux, was represented by his play, *Siegfried*. Eva was a heartsick maiden awaiting the return of her World War I soldier husband, who has developed amnesia and lost his identity. The press declared "she seemed sluggish, heavy-footed, restrained, and ill-prepared."[10] Ria was not in the cast.

The season's sensation, *Alison's House* by Susan Glaspell, opened on December 1. Unknown poems that tell of the poet Alison's thwarted love are discovered by her niece, played by Le Gallienne, who has upset the family by living with a married man. The manuscript reveals that Alison, too, has loved a married man she met at Harvard on a visit, and she suppressed her poems about that love until her death. While the illicit love is with a married man, and the locale is transferred to Ohio, everyone understood that the figure was meant to be taken for Emily Dickinson, widely known by this time to have been a lesbian. Here is a sample of Eva's dialogue as Elsa, the niece.[11]

> ELSA: I think she would be glad I am not alone. What could I do—alone? For you see, I am not enough. She would know that. She would be tolerant. She would be gentle—oh, so gentle. If she were here now—she would say—be happy, little Elsa, she would say.

Burns Mantle said that "*Alison's House* is what drama critics most frequently describe as a literary play. Meaning, usually, that it is burdened with intelligence, a generally undramatic story and a superabundance of stiff dialogue."[12] The critics attacked the play as sentimentality rendered in stiff prose and without any conflict. Worst of all, it was badly acted!

Le Gallienne followed this savage reception with a personal triumph in the old chestnut, *Camille*. Dressed in fluffy white organdy ruffles and lace, with a nosegay of blue cornflowers pinned at her waist, Eva played the last scene as a fragile, romantic, vulnerable Marguerite, a changed woman with a heart of gold. The celebrated actress Constance Collier directed the production, and Ria remembered a piece of business she gave the leading lady. During the letter scene, Collier interrupted Eva, and instructed her to play the scene as if she had the contents of the letter by heart. "When, under such excellent direction," said Ria, "Eva read the first couple of lines, and then let the paper fall to her side, speaking the rest of the lines by heart, a scene that had been played with intelligence and finesse, became suddenly heartbreaking."

For all her artistic and intellectual pretensions, Eva Le Gallienne never lost her sense of the theatre, and Ria Mooney recognized its effectiveness. The Civic's success with audiences was not in Russian art plays, however, but with melodramas like *Romeo and Juliet* and *Camille,* happy fantasies like *Peter Pan,* or in revivals that featured film stars like Nazimova. Furthermore, no matter how much theoretical speculation was expended upon Stanislavski, emotions were elicited from audiences by the technical application of color, coordinated movement of players, and thoughtful use of properties such as Mlle. Gautier's love letter. Ria was given caviar to eat in one of the Russian plays, but she noticed they did not supply vodka in scenes where it was referred to as the character's drink. At the Abbey, slices of ham were represented by pink blotting paper and lamb chops were painted pieces of wood. Reflecting upon these experiences, she began to realize that "the Abbey gained artistically as well as financially by forcing its players to use their imaginations in the matter of props."[13]

Ria may have admired Le Gallienne's courage in the face of the gossip that hounded her, but she also recognized the toll it took upon her concentration. Eva had missed rehearsals for *Camille,* and it was increasingly evident that she was drinking too much. Her bravado in the face of public condemnation caused her to react professionally rather than personally. She challenged the prevailing public moral sentiment by choosing to produce scripts that everyone conceded were badly crafted. *Alison's House* was a bad play. It had been produced for nontheatrical reasons, and it was painful to watch Eva struggling to make it work upon the stage.

If Ria Mooney felt that a performer's private life was her own business, she could not but observe that it might become detrimental to her performance on stage. Not only did Eva's notoriety focus attention on the actress rather than the character, it also hurt her concentration onstage and sapped her energy in rehearsals. *Siegfried* had flopped because Eva was distraught and distracted by Josie's divorce and the flap that followed. The art crowd might sneer at the last-act heroics of melodrama, but *Camille* came to the rescue of the Civic just in time. It might not be artistic, but it was good theater.

Camille became the greatest box office success the Civic ever had. Riding on that high, Eva announced she was taking a sabbatical for the 1931-32 season. She was exhausted and needed time to reconsider her position. Just as the surprise of that announcement began to subside, and to everyone's shock, *Alison's House* was awarded the Pulitzer Prize for drama! The critics were furious. Eva was being rewarded for her daring and not for the craftsmanship of her work. Once more, she had confounded her critics.

Where did that leave Ria Mooney? The surge of creative power brought on by her directorial assignment had quickly lost its momentum. She missed preparing each evening for a performance. She expressed her boredom during a Civic rehearsal to scene designer, Aline Bernstein. "Aline, I wish to God you'd fine me a rich husband. Provided he hasn't a fat stomach, I don't care what he is like, so long as he is rich." "The fat stomach isn't so bad, Ria," she replied, "when you get used to it."[14] Poor Ria, true to form, hadn't noticed that Aline's husband was on the portly side.

In any case, she was now not only bored but unemployed, and, in spite of some interest taken by Theresa Helburn of the Theatre Guild and Alla Nazimova, she couldn't find work. The summer was anxiously spent partying with a Dublin friend, Madeleine Boyd. Another friend, Englishman Stanley Naylor, introduced her to Helena Rubinstein, in whose apartment she remembered seeing her first Picasso.

In July 1931, journalist and Algonquin wit Heywood Broun assembled a revue called *Shoot the Works* for the purpose of giving a hundred or more out-of-work actors temporary jobs. The season saw the downfall of many producers, including the Shubert Theatrical Company, and rumor had it that Otto Kahn, a principal patron of the Civic, was having trouble paying his taxes. Broadway was not a hospitable place for an unemployed woman approaching 30, who had not appeared on the New York stage in almost two complete seasons. Someone even suggested that she might have a chance if the part of a madwoman needed casting. She thought the observation perceptive. Many of her apprentices, including Burgess Meredith and Robert Lewis, were cast in forthcoming productions, but Ria's name never appeared on any cast list.

Tired and defeated, she prepared to return home. Provident as ever, she had kept enough money to pay for a boat ticket. She hadn't the fortitude to take a temporary job as a waitress or domestic as so many of her unemployed actress friends were doing.

Just after the holidays, she got word that the Abbey, which had started on a gigantic 79-city tour of the states in October, needed a replacement for an actress who wished to return to Ireland. Ria agreed to join them in Atlanta, Georgia. Cheryl Crawford, casting director of the New York Theatre Guild, chose that moment to offer Ria a role in one of their productions, but she had already committed herself and had to refuse the part. She doesn't mention any foreknowledge of this event, and there is a dispirited tone in her recollections of the next couple of months. Miami was cold and all the good hotels were closed for the winter. The sink in her dressing room was occupied by a large beetle, and the only central heating she experienced was on the trains. The tour ended in Boston in April, and Ria found herself on her way back to Dublin after four crowded years of social and professional experience.

Almost 30, thinking herself dumpy and old, she had a feeling of inferiority about her person and her talent. Her American engagement had begun with promise. She had received good notices for her performance in *Le Bourgeois Gentilhomme* and *L'Invitation au Voyage*. She had been complimented by Dudley Digges, a former Abbey star and a fixture at the Theatre Guild, for doing so well among Le Gallienne's impressive company. But those were the last encouraging remarks she had received. After that, her acting just seemed to deteriorate, and she couldn't find a particular reason for it.

She had learned a great deal about theatre in general, and acting in particular, at the Civic Repertory Company. What had caused her to lose her naturalness and ease on stage? Le Gallienne had said that learning technique often destroyed instinct. She felt that she understood how an actress prepared for a role, what techniques of recall and movement, physical deportment and gesture were appropriate, and how to select them. She had seen expensive costumes and elaborate sets, and she had learned how to wear them and walk on them. She had observed the benefits of longer rehearsal periods for each play. Through it all, she had not lost her interest in playing, but somehow her confidence had deserted her. Clearly, it was important to have a strong and relaxed stage presence. She had unconsciously displayed that quality as Rosie Redmond. How was she to retrieve that uninhibited self-assurance after exposure to the bright lights of Broadway?

The first part she played upon returning to Dublin was a child of 13 named Duckey in Lennox Robinson's *The Far Off Hills*. She was so bad, it made her sister cry with shame. The dean of Dublin drama critics, Andrew E. Malone, said that the American theatre seemed to have made her very tired. Feeling the way she did, how could she hope to play an Irish 13 year old. Everything about the Abbey was cozy and familiar, including the kitchen comedies that were the staple of the repertory. How was she to fall into step with the ways of a theatre that had, after her four years of exile, become foreign to her?

Lady Augusta Gregory died early in the morning of May 23, 1932.[15] When a change of the Free State government occurred, the Abbey lost the support in political circles of Ernest Blythe. The new government was led by Eamon de Valera, whose attempt to make Ireland economically self-sufficient resulted in a cut of the Abbey subsidy to 750 pounds a year. Finally, there was a collision between a hostile government-appointed member of the Abbey board and Yeats, with the poet threatening to close the theatre should the appointment be confirmed.

Backstage, Ria observed the anarchy that had developed as Lady Gregory closed out her long watch. In 1930, Lennox Robinson found total artistic authority thrust upon him, and he was drinking too much to exercise strict control of the troupe. As if that wasn't bad enough, the more "serious-minded playgoers" began to create a competition between the National Theatre and the sophisticated new shop opened by MacLiammóir and Edwards in the Rotunda Assembly Rooms at the other end of O'Connell street. "The cult of decrying the Abbey to extol the Gate," wrote Holloway, "has become farcical to me. Both theatres make bad mistakes and both theatres accomplish great things frequently, and let us be thankful for that without belittling either."[16]

Ria knew and admired the Boys from earlier days, but, since her exile in America, two more names had been added to the Gate Theatre marquee, Edward and Christine, better known as Lord and Lady Longford. After two acclaimed seasons at the tiny Peacock, MacLiammóir and Edwards raised enough money to redecorate the Rotunda, and, in February of 1930, they opened their playhouse with Goethe's *Faust*. Committed from the outset to producing noncommercial plays, with Edwards proclaiming finances a bore, and MacLiammóir as extravagant with money as he was with words, the economic health of the operation quickly deteriorated, until it looked as if the theatre would have to close. At the first annual general meeting of the shareholders, on December 12, 1930, it was reported that the first year of production had created a shortfall of 700 pounds, no mean amount in 1930. Unless the Company could sell the remaining unsubscribed shares, which amounted to an astounding 1,200 pounds, the playhouse must close immediately.

At that moment, with superb timing and melodramatic élan, a nobleman on his charger rode in to save the day. "Rising from his seat in the audience," writes the Longfords' biographer, "a pink-faced rotund young man began struggling out of his overcoat. In an Oxford accent he announced that he would very much like to buy all the shares on offer, adding, 'and my cheque is ready whenever it is wanted.' The Gate Theatre was saved." Later, Lady Longford declared that "the moment of drama was unrehearsed. He knew that the Gate mustn't close, it was a necessity of life in Dublin and Ireland."[17] Soon after, Edward Pakenham (the Longford family name) was appointed a member of the Board of the Dublin Gate Theatre. He had everything that the financially irresponsible operation wanted: titled respectability, a classical education, plenty of money, and lots of time on his hands with no occupation!

Of course, the Longfords were Anglo-Irish, humorously defined by
Brendan Behan as "Protestant(s) on a horse." While Pakenham had Oxford
accented Irish, and took as his main residence a draughty old castle in
County Longford, he was bent on spending his money and energy liber-
alizing Ireland. Holloway remarked on this after *The Plough and the Stars*
brought Yeats to the stage to defend the Abbey's artistic freedom. "Now
that Ireland is getting reanglicized," he wrote, "O'Casey's plays just suit
the new class of audience who come to see them."[18] Lord and Lady Longford were devoted to the idea of "an uncommercial arts theatre," or, to
put it another way, a theatre that had little attraction for local Irish audiences. Since that was the case, it would be the Longfords' duty to re-edu-
cate the masses. Wasn't George Bernard Shaw doing the same for English
audiences, preaching through his plays the gospel of Fabian socialism?
The task would prove long and arduous, but the Longfords had plenty of
cash at their disposal, the support of a handful of intellectuals, and the
considerable theatrical talents of MacLiammóir and Edwards. MacLiammóir paints an interesting picture of the two Longfords in *All for Hecuba:*
Edward "with hands folded in dimpled content across his belly, motion-
less, watchful, absorbed," and Christine "in hunched-up curves, her head
a little on one side … drooped a little farther towards the end of the run."[19]
Neither planned on being a silent partner in the concern. In the beginning, they spent their late nights at a fashionable Dublin restaurant feed-
ing the Boys expensively, while the theatrical team supplied priceless
playhouse craft. Since Lord Longford consumed enough to feed both
actors, it was only right he should foot the bill. Unfortunately, the habit
of relying on his checkbook eventually opened a fissure in the relationship which none of the parties ever seemed capable of mending.

Ria regarded the Gate style as the Irish complement of the Civic
Repertory Company. While the Abbey was producing fourth-wall realism,
the Gate's style was more visual and actor-oriented. The Abbey's com-
mission was to produce new Irish plays, while the Gate was essentially an
actors' and directors' playhouse. As an actress, Ria longed to play exotic
characters in colorful costumes, as she had as a child in Madame Rock's
dance company. She hadn't had the opportunity in New York to apply all
that she had learned while standing in the wings or sitting in the director's chair at the Civic. The Gate was the only Dublin theatre that could
give her the materials to demonstrate the growth in her acting talent.

Before she could address that possibility, the Abbey took to the American road for the entire 1932-33 season, because the Depression of the
thirties and the loss of a portion of the government's subsidy made it necessary to bolster finances by another tour. The resident company was

The touring company (from l. to r.): Arthur Shields, Sara Allgood, Eric Gorman, Ria, Maureen Delaney, Christine Hayden, Gabriel Fallon, Eileen Crowe, F. J. McCormick, Barry Fitzgerald, M. J. Dolan. (University of Delaware Library, Special Collections.)

augmented by newcomers Denis O'Dea, Fred Johnson, W. O'Gorman, Cyril Cusack, Ann Clery, and Nora O'Mahony, who remained at home and were referred to as the second company. The touring players included Barry Fitzgerald, F. J. McCormick, Eileen Crowe, M. J. Dolan, P. J. Carolan, May Craig, Maureen Delaney, Arthur Shields, Kate Curling, and Ria.

This first company opened their American season on October 18, 1932, at the Martin Beck Theatre with Lennox Robinson's *The Far Off Hills*, and followed it on the 21st with George Shiels' popular comedy, *The New Gossoon.*[20] Shiels' previous hit, *Professor Tim*, had delighted Irish-American audiences the year before, and it was hoped that this cheerful comedy about a rebellious farm boy would distract the old critics who might raise a ruckus over the rest of the repertoire. The strategy didn't succeed. The New York United Irish–American Societies tried to get the Irish government to withdraw its subsidy from the Abbey players on the grounds that they were "at present touring America … giving wrong impressions of Irish life and character by presenting such plays as *The Playboy of the Western World* and *The Plough and the Stars.*" Synge's *Playboy* and O'Casey's *Juno* were the artistic centerpieces of the Abbey repertoire for foreign consumption, along with Lady Gregory's short piece about the Rebellion, *The Rising of the Moon*. The Fianna Fáil government, more responsive to Irish-American pressure than its predecessor, asked the Abbey directors to withdraw the two plays. Yeats countered by declaring he would forgo the subsidy altogether rather than submit to government censorship. Yeats was now the champion of artistic freedom in the eyes of the world press. What was lost in the argument was that the most popular Abbey plays were Robinson's *The Far Off Hills*, and Shiels' *Professor Tim* and *The New Gosoon*. Before the troupe departed New York, the Theatre Guild sponsored a single Sunday performance of William Butler Yeats' adaptation of *Oedipus Rex* with Eileen Crowe as Jocasta, Barry Fitzgerald as Creon, and F. J. McCormick as Oedipus.[21]

The three months spent in the cultural center of America gave Ria plenty of time to renew acquaintances and make new friends. Eva Le Gallienne brought her troupe back to Fourteenth Street in an adaptation of Lewis Carroll's *Alice in Wonderland* in a production that cost the unheard of figure of $23,000 and included 120 cast members. It was so complicated that the staging had to be worked out on paper.[22] The critics loved it and praised her "dauntless mood, tackling a task of superhuman difficulty, and succeeding where most of her uptown competitors, with much more time at their disposal, would fail." Ria's colleagues must have been impressed by the sheer spectacle, but, when it brought about financial crisis for the company, with Eva forced to announce the temporary closing of her theatre on January 19, 1933, they were already on the road. Did Ria read critic Richard Lockridge's observation in the New York Sun? "We have talked," he said, "over much, perhaps, of 'art' in relation to the Civic. We have given the impression that it is all very high-minded and worthy, but not on the whole much fun.... A visit to 'Alice' has been held up too much in the light of a duty, and not enough in the light of a lark."

Ria was invited to a reception given by Irish-American lawyer Judge Kinkead. It was her first contact with "lace-curtain Irish." That derogatory term stigmatized those emigrant millionaires, whose wives gossiped "about each other, about clothes," and about troubles with servants, while the menfolk talked stocks and shares and business deals. Ria found herself siding with the servants of these "Irish American gombeen men." These were not the sophisticated people she had met in artistic American circles, but were they much different from most of the big house occupants in her own land, who talked about racing, the servants, and each other? She must have been acquainted with Lennox Robinson's play *The Big House*, in which an elderly Anglo-Irish couple are utterly lost in the turbulent world around them. Inherited money apparently provided a patina of respectability for the class-conscious Ria Mooney.

It particularly annoyed her that Yeats was holding court in the corner of the large L-shaped room surrounded by only a small group of admirers, while the majority "were gossiping among themselves." On the other hand, her good friend, Denis Johnston, said that to him "Yeats was a major poet with a floppy tie…. George Russell was just a nice old man with a beard: the 'hairy fairy' as he was called." Johnston taught in America for many years, and was regarded with awe by people who asked him: "Did you actually know Yeats? Did you really have lunch with Shaw?" He thought, then, that "it must have been an unusually interesting time."[23] Ria can't be faulted for trading on her acquaintance with O'Casey, Yeats, and Lady Gregory, but she doesn't appear to have been aware that such talk was a form of gossip and might be considered snobbish.

During this tour, Ria took riding lessons, and she persuaded Barry Fitzgerald and Kate Curling to join her.[24] The company visited the White House and was photographed on the front steps. Ria thought she might be of help to Irish industries by taking samples of their work to department stores in America's big cities. She carried her package of hand-woven tweeds and Dun Emer carpets to executives at Gimbel Brothers, Peck and Peck, and Marshall Fields of Chicago. She discovered that duty was assessed by pound weight, as well as by the yard, that bulk sales would be too expensive to import, and that highly priced single items might not be sophisticated enough in style to entice those who could afford them. Her American contacts secured her entry into these executive suites, but her salesmanship was more patriotic than businesslike. She might have done much better for native Irish industries if she could have enlisted the support of those "lace curtain" Irish she so scorned at Judge Kinkead's soiree. In any case, "it was a great disappointment," she said, "that my efforts were not successful."

When Ria returned to Ireland in the late spring of 1933, she had just passed her 30th birthday. Pictures of her reveal a comely young woman given to wearing head scarfs and broad-brimmed hats, her round face lit up by a pleasing smile, sometimes with a cigarette dangling from an extended hand.

By now, she had a wide acquaintance in artistic circles in both Dublin and New York, and the celebrity that went with her association with two world renowned English-speaking theaters. What did she think of her five years of touring and playing in England, Ireland and America? What opinions had she formed about playhouse procedures?

Clearly, she had a taste for contemporary poetry and art. She was already friends with a well-known dealer and art patron, Victor Waddington, from whom she purchased two Jack Yeats paintings on the installment plan. She idolized the Russian actress Nazimova because of her glamour and technique, and, for a while, imitated her make-up. Most of her theatrical models were either European or Anglo-Irish, and, since she had no Irish, it is not surprising that she was attracted to the members of Dublin's English-speaking literary and social elite, such as Mary Manning, Denis Johnston, and Sean O'Casey. In New York, where aristocracy had no history, she moved among the literary, political, and social intelligentsia from the fashionable world of Greenwich Village.

Ria Mooney was a serious woman, "high-minded and worthy," who thought more of duty than of fun.[25] She divided her life into two parts— the professional, and the personal. It is moot whether or not the gossip about the private lives of Eva Le Gallienne and MacLiammóir and Edwards influenced her theatrical judgment. Certainly, her approval of life at the Civic, her veiled references to her "patron," Mrs. Eleanor (Kick) Erlanger, to whom she dedicated her memoirs, her admiration for the Boys, her dropping of the names of sophisticated artistic leaders of society throughout her autobiography and her ambition to be counted among them, are obviously significant factors in her life on the stage.

It is noteworthy that she makes only passing reference to her brothers and sisters in her memoirs. According to Mary Manning, she never invited her playhouse friends home, although she often visited *them*. Mary Manning's mother took a great liking to Ria, who visited the Mannings frequently. Ria lost her mother at 14, and her father left her to her own devices from then on. It must have put a strain on her social relationships to be unable — or unwilling — because of domestic circumstances, to invite friends to her house. Later, when she found herself at the center of the *Plough* fracas, the separation of her private and professional lives helped to protect her family from the scandal it created. Dublin was a small provincial city. Social pressure on a local Catholic family whose daughter was portraying a prostitute at the National Theatre might have caused pain to her relatives.

These considerations did not cool her ambition to be a leading player, but they made her cautious about confiding in anyone, and reluctant to accept financial help even from the older Sean O'Casey. They also highlighted a spirit of determination in her character that caused Theresa Helburn to think of her as "tall personality with a small body." She had borrowed ten pounds to try her hand in the London theater. When on tour in America, she had auditioned for Eva Le Gallienne, a leading lady in Bohemian New York. Without previous professional experience as a director, and almost totally on her own, she had developed staging techniques and displayed a gift for command.

At the same time, she felt that her appearance limited her scope as an actress. Lennox Robinson thought she had the skill as a 30 year old to play a 13-year-old girl, but Ria did not, and it made her critical of his judgment. Meanwhile, her intellectual Dublin acquaintances had taken to comparing the Abbey unfavorably with the new, exotic, magical world of the Gate. One playhouse reflected the "dull reality" of quotidian contemporary Irish life, while the other featured the poetry and glamour of the European artistic world.[26]

Ria's attraction to aristocracy, whether titled or talented, European or American, is evident in her name-dropping. At the same time, she took pains to make her private life appear respectably bourgeois. She lived in a country with a small but culturally influential, Anglo-Irish, English-speaking, artistic elite, who had a distaste for the censorious puritanism imposed on them by the Free State and the Catholic Church. Although British in outlook and education, they were born in Ireland and thought of themselves as Irish. Too small numerically to have much political influence, they sought to preserve their ascendancy culturally.

Ria was born a Catholic, although there is nothing in her memoirs to suggest that she had a strong commitment to that faith. In fact, she never refers to it at all. But she could not have lived through the *Plough* riots without understanding the importance of Catholic beliefs for Abbey patrons. As a result, she found herself in a dilemma. If a playhouse in Ireland was to make its way, it must appeal to Catholic sensibilities or at least not offend them. At the same time, the tastes of the cultural trendsetters—their eloquence, learning, cosmopolitanism, and influence in London and New York—attracted her. She could see, though, that the plays they praised had little box office life, while those they dismissed proved popular with local Irish audiences.

Caught between these conflicting cultures, Ria Mooney appeased both by never breathing a censorious word about either, while being careful to keep her own opinions private. Onstage in Dublin, she tried to please her audience; offstage, she cultivated the fashionable Anglo-Irish world. The effort seemed to lower her spirits as the Depression devastated the New York theatre. She knew she was lucky to have a secure position at the Abbey, but she was also convinced she would never develop within its confines. Gradually, her hopes focused on gaining entrance to the Gate, and, up to that point, whatever Ria Mooney had wanted, she had gotten.

CHAPTER FOUR

"The Jilted Lover" and "The Unwanted Gifts"

In September 1933, Ria Mooney joined a Gate Company struggling with money problems and wounded by the temporary loss of one of its most talented leading ladies, Meriel Moore. Business the previous season had been bad. Furthermore, the financial exigencies were creating personal problems that promised trouble in the future. "No," said Micheál MacLiammóir, "theatrical gloom ... is never financial merely. It is the gloom of the bringer of unwanted gifts, the despair of the ardent jilted lover."[1] In time, this would prove to be an apt summary of Lord Longford's romance with the Gate Theatre.

MacLiammóir increasingly regarded his theatrical landscape as "shrouded in a rain of hard work and quarrels and bills for canvas and paint and timber and costumes, with no money to pay for them." No box-office money, anyway. Edward, Lord Longford, "nobly stood over the losses of *Agamemnon*, and he was ready with a loan for the Johnston play." He also gave free casting advice, until Hilton Edwards lost his temper and called him "a dilettante."

"You're trying to force the theatre where I don't see it can go," cried the frustrated director, "and lending your own Board the money for your amusement. If a theatre can't pay its own way, let it bloody well close down, and let's do something honest. It's a lousy game anyway. Of course it is! I won't be dictated to about casting, and I won't engage people I don't believe in, and I ... oh, but I suppose I must, I suppose I've got to."

Meanwhile, the comedy of manners onstage was Oscar Wilde's *The Importance of Being Earnest* with MacLiammóir as Algernon and Cyril Cusack as John. Their female counterparts were Betty Chancellor as Cecily

and Ria as Gwendolen. Backstage gossip was never a Mooney characteristic, and her memoirs breathe nary a word about greenroom storm and
strife. She found the "same magic windows on to different places, people
and periods"[2] at the Gate, as she had as a child at Mme. Rock's, in the Rathmines and Rathgar Musical Society as a girl, and in her first years in New
York City with the Civic Repertory Company.

On Tuesday, October 31, Ria played Lady Anne to Hilton Edwards'
lead in *Richard III*. At Christmas, she was one of the fairies in *A Mid-
summer Night's Dream*. She seems to have overcome her fears about
appearing at her age and with her figure in such roles. Holloway heard
from his friend, T. C. Murray, that the playwright's daughter knew one of
the ladies playing a fairy, and she said that they all objected to the costumes they had to wear — a kind of Greek robe — but Hilton Edwards
ignored them. "His word is law," the girl told her father, "and he marshals
them about like puppets."[3] The director had the reputation for being imperious, but Ria responded to his instructions with faith in his judgment
and comfort in his precision.

The first new Gate production of 1934 was Ria's adaptation of the
Brontë novel *Wuthering Heights* with MacLiammóir as Heathcliff, herself
as Catherine Earnshaw, and Edwards directing. She felt that Hilton's direction saved her performance. "I was stilted and stiff from the beginning,"
she said. "One day at rehearsal, having been through the first Act, Hilton
came up to me before we went through it again, 'when you run on for
your first entrance, have nothing on your mind except that you want Nellie to fasten your dress. As it is, in your first lines, you are anticipating
Catherine Earnshaw's reactions throughout the entire play. We'll start
again.' From that entrance until the end I took each scene as it came, and
so, thanks to Hilton's correct observation and helpful direction, I gave
one of my best performances."[4]

It seemed so simple, but it was just the advice she needed. She had
to let go, risk drying up, listen to what others said to her and respond to
them as if she had never heard them say those words before. It helped her
to recover her old sense of ease, naturalness, spontaneity and assurance.
MacLiammóir found she lacked Meriel's "lightness and grace," but she had
"a curious intensity like a steadily burning inner fire, and her acting was
poised, shapely, and full of intelligence."[5] Her head was full of Le Gallienne and Nazimova theories, and "she would labor at some small technical points for hours together and be ready for endless discussion about
the theatre," but she gave "a dark and radiant performance" as Catherine
"that seemed aglow with flame." She loved the novel and delighted in
Micheál's Heathcliff, even though she still believed she wasn't ideally cast

Ria appearing in this early Gate production seems to have overcome her depression about her figure. (Gate Theatre Archive, *McCormick Library of Special Collections*, Northwestern University Library.)

as Catherine, because she felt too small. Holloway wrote in his journal that she "put in some fine acting," as Catherine, and, "as Heathcliff, Micheál MacLiammóir put on a fine piece of creepy acting — speaking his long descriptive speech with thrilling effectiveness."[6]

Two weeks later, Ria played the Bride in Denis Johnston's *Storm Song*, and Holloway found her "one of the gentlest and most lovable old homely women I have ever seen on the stage, and in Scene 4 on making her exit, she gained a round of spontaneous applause, richly deserved...."[7] At the end of February, the Gate featured four one-act plays, including Shaw's *Dark Lady of the Sonnets* with Edwards as Shakespeare, and Eugene O'Neill's *Before Breakfast* with Ria as Mrs. Rowland, the drab nagging wife. She got four curtain calls at the end of her performance. She was back! The season had given her the opportunity to play romantic parts in

Ria as Catherine and Micheál MacLiammóir as Heathcliff in the Gate production of *Wuthering Heights*. (Gate Theatre Archive, *McCormick Library of Special Collections*, Northwestern University Library.)

plays by Shakespeare and Shaw, and best of all, to play the leading role in her own adaptation of *Wuthering Heights*. Her versatility as an actress was evident to all.

Meanwhile, her friends at the Abbey were lamenting the fact that they must go on another extended tour of the States in the fall. Most said they would prefer to remain at home, but they felt compelled to go because they made so much more money touring. Holloway told actress May Craig that "the Dublin public haven't forgiven the Abbey for the Company's last trip to the States, and they leaving the Abbey deserted almost while away. Going again this year for over ten months will be the last straw, I imagine! The Gate has become Dublin's artistic center, and the Abbey merely a visitor's theatre!"[8]

Still, in spite of appearances, things weren't much better at the Gate. Hilton Edwards obviously objected to a wealthy playboy taking over his theatre. He saw Pakenham as an interfering, spoiled amateur with the Gate as his new toy. Ironically, Lord Longford couldn't forgive Hilton Edwards his British nationality! Backstage at the playhouse was explosive. Regulars told a tale of Hilton pulling the paint ladder out from under Micheál because he had tipped a bucket of green paint over him.[9] Rolling around the floor in furious combat, they brought Christine, Lady Longford, down with them. Edward stopped the fight, waving a prop shillelagh over his head and crying out, "The next man to move, I fell to the ground." The Boys were mercurial—flamboyant. Everyone connected with the Gate saw an explosion in the making, but nobody was able to predict when it would come. All Ria could do was enjoy her momentary success and keep a watchful eye.

During the summer of 1934, Dublin was alive with rumors of a power struggle among members of the Abbey board for control of the National Theatre.[10] When the first company of players left for America at the end of September, Lennox Robinson with them, Yeats was persuaded to appoint Blado Peake, an Englishman who had trained at Norwich, as temporary director of production. He opened his reign with a misconceived mounting of *Macbeth*, followed it with Molière's *School for Wives*, Schnitzler's *Gallant Cassian*, and Pirandello's *Six Characters in Search of an Author*. Obviously, the comparisons made by Dublin critics between the Gate and the Abbey repertoires, which always seemed to belittle the Abbey, had forced the Abbey Board into changing its policy. "I doubt if it ever crossed their minds," wrote Frank O'Connor, "that what attracted younger people like myself to that pair of rascals [MacLiammóir and Edwards] was not that they had discovered the key to wealth, but that they were nearly as crazy as Yeats himself had been in his youth and produced what they wanted to produce regardless of anyone's opinion."[11] In any case, the change was a major miscalculation. Receipts fell disastrously, Peake was terminated in January 1935, and the playhouse closed down temporarily.

During that summer of '34, the Gate lost the young and promising Cyril Cusack to the National Theatre, but it retained the services of Ria and added the strikingly handsome James Mason to its ranks. In the fall, when the two playhouses offered competing productions of *Macbeth* and *Julius Caesar*, in Dogberry's words, "the comparisons were 'odorous'" and critical approval went exclusively to the Gate. As Brutus, James Mason made a favorable impact on the Gate's patrons, and, despite MacLiammóir in a leopard-skin leotard as Mark Antony, the acting, direction and settings won unstinting praise.[12]

Ria's first appearance of the season came on Tuesday, November 20, 1934, in *The Provoked Wife*. Holloway thought her impersonation of the role of Belinda "delightfully played." One critic found the 25-year-old Mason "gay, witty, satirical, affectionate by turns." Another reviewer noted that MacLiammóir, who played the bright young spark seeking the affections of Coralie Carmichael, "gave a familiar picture of mincing vivaciousness."[13] Harry Fine, business manager for the Gate, said that "Micheál hated [Mason's] guts, and did everything to make his life miserable."[14] There wasn't room at the Gate for two leading men. For her part, Ria never mentions the backstage tensions of the moment. She was concentrating on preparing for her leading role in *Lady Precious Stream*. It was one of her fondest memories of her time at the Gate.

"When I played Lady Precious Stream," she remembered 35 years later, "I had the wardrobe mistress, Chris Keely, make me long sleeves of white silk, which I wore under those of the embroidered Chinese coat. When I wished to depict sorrow, I would drop my hands from the wrist, allowing the white silk sleeves to cover them as I had seen that wonderful actor — China's greatest — Mei-lang-Fang do when he visited New York at the beginning of the thirties to give his first performance outside China's State Theatre. For joy and laughter the white sleeves were shaken back, hands raised with palms outwards, the face remained expressionless throughout, while the eyes were kept modestly concealed behind lowered lids. I don't think I have ever enjoyed a part so much...."[15]

The authentic embroidered Chinese coat was lent to her by Lord Longford, and, among that huge cast, Holloway found "Ria Mooney's impersonation of 'Precious Stream' the one that reached nearest perfection."[16] James Mason sat to one side of the stage dressed in evening attire, and as "The Honourable Reader" explained all that was taking place on stage. For Ria, this strange play had everything she loved about the theatre:

"characters through whom one could escape from the ordinary, everyday atmosphere. I suppose it is this desire to escape from the realities of day-to-day living which drives many people into the life of the theatre. In the Abbey there was seldom such escape."

Why, then, did she choose this of all moments to abandon the Gate Theatre where she had been so much at home, and return to the Abbey which was experiencing its most severe crisis? "One evening," wrote Ria, "at one of Mrs. Reddin's 'At Homes,' I was approached by F. R. Higgins, who had just been appointed Managing Director of the Abbey. He asked me if I'd be interested in coming back to that theatre in leading parts."[17] Therein lies an important tale untold. "I was temporarily annoyed with Hilton and Micheál," she wrote, "because they were going to visit London, and for the visit they were taking my biggest parts from me. I was therefore wickedly pleased to accept Higgins' offer, and returned to the Abbey on top salary, which, though not very large, and by present-day standards, a mere pittance, was then the best I could receive in Ireland." The Gate's London repertoire consisted of Longford's *Yahoo*, *Hamlet* with MacLiammóir in the lead, and Denis Johnston's *The Old Lady Says "No!"*, all of which had been produced by the troupe before Ria joined them, and in none of which had she any important part. The most plausible reason for her otherwise unaccountable return to the Abbey was attachment to F. R. Higgins.

"In Fred Higgins there entered upon the scene," wrote Hugh Hunt, "a genial, witty and lovable personality; a master of intrigue and a man of considerable ambition. Higgins set out to wean Yeats from his loyalty to Robinson, for if a successor had to be found to the aging poet, there was none more suitable than the man whom Yeats had described as 'undoubtedly the finest of our young poets.'"[18]

"Yeats," wrote Frank O'Connor, "was one of the most devious men I have ever known.... Still, in the matter of deviousness, he was

Sean O'Sullivan's portrait of F. R. Higgins dated 1928. (Julien O'Sullivan and the National Gallery of Ireland.)

a child compared with Higgins. If I had the talent of a comic novelist I should love to describe how that brilliant and delightful man put us all by the ears. Higgins didn't even make a secret of it. He lived in what seemed to be an almost enchanted world of extemporization, imagination, and intrigue."[19]

Holloway tells us he was "speaking to F. R. Higgins and Mrs. at the Abbey. Fred gives a very good imitation of a stout W. B. Yeats in his manner and bearing, and becomes more and more like his model every day."[20] At one point, Holloway thought Higgins had "become as big as the side of a house."

Pictures of Higgins reveal a man of Johnsonian stature with a dark mop of unruly hair, an unsmiling, full face, a cigarette stuck in the left side of his mouth. In the appendix of Ria's memoirs, her editor, Val Mulkerns, has included a Higgins poem entitled *The Ring Maker*, which was missing from the published edition of his last book of poetry, *The Gap of Brightness*. Ria gave Mulkerns a proof copy of that book, which contained the inscription: "To and for dear Ria this only copy of my unexpurgated first edition from Fred Higgins 4.4.40." The final verse of that poem is of special interest.

> "My thanks! For unto her — who yearns with heart
> All reverence for our hushed holy land —
> Whose mind is gentle, passionate and wise
> Deeply in things that share earth's darkest hints—
> For her, this ring; to keep the artist mind
> The stamina of Ireland, upon her hand."[21]

"In the note to me," writes Mulkerns, "which accompanied that proof volume, Ria Mooney wrote: 'I gave up wearing the ring 20 years ago because the silver of that "grey circuit" grew so thin the ring became an oval.'"

Mervyn Wall, playwright and novelist, wrote the following note to Mulkerns on April 16, 1980, shortly after the publication of Ria's autobiography. "I enclose a copy of a poem written for Ria and hung by her on the wall of her 'hut' in Glencree. It was written by F. R. Higgins during their long affair."[22] The poem is dated March 9, 1938.

A Wish for Ria
by F. R. Higgins

> These hills and glens this evening pour
> Their tides of peace toward Ria's door.

O may they for a lifetime shut
Their sunset wealth in Ria's hut.

So, it would appear that Ria returned to the Abbey because of her attachment to F. R. Higgins. She came upon the scene just as the directors were about to begin their offstage version of King Lear and his daughters, with Yeats as the monarch, Higgins and O'Connor as the ungrateful offspring, and the newly appointed director, Hugh Hunt, in a curious piece of miscasting, as Cordelia. Ria's part in the plot was as the silent partner of F. R. Higgins.

Higgins was a poet and heir apparent of W. B. Yeats, and Ria admired Yeats and poets above all others in the theatre. Witty, genial, imaginative, the 39-year-old Higgins was at the beginning of what promised to be an important poetic career. His first book of poetry, *Arable Holdings*, had been put out by Yeats' house organ, the Cuala Press, in 1933. His vision of the Abbey was as a museum created by and for the poetry of Yeats. He had no theatrical background or training, and it seems likely that he consulted Ria about technical matters throughout his campaign to remake the Abbey in a poetic image. There was, however, one drawback to their alliance: Higgins was a married man.

On Monday, April 29, 1935, barely three weeks after her departure from the Gate, Ria appeared in Teresa Deevy's one-act play *The King of Spain's Daughter*. As Annie Kinsella, Ria played a laborer's child with romantic ideas who nearly meets a pitiable end at the hands of a brutal father. Holloway thought she laid "bare the fluttering thoughts that filled her head with great artistry and tact."[23] Cyril Cusack played her lover effectively, but Ann Clery, in a small part, had often to resort to the prompter and it marred the performance. It was evident that the Abbey had few character actors to draw upon with the first company still on tour in the states.

Soon after rejoining the Abbey company that spring, Ria approached Yeats at a directors' meeting with the proposal that she be given the post of teacher of the School of Acting. On August 30, 1935, Holloway was told she had been appointed teacher instead of Michael J. Dolan, and he was surprised. Part of her application was a proposal that the female students dress in simple cotton uniforms, because "self-consciousness could be the main stumbling-block.... Many girls wore expensive and tasteful garments, while some, due to circumstances, could not, and were overcome by embarrassment when they had to stand in front of the others."[24] Ria had accumulated a great deal of experience and knowledge in her first decade of performing. She remembered her own feeling of inferiority as a child of lower middle-class background, required by Abbey custom to use her own attire in contemporary parts. Her teaching instincts had been developed at Le Gallienne's Civic Repertory Theatre; her theories of acting reflected the conversations she had had with the Russian-trained Nazimova.

She tells us that her "plans for an Experimental Theatre ... were accepted unanimously at a General Meeting of the students, and eventually approved by the Board of Directors." She eventually produced Jack Yeats' first play, *Harlequin's Positions*, and she taught her students to speak with intelligence and conviction but with a minimum of movement. Settings were not a vehicle for a stage designer's ego. "Nothing should distract attention from the play as conceived by the writer."[25] Her experience as an actress in three separate theatrical organizations, and her work as Eva Le Gallienne's assistant, had given her an appreciation of how difficult it could be to blend all the elements of play production together.

At the same time, Yeats had resolved his differences with O'Casey and, on August 12, the Abbey produced *The Silver Tassie*. The production created another row: Brinsley MacNamara was forced to resign from the board as a result of some insulting remarks he made about O'Casey, and the Abbey was once again the center of Dublin's attention. It was the last production before Hugh Hunt assumed control of play production.

In September, *A Deuce o' Jacks*, a one-act play by F. R. Higgins, attracted a fashionable crowd. Holloway thought that "a few more such performances and the traditions of the Abbey would be no more."[26] At the end of the month, Hunt gave Dublin two Shaw plays, *Village Wooing*, which featured F. J. McCormick and Ria in three short scenes, as a curtain raiser to the full-length *Candida*. At the Gate, MacLiammóir was appearing in *The Marriage of St. Francis*, which Dublin wits insisted upon referring to as "the St. Francis of a Sissy."[27] Obey's *Noah* arrived in the middle of November but failed to impress, and the promising young writer Frank O'Connor was appointed to the board to replace the departed MacNamara.

The first production of the new year was Shakespeare's *Coriolanus* with the English actor, Reginald Jarman, in the title role. With an English director, and a Russian lady as scene designer, the addition of Jarman to play the lead seemed a clear insult to Abbey actors. Critics complained that Irish plays perfectly played by Irish actors were what was wanted. *Coriolanus* was withdrawn after a week and replaced by George Shiels' *Paul Twyning*. The venture had cost 350 pounds, and receipts for any night rarely exceeded 10 pounds and for the two final performances four pounds and four pounds seven shillings. It was evident even to Hugh Hunt that the current policy "neither recaptured the so-called 'lively minds' who had deserted to the Gate, nor pleased the groundlings of the Abbey."[28] It is interesting that Hunt felt the need to put quotation marks around the lively minds, but not the pejorative "groundlings."

In February, Ria appeared in St. John Ervine's *Boyd Shop* as one of four gossips; the other three included Eileen Crowe, Maureen Delaney, and May Craig. Holloway acknowledged the reassertion of the first company's strength by remarking that "the four made a clucking hen party hard to beat."[29]

Teresa Deevy's play in three acts, *Katie Roche*, opened with some fanfare in the middle of March. The plot concerns a girl of irregular parentage who marries a much older man and continues to philander with her young lover, while retaining a fondness for the elderly man. Though the play was sensational in content, greenroom gossip seemed mostly taken up with the angry split at the Gate between Lord Longford and MacLiammóir and Edwards over the Boys' projected tour to Egypt. The troupe left Dublin on February 20 warned by Longford that they must bear the entire financial risk of the tour themselves.[30] They planned on opening in Cairo on March 10. In an attempt to gain financial independence from Longford, the Boys were now forced to tour just as the Abbey had done in order to make ends meet. The acrimony of the split forced Dublin's theatrical community to take sides. Ria seems to have remained aloof, engrossed by her romance and the intrigues behind the scenes at the Abbey.

In fact, the conflict backstage at the Abbey appears to have been far more exciting than the action onstage. Hunt wore a red, white, and blue rosette in the theatre on King George's jubilee day, infuriating Higgins. Hunt gave an interview to an English paper and described Higgins and O'Connor as Red revolutionaries, "determined on turning the theatre towards [their] own political aims." O'Connor had turned on his old friend and supporter, Lennox Robinson, because he had come to believe that most of the theatre's mismanagement was traceable to him. The playhouse had two directors, Robinson for the Irish plays and Hunt for the European. The imported classics failed to attract attention, and Robinson insisted there weren't any new Irish plays worth mounting. Such an attack upon Irish writing was bound to offend the feelings of writers like O'Connor and O'Faolain. Everyone seemed bent on offending everyone else.[31]

On Monday night, August 10, 1936, Yeats came to the Abbey to see his play *Deirdre* performed as the curtain raiser before Deevy's *The King of Spain's Daughter*. Ria played the first musician and Holloway thought that she "spoke the opening lines with clearness and beauty, and set all that followed a headline of clear articulation in which they strictly followed."[32] Unfortunately, Yeats missed the diction and intoning of the original Abbey production and scolded Hunt for emphasizing the play's worth as theatre at the expense of its verse. The production was not retained for a second week even though it was profitable. Hunt blamed Higgins and O'Connor for thwarting him at every turn. Ria was said to be disheartened by the way Frank O'Connor interfered with her work in the School of Acting, and O'Connor maintained he was just trying to get Robinson a job since he was no longer managing the main company. Holloway was philosophical about the rumors of the Abbey's imminent demise. "The Abbey has seen many ups and downs," he wrote, "and has come through them all."[33]

Hunt summed up the situation as follows: "Higgins and O'Connor set out to neutralize Robinson, and at the same time to neutralize each other.... Although intent on playing a martyr's part, Robinson was quite capable of emerging from his despondency to strike an effective — and surprisingly venomous— blow at his warring colleagues. Meanwhile, Blythe the inscrutable watched and waited."[34] It was pure melodrama, and, as the Abbey seemed to be crumbling about them, the participants appeared to be having the time of their lives.

The fall season of 1936 began with a new play by Cormac O'Daly entitled *The Silver Jubilee*. It failed and was immediately replaced by a revival of *The Plough and the Stars*. The second week in October brought George Shiels' hit comedy, *The Jailbird*, which was succeeded by Teresa Deevy's new play, *The Wild Goose*. The Abbey had two crowd-pleasers in a row, relieving the strain on the production budget.

Deevy's plot hinges upon the decision of a young man whether to be a priest, get married or go to France. Ria played the wild young girl who has fallen madly in love with "Martin." She was praised for her performance in a part that many thought suited her style. During Christmas week, the Abbey opened Denis Johnston's *Blind Man's Buff*, a murder mystery, with a wonderfully tense trial sequence, that seemed to grip the audience interest throughout its three acts. Three new plays in three months had found favor with Dublin audiences. The acting was uniformly praised, the box office booming, and the backstage bickering overshadowed by the abrupt reversal of playhouse fortunes.

On Monday, January 25, 1937, Paul Vincent Carroll's *Shadow and Substance* cast its spell over the city and promised to run forever.[35] The plot revolves around a little girl servant of a foreign-trained and sophisticated Irish canon, who stuns the priest by her testimony that she has visions of St. Brigid. As the servant, 16-year-old Phyllis Ryan captured the hearts of Abbey regulars, and Arthur Shields astonished them with his transforming make-up and austere comportment as Canon Sherrit. Ria received praise for her portrait of the scheming Jemima Cooney, and Cyril Cusack was a successful schoolmaster. In all, the Abbey had an undisputed triumph on its hands just as the Gate Company was deserting the city for another tour of Cairo.

What better time for Fred Higgins to reverse the happy trend by taking off *Shadow and Substance* and replacing it with *Songs and Poems*, which was not even a play but a recital of works by Yeats, James Stephens, and, of course, F. R. Higgins. Thus was failure snatched from the jaws of success!

O'Casey's farce, *The End of the Beginning*, opened in the first week of February and disappointed an expectant and socially prominent crowd. When the *Irish Times* critic panned the play, O'Casey dashed off another of his epistolary salvos that delighted the city's gossips and kept the Abbey's name before the public. Easter week witnessed the opening of Shiels' *Quin's Secret*, another delightful comedy that packed the houses and amused everyone. Lennox Robinson's *Killycreggs in Twilight*, a Big House play about two sisters and nephew clinging to the old order of things, opened on Monday evening, April 19, 1937, with Ria and Christine Hayden as the sisters and Cyril Cusack as the nephew. Three weeks later, Maura Molloy's melodrama, *Who Will Remember...?* attracted "a great gathering of the clans at the Abbey."[36] Valerian Hall, the family seat of the "Pommerys," is a haunted house with strange inmates. Ria was "Cressida Pommery," a woman with a mad streak who becomes vindictive when those around her oppose her wild love affairs. It was a large, physically and emotionally taxing role in which Ria was generally agreed to have acquitted herself well.

It had been a busy and prosperous fall, winter, 1936, and spring, 1937, for Ria and her colleagues at the Abbey. In all, from October till May, the Abbey had mounted nine new plays by eight different playwrights, three of whom, O'Casey, Shiels, and Robinson, were established Abbey playwrights; and three others, Deevy, Carroll, and Johnston, had given the theatre their first popular efforts. Ria had played leading roles in three of the nine new productions, and had appeared in significant character parts in two others. Was she surprised when she heard the Abbey was to go on another American tour from August 1937 to April 1938, or had Higgins arranged the trip himself? Was it an accident that he went out with the touring company as manager?

"On the way out to America," Ria wrote in her memoirs, "I hung over the rail one day, watching the sea and talking to F. R. Higgins. From this conversation, we discovered we were related."[37] The next two pages of her memoirs provide an elaborate deception which appears to have been created by her need to speak about her love for Higgins. It is both difficult to follow and seems a melancholy form of self-justification. A reader unacquainted with the subtext might pause and wonder why such a dull and unimportant story is inserted so late in the book, while anyone acquainted with the affair can hardly help smiling at, and perhaps empathizing with, this forlorn attempt at memorializing Higgins.

In any case, the company opened its American tour in New York City on October 2, 1937, and remained there, playing its seven play repertoire through the new year.[38] Ria was now playing Pegeen Mike in Synge's *Playboy*. Her interpretation of the Mayo termagant leaned toward the hard and aggressive peasant girl, rather than the conventional vivacious and vulnerable beauty. Yeats and Sinclair Lewis, the successful American novelist, "seemed to see beneath the player's personality to the mental interpretation." They approved of her portrait, but the critics ignored her and concentrated their attention on F. J. McCormick.

The rest of the repertoire consisted of two plays each by O'Casey and Robinson, and one each by Deevy and Shiels. Ria played Rosie Redmond again in *The Plough and the Stars*, and Amelia Gregg in *Katie Roche*. In *Drama at Inish*, Robinson's satirical portrait of a self-dramatizing Russian leading lady, a la Nazimova, Ria had fun with Constance Constantia, the queen of a summer resort theatre. For the fifth offering, she played a small character part in Hunt's adaptation of Frank O'Connor's short story, *In a Train*. The continental tour left her with memories of a "sandy desert near Phoenix, Arizona: great ships at rest in the Harbour of San Diego; luncheon at Paramount Studios in Hollywood; the atmosphere of old-time Charleston, where we had lunch with Marc Connelly," who was enjoying the success of his recent Broadway hit, *Green Pastures*.[39]

She remembered traveling by train across what seemed the endlessly flat and monotonous prairies, until she awoke one morning high in the Sierra Nevada mountains, which were "deep in snow. We could sometimes see crawling along the delicate-looking wooden trestles that carried the rails over ravines ... men in trucks ... in front of our engine, tapping the rails to make sure they were secure...." She was terrified and resolved to get drunk before the return passage began. She adored San Francisco, the redwood forest, visiting Chinatown, and Fisherman's Wharf. She credited Higgins with promoting F. J. McCormick, who had previously stood in Barry Fitzgerald's shadow. Ria was happy to see that great actor receiving his due at last.

The leisurely days on trains and ships are referred to only once in

her memoirs, and then in relation
to her discovery that she and Higgins were related. She appears to
have enjoyed her travels in America, and one can only suppose
that Higgins had something to do
with her happy memories. The
relations between F. R. Higgins
and the Abbey board back home
were nothing like so cordial.

"In America," O'Connor
tells us, "Higgins simply ignored
our cables, though after a month
or so I got one report from him
which was a masterpiece of wild
humour, but told me nothing we
really wanted to know." Blythe
wanted to fire Higgins, but Yeats
objected, saying that "you can't
buy a genius for three pounds
a week." O'Connor said Yeats

Frank O'Connor is best known as one of
Ireland's premier authors of the short
story. (G. A. Duncan.)

"merely wanted someone to keep that wretched touring company out of
our hair while Hunt went on with the real business of the theatre."[40]

Higgins was not the only member of the board having trouble keeping his eye on theatrical affairs. While the December production of Sean
O'Faolain's first play, *She Had to Do Something* was being rehearsed,
O'Connor also felt the need to do something, but it only peripherally
related to acting. Evelyn Bowen was the attractive and talented wife of the
actor and author, Robert Speaight. Though her stage experience was
confined to amateur theatre, she was hired to play the part of a French-
woman who invites a company of Russian ballet dancers to visit an Irish
provincial town.[41] The players threatened a strike over this suggestion that
they were capable of playing nothing but Irish parts. O'Connor dissuaded
them from taking the action, arguing that such a public act would be dis-
courteous to a guest. When he eloped with the Mrs. Speaight, he managed to not only shock Dublin's sense of propriety, but he undermined
his position on the board and, eventually, was forced to withdraw from
the playhouse and Ireland. It is not surprising that O'Connor failed to
develop this incident in his own account of the Abbey wars.

Events now began to take on a life of their own. On 12 successive
evenings in August 1938, 17 plays, lectures on the Abbey and its dramatists,

and exhibitions of pictures and manuscripts connected with the theatre were presented to an admiring American, British, and Continental public. On August 10, Yeats' *Purgatory* was presented, and, "when, at the end, the familiar white-haired figure walked onto the stage, no longer as upright as in former days, a wave of emotion seemed to sweep through the audience, for the Festival was a salute to the theatre he had inspired, and *Purgatory* was his farewell to Ireland."[42]

In September, the board agreed to acknowledge Higgins as Yeats' heir, appointing him managing director. The first sign that there was trouble in the Abbey boardroom appeared on the night Lennox Robinson's new play, *Bird's Nest,* opened that same month. Robinson came on stage for the usual curtain speech. "Alas," wrote Holloway, "he was well oiled as usual!"[43] In October, Yeats left Ireland for the more salubrious climate of the French Riviera. With Yeats away in Menton, Robinson in his cups, and O'Connor's influence waning, a divided board decided to reject Paul Vincent Carroll's new play, *The White Steed,* because it might prove offensive to the priesthood. The board next rejected Yeats' *The Herne's Egg* on the grounds of obscenity. O'Connor opposed the rejection, and Ernest Blythe voted with him. He did so, he said, because the play was so obscure that no one would notice that it was obscene.[44]

Hunt resigned his position at the Abbey in November to direct *The White Steed* in New York with Barry Fitzgerald, Jessica Tandy, and Liam Redmond. The final blow came on Saturday, January 29, 1939. On that day, William Butler Yeats died in southern France at the age of 73.

"With Yeats permanently gone," wrote Frank O'Connor, "I began now to realize that mediocrity was in control, and against mediocrity there is no challenge or appeal. Higgins was a good poet, but he couldn't produce a child's recitation."[45] Ria and her poet must have been saddened by the loss of their hero, but they were probably consoled by the knowledge that Higgins had inherited the leader's mantle, and with it control of the theatre he was said to have created. They stood together now at the head of the Abbey, Ireland's National Theatre.

In March 1939, Holloway wrote the following in his journal. "I greatly fear there is nobody in Ireland today fit to step into the shoes of the late W. B. Yeats. We have a young poet here, who is Managing Director of the Abbey Theatre just now, who apes all the outward mannerisms of the late poet: wears his hair similarly, dresses like him, and walks and gesticulates like him. But as he is bulky of frame, his figure only bears an inflated version of W. B. Yeats. F. R. Higgins is his name and he has written some quite good poetry, but it takes more than a clever impersonation of genius to be mistaken for one."[46]

The death of Yeats was not the only trouble to descend upon the play-house that year. F. J. McCormick's health seems to have broken down, and he had to give up a principal part in Louis D'Alton's new play, *Tomorrow Never Comes*, which opened on March 16. On September 3, 1939, war broke out on the Continent and the Irish government declared its neutrality. Now began the dreary round of shortages of electricity, coal, gasoline and clothing that plagued civilian life for the next five years. Paul Vincent Carroll's new play, *Kindred*, opened at the end of September, but it failed to impress the crowd of celebrities assembled to welcome back the rejected author. George Shiels' *Give Him a House* opened at the end of October, and it was the first Shiels play in several years to fail to find an audience. The depressing year ended with the loss of one of the Abbey's most talented actresses, Miss Frolie Mulhern, who died suddenly on Friday, November 17.

With Europe in flames, Louis D'Alton's *A Spanish Soldier* seemed a fitting first new play of 1940. The plot conflict revolves around the return of a young husband from the Spanish war, who discovers his brother has fallen in love with his wife during his absence. Ria played the young wife, Hessy, and Cyril Cusack her husband. The generally good notices for players and playwright relieved some of the gloom produced by the recent run of bad luck. In mid–April Elizabeth Connon's *Mount Prospect*, adapted from her novel which had been banned in the Free State, brought controversy once again to the playhouse. Stepbrothers love the same girl, and, after one of them seduces her, she dies in a car crash, one brother kills the other, and almost does away with the stepmother. "Ria Mooney," wrote Holloway, after witnessing the opening night performance, "[as Mrs. Kennefick] dominated the play as she did the family. Hers was a great achievement and one to go down in the stage history of the Abbey."[47] When, on August 5, 1940, the Abbey opened George Shiels' mystery, *The Rugged Path*, the National Theatre seemed to be back on track.

Holloway thought that *The Rugged Path* proclaimed George Shiels a great dramatist.[48] Always good at character study, with dialogue that "was ever witty and wise, in his latest he is a clear thinker as well." By the end of September, the play had played to 20,000 patrons, double the attendance of the Abbey's previous longest-running hit, *Blind Man's Buff*. The play continued until October 26, 1940, filling the house even on its closing night. F. J. McCormick, who had a leading role in the piece, was happy at the continued success of the play, which he thought was creating a new audience for the playhouse. The old Abbey crowd had dropped off or died out, and the war had closed off British road companies to Dublin, so the local theatre was the only entertainment open to isolated Ireland.

On Monday, December 9, Francis Stuart's *Strange Guest* was hailed as a fine play "supremely well played by the entire cast of eight."[49] The strange guest of the title is a nun who has been turned out of her community and finds a place in the house of a wealthy family. It is the reaction of each member of the family as they come into contact with this saintly figure that provides the action of the play. Ria was praised for her "beautiful rendering of the character of the nun." Holloway reported in his journal that "the dialogue was splendid and the thronged audience listened to it with rapt silence that was eloquent — a stillness that could be felt."

In spite of the wartime conditions and isolation imposed upon Ireland by the European conflict, Ria had a right to be pleased with her theatrical life. She had received great praise for her last two leading roles, had a good part in Shiels' long-running hit, and her poet, despite intense criticism by Dublin's artistic insiders, was presiding over one of the Abbey's most successful seasons.

On Wednesday, January 8, 1941, Holloway called at the film censor's office and met Dr. Richard Hayes, longtime member of the Abbey governing board and an old friend. His greeting profoundly shocked the Abbey regular.

"I suppose you heard," he said, "that F. R. Higgins died this morning?"[50]

CHAPTER FIVE

"Even the Spring Is Old"

The demise of F. R. Higgins surprised and shocked Dublin Society. "The old laugh was still with him," said his playwright friend, Brinsley MacNamara, "and it is only a week ago that I found him almost as gay as ever, and all for making light of his illness."[1]

Beneath a thin-faced portrait of the poet, the *Irish Times* of Thursday, January 9, 1941, described his passing. "Mr. Higgins, who had been suffering from heart trouble for some time, collapsed on Tuesday morning while transacting business near Jervis Street Hospital, and he was taken to the hospital in a very serious condition. Shortly after admission he became unconscious. He died shortly before four o'clock yesterday morning."[2]

Born Frederick Robert Higgins in April 1896, he had spent his formative years in Meath, where he was to be buried. His poem entitled "Auction" had recounted the sale of his beloved home in Higginsbrook, County Meath.

> A house of ghosts and that among
> Gardens where even the Spring is old;
> So gather round, the sale is on,
> And nods and winks spell out in gold,
> Going, going, gone.

Now, *he* was gone. The *Times* credited him with changing Abbey policy from frequent revivals to the almost exclusive production of new plays. "Mr. Higgins," it said, "expressed the opinion that there were enough plays being written to enable the Abbey to continue almost indefinitely without ever repeating anything of more than a year old." There was praise for the 12-week run of George Shiels' *The Rugged Path*, and acknowledgment of the appeal Higgins made to young audiences.

The obituary concluded with a list of Higgins' writings and awards, and the simple statement of those left behind to mourn. "In 1921, he married Miss Beatrice May, only daughter of the late James Moore, of Clontarf, who survives him. Both his mother and his wife were with him when he died."

On Thursday evening, the cortege left Jervis Street Hospital for St. Mary's Church, Mary Street, Dublin, passing the Abbey, where it was joined by many of Higgins' literary and

Frank Dermody

artistic associates. Following the hearse were his widow, mother, brother, sisters, and niece; then the Abbey directors, Robinson, Hayes, Blythe, and O'Farachain; the playwrights T. C. Murray, Rutherford Mayne, Austin Clarke, and Brinsley MacNamara; the painter Jack Yeats and Judge K. Reddin; Sean O'Faolain and Frank O'Connor; the acting company of F. J. McCormick, Eileen Crowe, Denis O'Dea, M. J. Dolan and Frank Dermody.[3] Lost in the crowd was Ria Mooney. It was the only public expression of sorrow given to her to make.

Higgins had written a memorial poem for Padraic O Conaire, a writer he loved. Did Ria hear the broadcast on Radio Eireann in which MacNamara read it as an elegy for the poet himself?

> Alas, death mars the parchment of his forehead;
> And yet for him, I know, the earth is mild—
> The windy fidgets of September grasses
> Can never tease a mind that loved the wild;
> So drink his peace—this grey juice of the barley
> Runs with a light that ever pleased his eye—
> While old flames nod and gossip on the hearthstone
> And only the young winds cry.[4]

Ria Mooney was not one "to nod and gossip on the hearthstone." She had lost a romantic escort, also a friend at court in the National Theatre. It was a severe personal and professional blow.

In her memoirs, she encapsulates significant developments in her theatrical life in one confusing page. "W. B. Yeats died in France in 1939," she wrote, "and Fred Higgins, who had conscientiously tried to carry on the theatre in the way that Yeats would have wished, died in 1941. The new Managing Director was Ernest Blythe."[5] The contrast between Higgins and Blythe could not have been more pronounced. Higgins was a romantic Anglophile poet; Blythe a dour Gaelic lover.

"Some little time after" the mourning of these January days, Ria noted a sad conversation that took place in the Abbey greenroom one evening during an interval. "We were all very depressed. George Moore's words, we felt, were coming true. He had said that the Abbey would last only as long as Yeats lived, and rightly or wrongly, we all thought that the Abbey would cease to be the Theatre that Yeats had visualized, now that Higgins, too, had gone."

When the next act was announced, she "began talking to F. J. McCormick who, like myself, did not yet have to appear on the stage. He had taken no part in the previous discussion, but I refused to be put off by his silence and asked him, for the sake of an old friendship, to tell me if we were all quite wrong in believing that the Abbey Theatre was coming to the end of its days. He rose from his chair, this man whose nature was completely free of rancour, and said, deeply moved: 'Ria, I have ceased to care what happens to the Abbey Theatre,' and quickly left the room. I felt this was the end. After that discussion in the greenroom, I left the Abbey...."

The conversation captured her despair about the future of the Abbey without Higgins and W. B. Yeats. McCormick was not alone. Frank O'Connor remarked that, with Yeats "permanently gone, I began now to realize that mediocrity was in control...." Of course, one might observe that Higgins had beaten O'Connor for control of the Abbey, embittering him in the process. Now Ria was forced to watch Higgins' place being taken by a man with whom she had nothing in common, personally or professionally. Once Blythe got control, she felt no longer welcome, even though she remained with the company until 1944.

Blythe's critics blamed his presence on "the Nationalist-Catholic establishment — Christmas pantomimes in Gaelic guying the ancient sagas that Yeats had restored, and enlivened with Blythe's Gaelic versions of popular songs and vulgar farces."[6] Blythe, genuinely attached to the Irish language, thought it could be revived if people could be induced to sing popular songs in it. O'Connor found Blythe's Irish translation of "I Got a Gal in Kalamazoo" "peculiar." O'Connor complained that "one by one they lost their great actors and replaced them with Irish speakers; one by one, as the members of the Board died or resigned, they replaced these with civil servants and lesser party politicians."

Whether Blythe's ascendancy blighted the theatrical landscape, there is no doubt that Higgins's passing left Ria unprotected at the Abbey. Her feelings of isolation were further exacerbated by Ireland's neutrality in the war. The "emergency" contributed to a general malaise throughout the country, and it had an especially adverse effect upon Dublin's artistic community.

Betty Chancellor, a leading lady at the Gate, wrote colorful descriptions of Dublin in those early years of the "emergency" to Denis Johnston, now a BBC war correspondent. "Life is so drab here, and the country does get one down a bit. Things like scabies, a skin disease got from dirt, are rife in Dublin. The gas goes off at 7 at night. The buses stop at 9.30. We have barley flour which is nearly white and madly constipating."[7]

The monthly periodical *The Bell* in 1942 predicted "scurvy, rickets and kindred diseases because we are unable to get a properly balanced diet."[8] While there was enough meat for anyone able to pay for it on the black market, the unavailability of tobacco was depressing. Rural Ireland suffered less from food shortages. Some even found the isolation attractive. "Looking back on it," wrote John Ryan, "there was a lot to be said for the times.... The goodness of simple things was emphasised rather than diminished by the absence of superfluous luxuries. The country was clean, uncluttered and unhurried."[9]

During the war years, European and English exiles gave Dublin "a certain international atmosphere." Patrick Campbell thought "Dublin almost seemed to have a special duty, in a world gone grey and regimented, to preserve the gaieties and pleasures that we felt had vanished from everywhere else."[10]

Against these ameliorating circumstances must be placed the alienation experienced by Anglo-Irishmen who joined with the British to fight in World War II. Casting their loyalties with England, they felt neutrality placed them in a false position. Betty Chancellor adopted Denis Johnston's ambiguous nationality when she wrote to him that "this city is dying. The frightful censorship and narrowness is sapping the life out of everything, and there is nobody to fight a battle because the place is full of drunken Blitz Gaels and Queens...."[11]

The Gaiety Theatre, which in normal times would have played host to English touring companies, brought Gate productions of West End and

Broadway comedies and thrillers to its patrons.[12] As with *The Rugged Path* at the Abbey, Gate productions of American comedies like *Arsenic and Old Lace* and *The Man Who Came to Dinner* played long runs to large audiences attracting customers who had never been to the theatre before. The Dublin theatre public was changing. Isolation from international productions of plays and films forced those seeking entertainment to try their luck with the Dublin stage.

Meanwhile, the Abbey found a new favorite in Louis D'Alton, son of Charles D'Alton, a comedian and actor-manager. His play, *The Money Doesn't Matter*, ran for eight weeks and remained in the Abbey's repertory as one of the company's great successes. Five months later, D'Alton's *Lovers' Meeting* scored another success. With the successful Shiels sequel to *The Rugged Path* entitled *The Summit*, and new plays by MacNamara and Robinson, the playhouse seemed, despite Ria's gloomy greenroom predictions, to be doing quite well.

Perhaps to assuage her grief, or because the Abbey's regular patrons were complaining of being shut out by the policy of long runs, Ria was asked in 1942 to stage a revival of Padraic Colum's *The Fiddler's House*.[13] Although the play was to have a single Sunday night performance, she threw herself into the mounting of the piece, introducing color to match the poet's conception of Irish farm life. She asked scene designer, Michael Clarke, to give her a realistic farmhouse, and the kitchen scene was decorated by a buttercup yellow cotton table cloth that she brought from home. Stimulated by that splash of color, Clarke painted the wooden settle beside the fire with rose tints, "on which the flames reflected a warm glow." Violet curtains on the windows, a dresser painted black, two girls in colored skirts "with bodices of blue and purple, green and red," and a Fiddler in a "corduroy cut-away that had become golden from age" completed the color scheme. When Ria heard that a revival of *The Playboy* was planned, she went to Blythe with the suggestion that Sean Keating, of the Royal Hibernian Academy, be asked to do the designs for the sets and costumes. The management agreed, and director Frank Dermody made no protest. Ria remembered the brightness of the production with great fondness.

She was delighted by murmurs from the audience when, as the Widow Quinn, she made her first entrance wearing "a large tortoise-shell comb stuck in my straight black hair, and an embroidered Spanish shawl around my shoulders." She ignored criticism that she had gone outside the traditional costume to show off. Her father recalled that, as a young man, he had seen in Galway "some gayer females arriving into the city with Spanish combs and embroidered shawls, worn with their red homespun petticoats."

Whether as a result of her achievement with this special performance, or because the playwright, Roibeard O Farachain, was playing the lead in his own verse play, *Assembly at Druim Ceat*, and wanted Ria's sympathetic hand at the helm, she was asked to prepare the play for March 1943. During that season, Ria also agreed to help poet and playwright Austin Clarke and O Farachain direct verse drama at the Dublin Verse Speaking Society.[14] They knew of her love of drama in verse, and they persuaded her that her charge would merely be "to make out movements and act in the capacity of stage-manager." Clarke helped with the casting, but otherwise she was left to make all the theatrical decisions herself.

Although surrounded by enthusiastic and dedicated members, Ria discovered that integrity and talent were not enough in actors playing large roles. They must have that "elusive quality called stage personality which enables one person more than the other to reach over the footlights and attract the public." Since there wasn't even enough money to buy tea for the cast, they were unable to mount strong physical presentations. Ria was convinced that the only solution rested in replacing poets with actors in the leading roles.

Despite all her theatrical acumen, Ria was disappointed in the final product. "I must confess," she wrote, "I found them — or some of them — very dull." Her happiest memories of her work in what became the Dublin Lyric Theatre were first productions of Donagh McDonagh's *Happy as Larry* and T. S. Eliot's *Sweeney Agonistes*.

March 1944 found her once again in the Abbey director's chair for George Shiels' comedy *The New Regime*, a play she thought "not particularly good." The Abbey play list of the period shows an enormous increase in the production of plays in Irish. Obviously, Blythe's influence in choosing scripts and actors emphasized a language which was foreign to Ria. At the same time, her forays into directing reawakened an interest that had lain dormant for a decade. So, when Louis Elliman, managing director of Dublin's Gaiety Theatre, asked her to direct plays and form a Gaiety School of Acting, she had no trouble making the choice. Her heart had left the Abbey in January 1941.

Louis Elliman owned and operated the 1,200 seat Gaiety Theatre.[15] Before the war, the Gaiety had been home to English professional touring companies, now excluded by visa difficulties and the dangers of sea travel. Elliman wisely signed MacLiammóir and Edwards to six week engagements in the fall and the spring to supplement the local musical presentations of the Rathmines and Rathgar Musical Society. Ria had the pleasure of seeing her adaptation of *Wuthering Heights* revived by the Boys at the Gaiety with great popular success.

Ria as Lady Kitty in the Gaiety Theatre production of Somerset Maugham's *The Circle.* (University of Delaware Library Special Collections.)

Ria's renewed zest for theatre was immediately felt backstage at the Gaiety. She auditioned 500 applicants for the acting school, staged a full-scale production of Heijermann's *The Good Hope*, and, because there were some students left over, she threw in Robinson's one-act play, *Crabbed Youth and Age* for good measure. As if that weren't enough, she rehearsed the bill with two different casts, one to play a Sunday matinee and the other the evening performance. Ria's efforts won approval from Elliman, who chided his son for practicing deception on the public. The old man considered the players professionals. When Louis saw the evening presentation, he was embarrassed by people "coming to him and congratulating him on the wonderful players he had gathered together." Among the new faces Ria selected and trained were Milo O'Shea, Anna Manahan, Marie Keane, and Jack McGowran. All distinguished themselves in the entertainment world in the next two decades.[16]

When the war ended, Ria expected Elliman would again re-enlist cross-channel companies for the Gaiety. Audiences would be unlikely to accept her young students on the main stage once London theatre arrived in Dublin. In any case, an actors' union had been organized in Dublin in 1942, and, with the emergency over, they would not allow poorly paid apprentices to drive down the wages of seasoned performers. However, if London theatre folk were about to invade Ireland, there seemed every reason to suppose that Irish actors might return the favor. It was clear that the relative stability of the war years was to be radically altered.

In 1946, Ria received a visit backstage at the Gaiety from Bronson Albery and his wife, Una. "She was the daughter of T. W. Rolleston," Ria recalled. Rolleston was "one of those Anglo-Irish, like Yeats, Synge and the Countess Markiewicz who were ready to give up everything for Ireland."[17] Ria was still impressed by social pedigree, though what was left of it after the Civil War was in ruins after World War II. They had come to Dublin to engage a director for the London production of Sean O'Casey's play, *Red Roses for Me*, and they wanted her to undertake the task.

The irascible but kindly Sean O'Casey, who had given her five pounds to remain a week longer in London two decades before, had become a belligerent hermit in Devon. Perhaps her memory of his generosity to her accounts for Ria's temerity in daring to suggest cuts in his dialogue. Whatever her thoughts in the matter, after studying the script and before starting rehearsals, Ria wrote the playwright suggesting excisions. While she loved his "grinding our bums to power on the pavements of Dublin streets," she found "the face, the dear face that once was smooth is wrinkled now" embarrassingly sentimental. She apparently hadn't satisfied O'Casey that her reasons for wanting to cut his lines were valid, because he sent her "lengthy letters of vituperation, ... each letter stamped with the words, 'Friends of the Soviet Union.'"

Bronson Albery suggested that Ria visit O'Casey in Totnes for a few days before beginning rehearsals, but the playwright wrote her a "vicious letter" declaring he had no desire to see her. Undeterred, Ria asserted that as her "aim was the success of the production, and as his must be the success of the play," she had better see him before rehearsals began. The invitation, as short as the other letters were long, was grudgingly renewed.

She was met at the station by Eileen O'Casey and one of her sons. Once at the "comfortable, well-run Irish middle-class home," she was escorted to a large table set for tea. There was no sign of O'Casey himself. Eileen explained that he was resting. When he appeared without introduction, she was so glad to see him that she forgot herself and threw her arms around his neck. Obviously touched, O'Casey reverted to the kind curmudgeon she had known in her youth.

They talked about the play, got through a costume problem about color, which the author explained away by declaring that he was "color-blind." When she checked her script the next day, she discovered that the misunderstanding had been her fault and not O'Casey's.

After tea, they retired to his study and Ria told him what she wanted in the production, describing a scene in Act II "where a stone shatters the window, and Mullcanny, Roory and Brennan dive for cover...." She thought they should leave their hiding places in positions that mimicked the animals they spoke of in their dialogue: "Mullcanny with bent knees and arms dangling by his sides, Roory like a hobbled goat, and Brennan wriggling like a python on the floor."

"You needn't say another word," said O'Casey. "You understand my play."

Although Ria appeared to have bearded the lion in his den, O'Casey's intimidating spirit hung ominously over rehearsals. Act III of *Red Roses for Me*, composed in the playwright's most uncompromisingly expressionistic style, is a disturbing mood swing from the other three realistic acts. Ria knew it retarded the play's pace and did nothing for the plot itself, but she "hadn't the courage to face Sean and tell him." Some of her hard-won confidence seemed to be fading away, and she even worried that maybe it was her own fault.

Bronson Albery told her that, if the scene remained as it was, the play's failure was guaranteed. Eileen O'Casey, her husband's surrogate at rehearsals, was enlisted to phone and break the news of further cuts to her spouse, and, to everyone's great relief, he gave his consent.

The play was not expected to be a commercial success. The most anyone predicted was a two or three week run. When the play continued to attract audiences for 17 weeks, Ria acquired a reputation as an effective director, one who could handle a difficult playwright and demonstrate a sophisticated grasp of the director's craft.

To her delight, Ria was invited to spend every weekend during the preparation for *Red Roses for Me* at the Tudor farmhouse of the Alberys' in Hertfordshire. "It was my first experience of living in ideal circumstances in a 'bit of old England.' I adored it!" After the opening, she "did the rounds of Chelsea's nightlife with dear Ethel Mannin's husband." Ethel was a popular novelist of the day, who had lived for many years in Connemara.

One disappointment she had to deal with was the lack of discipline in the company. Some of the backstage staff had been entertaining friends in the club attached to the theatre, and had missed lighting and sound cues. She called a Saturday morning run-through and restored the production to opening-night standard. Again, after a short tour, when the production returned to the New Theatre, she was horrified to find overacting and the tossing off of lines with apparent disinterest in the audience's reaction. Since it would cost too much to replace the offenders, there was nothing she could do about it. While these developments onstage did not diminish her reputation as a rising star, they sent her back to Dublin and the Gaiety Theatre "utterly depressed."

Soon after her return to the Gaiety, Louis Elliman asked her to put on *Red Roses for Me*. Remembering the expensive and authentic treatment

Byrd had given the London production, Ria was reluctant to return to the modest settings available in Dublin playhouses. Unable to alter the scenic circumstances, she stirred things up by casting Noel Purcell as Brennan of the Moor. A popular female impersonator as a vaudeville performer, Purcell had little experience in straight plays. Even his friends thought this casting would do both the player and the play irreparable harm. As it turned out, his performance proved Ria's intuition correct, and provided him with an audition for a very successful film career.

Her English sojourn had established Ria Mooney as a gifted director. No one seemed surprised when she was given the assignment of directing the American play *Winterset* with Broadway and screen star Burgess Meredith and his glamorous wife Paulette Goddard in the leading roles. She hadn't seen much of Meredith since their youthful endeavors at Eva Le Gallienne's Civic Theater, but he had not forgotten that it was Ria who had given him his first theatrical opportunity. Mercurial Micheál MacLiammóir was also in the cast, but the only player that gave her heart palpitations when she thought of directing him was MacLiammóir's brother-in-law, Anew McMaster.

A theatrical legend in rural Ireland, the actor known simply as Mac had headed his own company, playing the great Shakespearean roles for a quarter century. Dublin cognoscenti called him the world's worst "ham." Ria wondered how she might give him even the most timid of suggestions on how to play a scene. She needn't have worried. She was genuinely touched by his humility and surprised at the gratitude he showed for any direction she offered him. "The only difficulty I had with him," she said, "was convincing him that he could certainly act." She thought of him afterwards as "possibly one of the world's great actors" and paid him a generous tribute in her memoirs: "...as usual in Ireland, he died without hearing or reading the word 'great' used by a critic to describe him — at least, I never read in a Dublin newspaper this just verdict on him, from those who could have helped him to the position he deserved."[18]

While Ria resented this Dublin snub of a dedicated actor who had haunted the Irish countryside with his bravura Shakespearean renditions, delighting the common Irish folk. She also expressed annoyance at the lack of recognition scenic and lighting designers received from critics and audiences. Interested in scenic and lighting details of her productions, Ria never failed to praise those who helped her achieve the desired effect. She recalled with special delight the mood Gaiety lighting director Harry Morrison produced for her production of *The Dybbuk*. "I had told him I wanted the first scene so dimly lit," she remembered, "that it was only when the characters spoke that I would like their faces to be seen — I directed them to sway in and out of the light, their bodies creating shadows on the walls."

Ria tried to achieve the effect by setting baby spotlights behind books piled on small tables. Harry Morrison had other ideas. When she arrived for the dress rehearsal, she discovered the books had been disposed of without her permission. Furious, she accosted Morrison and demanded an explanation. He escorted her to the auditorium, switched off the lights, plunging the stage into darkness. Suddenly, light emerged from a carefully carved recess in the table top into which he had fitted a small lighting fixture. Then, he slowly moved his face in and out of the light, achieving the exact effect she had been hoping to attain. Later, when she realized that she was being given credit for Harry's work, she insisted his name appear with that of the scenic designer on all programs of plays she directed.

In 1947, Ria heard that Frank Dermody, who had borne the brunt of Abbey production responsibilities for most of the last decade, was mentally and physically exhausted and about to retire from the theatre.[19] Rumors said that he was forced to leave because of an impending scandal, while others insisted he was joining an Irish film company in Britain.[20] Dermody had taken the critical heat for what was perceived to be the loss of Abbey production standards expressed in so public and vociferous a manner by Valentin Iremonger. He had been forced to stand by as the cream of the Abbey troupe was wooed away by big motion picture salaries. In the previous year, Eileen Crowe, F. J. McCormick, Cyril Cusack, M. J. Dolan, Denis O'Dea and Siobhan McKenna had signed contracts to appear in films in Ireland and England. In a belated attempt to prevent a mass exodus of players, the Abbey board raised performers' salaries to ten guineas (ten pounds ten shillings) a week, and, in a related action, the annual government subsidy was increased to 3,000 pounds a year. Added to that grant was a jump in support for plays performed in Irish from 500 to 2,500 pounds a year. The final, unexpected — and, no doubt, most telling — blow to the company was the sudden loss of one of its oldest and most faithful players.

On April 24, as Ria approached her 44th birthday, she was stunned by the announcement that F. J. McCormick was dead. It was the passing of a theatrical era. She could not remember a time when his name had not dominated the cast lists of the National Theatre. It seemed that, with his departure, most of the beloved characters from Irish dramatic literature had taken their final bow and forever deserted the Abbey stage. In many ways, it was a greater blow to Dublin theatre than the passing of W. B. Yeats, for the poet had left a body of work behind to be savored by succeeding generations. McCormick's creative presence, apart from glimpses of his craft available on films of the period, disappeared with him.

It was time to take stock of her own current theatrical position. She had spent two wandering decades in Dublin, London and New York. During that time, she had been almost constantly employed. Her career had traversed a decade of disastrous economic depression, and been held hostage for six years by the hostilities of a world war.

As an actress, she had been prominently featured in the most important Irish plays of that period from the pens of playwrights O'Casey, Carroll, Shiels, Robinson, Yeats, Lady Gregory, and Synge. She had appeared in New York City with an internationally known repertory theatre under the direction of Eva Le Gallienne in plays by Chekhov, O'Neill, and Giraudoux. She had written a successful adaptation of *Wuthering Heights*, and she had been a featured actress with MacLiammóir and Edwards in such exotic pieces as the traditional Chinese play, *Lady Precious Stream*.

As a director, she had assisted at the Civic Repertory Theater in New York City, staged several plays for the Abbey, assisted at the founding of the Dublin Lyric Theatre, and successfully mounted O'Casey's *Red Roses for Me* in London. She had been the director of both the Abbey and the Gaiety acting schools, where she had helped discover and develop the next generation of Irish actors.

It was an impressive record of achievement. Where should she direct her next steps? She was tired of teaching, and felt that her usefulness to the Gaiety was at an end.

Then, her direction was determined for her by unsolicited offers made for her theatrical services.[21] They indicated the task to which she was best suited, and acknowledged her achievement as a director. As a result of her work on the London production of the O'Casey play, she was offered a position at the Embassy Theatre to organize an acting school and direct every third play.

Burgess Meredith, playing under her direction at the Gaiety, told her he was thinking of starting an Art Theater in Hollywood. Would she like to join him in the project, directing some of the plays and running an acting school at the same time?

While she weighed the good and bad aspects of both offers, she was phoned by O Farachain, one of four Abbey directors and the poet with whom she had helped start the Lyric Theatre. He and his wife wanted her to spend an evening with them at their Dublin home. She turned down the invitation, explaining that she was distracted by her state of indecision and would not be pleasant company. O Farachain was surprised at her quandary, and asked if she really was leaving the Gaiety. Although he was in no position to offer her a job, he asked would she be interested in coming back to the Abbey. The thought that she might contribute from her considerable theatrical experience to the further enhancement of the reputation of the National Theatre obviously flattered her, but it was out of the question. After all, she hadn't the Irish language. It was silly, of course, because almost all of the repertoire performed at the Abbey was in the English language, but, nonetheless, Blythe would want the director to be an Irish-speaker.

She was convinced that her knowledge of the theatre was more important to the Abbey director's position than an ability to speak Irish, but could O Farachain successfully persuade Blythe to agree to make her an offer? In her memoirs, she does not tell the reader how long or how difficult a time her poet friend had with the hard-nosed Blythe, or whether Blythe actually offered opposition to a director who had no Irish. Whatever the circumstances of the deliberation between Robinson, Hayes, O Farachain and Blythe, the offer finally was made.

Ultimately, though, why would she accept the position of resident director of the Abbey Theatre? It's true, she said she was tired of teaching students to act and had nothing left to give the Gaiety Theatre. However, there wasn't much to choose among the three offers she had in hand. The London, Dublin, and Hollywood offers were for the same kind of position. Nonetheless, she felt challenged to take on, and flattered to be given, the artistic control of what was, after all, her theatrical home. There she had started and to that place she always seemed to return. Maybe she could contribute something to her native place from her broad experience of the English-speaking theatre. Beneath all these theatrical considerations one senses a powerful though private and personal issue. She obviously hated the thought of leaving Dublin. The other offers would force her to go into exile.

"I therefore accepted the Abbey offer with enthusiasm," she wrote in her memoirs, "saying no to my friends in England and America, for the privilege of working for my own country."[22]

— PART TWO —

The Director

CHAPTER SIX

"Picked Amongst the King of Friday's Men"

Ria Mooney was uniquely qualified to perform the task she was about to assume. To begin with, she had come upon Abbey production techniques just as the first generation of Abbey actors were about to leave the scene. In a sense, it was given to her to be a witness to a living tradition, to listen to descriptions of the Abbey's foundation from the lips of those who were there at the creation. Her backstage lore demonstrated, if any demonstration was needed, the pitfalls a director must try to avoid. She had seen for herself how others grappled with the personality problems, the technical limitations, and the dangers notoriety posed for the director. The struggles for power among Hunt, Higgins, O'Connor and Robinson, and their effects upon the players were reflected in her recorded conversation with F. J. McCormick. He had as much as declared a pox upon both houses. McCormick seemed to be saying that such backstage gossip merely interfered with the business of the stage.

Then, there was the scandal that had all but destroyed Eva Le Gallienne's Civic Repertory Company, in spite of that lady's extraordinary energy and manifest theatrical talent. There could be little doubt that press preoccupation with Eva's private life created stress onstage that obscured her theatrical accomplishments. Maybe directors were better off being overlooked. At any rate, it was difficult for anyone not involved in the production itself to tell exactly what it was a director actually did. It was easy to see the results of the efforts of playwrights and actors, and of scene, costume and lighting designers, but the input and influence of the director in each of those endeavors was impossible for the untrained eye to discern.

Finally, Ria's sojourn at the Gate Theatre exposed her to the manic methods of two gifted egoists. Wherever they went, the Boys left a trail of hostility and neuroses in their production wake. MacLiammóir and Edwards forced divided loyalties on Gate performers when they split with the Longfords. That rift was never healed.

So Ria had vivid memories of backstage feuds and the effect such infighting had upon the work the public viewed on the stage. She knew the situation she was entering from long and, sometimes, bitter experience. With these examples fresh in her mind, Ria Mooney could not have underestimated the difficulty of the challenge she was accepting.

It would be her first task to collaborate with management, and that meant Ernest Blythe, in choosing scripts for mounting. Blythe's emphasis on the Irish language had created open hostility in the Dublin acting community, and it might have scuttled her own appointment as director. It would be no small task to meet and collaborate with such a manager. Choosing scripts for production was a question of discerning stageworthiness in the dialogue. Did Blythe understand what an actor and designers could do to help tell the story?

Once the script was selected, she must turn her attention to casting the best actors available for the parts, arrange the movement of the players, coordinate their costume selections for color and character type, set the lighting and scenic effects indicated by the action and atmosphere of the story, drill the complicated sequences that required swift physical interaction among many characters, and insist that everyone concentrate, in spite of personality conflicts, on representing the author's intention in telling their tale.

Ria had tried her hand at adaptation for the stage, and her rendering of *Wuthering Heights* passed the stagecraft test administered by Edwards and MacLiammóir. In that exercise, she had demonstrated her knowledge of the stage as it applied to playwriting. When she wrote or read a script, Ria tried to visualize the actors and setting and movement of a staged piece.

Furthermore, she had labored over scripts of the two apparently incompatible schools of playwriting, the Poetic and the Naturalistic, and had managed to excel in both. She had learned the poetic lessons of W. B. Yeats from the poet himself. It was Yeats' ambition "to restore words to their sovereignty" in the theater. "We must make speech even more important than gesture on the stage."[1] "I taught my students," she recounts in her memoirs, "to speak [Yeats'] plays with intelligence and conviction, within the characterization given them by the author, and with no more than the minimum movement necessary."

In contrast to this emphasis on the spoken word, Ria, in the title role of the Gate production of *Lady Precious Stream*, achieved character effects through the mechanical manipulation of "long sleeves of white silk." In addition, although her performance as the gritty but sympathetic prostitute in O'Casey's *The Plough and The Stars* was a faithful copy of the physical appearance of prostitutes as she had observed them in the lane behind the Abbey, Ria was completely ignorant of the nature of the character she was supposed to be playing. Yet, O'Casey told her she had saved his play. The contrast between her innocence and her appearance had created her characterization.

There is nothing actors, especially young enthusiastic actors learning their craft, enjoy more than a passionate discussion about theories of playing. Ria was no exception. As an actress, she had worked with and learned from the most distinguished Abbey performers. She had heard and participated in the backstage discussions on the actor's craft with Frank Fay, Sara Allgood, M. J. Dolan, and Lennox Robinson. During her years with the Civic Theater in New York City, she had listened to Nazimova's firsthand account of her experience with Stanislavski's theory. The "Method," a style of teaching acting that insisted the actor must become

Barry Fitzgerald, Gabriel Fallon, and Ria Mooney backstage in the Abbey greenroom in the early years of Ria's reign as artistic director. (G. A. Duncan.)

the character they were playing, was the rage among prominent members of New York City's art community. For a while at least, Ria had modeled herself after Nazimova, the glamorous Russian star.

Barry Fitzgerald, returning to Hollywood after a holiday in Ireland, was accosted by a journalist and asked if he used the Stanislavski Method. "Look," he replied, "we've been using the method ever since the foundation of the Abbey Theater; but we never called it by that name!"[2] Also, hadn't Ria heard F. J. McCormick's acting described as "akin to mediumship?"[3] It was said that, as he stood in the wings about to go on, he "ceased to be and the character he was playing took over." To a certain extent, she was sympathetic to that image. After all, she flirted throughout her life with spiritualism. At the same time, however, she struggled as an actress with the fact that her medium, however much her spiritual part was in touch with the role she was playing, was quite simply herself. Her face, her body, her life must be molded to bring out the creation of character. Acting was not a question of altering internal states alone. An actress's appearance, with all its limitations, her body and the way she dressed and moved, was to her audience an external reflection of an interior disposition.

Ria Mooney enjoyed Mme. Rock's Academy as a child, the Rathmines and Rathgar Musical Society as a girl, and the Gate and the Civic theatres as a professional, because of what she called "the 'poetry' of theatre in each of those quite different organizations; the same escape from dull reality." For her, poetry was nothing less than the total art of the theatre.

Although she took delight in discussing these theories, she knew that's all they were, abstract reflections on what was, after all, a very practical craft. She recognized the different techniques that actors used to play their parts. She loved the plays of Yeats, but her performer's instincts told her that they would not benefit from Stanislavski's Method. Ria believed passionately in the literary genre of poetry in the theatre, but poetry had conventions of its own, not necessarily or exclusively related to theatrical performance. She was willing and able to elevate the spoken word to the first place of theatrical importance, but, at the same time, as an actress she made subtle use of make-up and costume, and consciously employed lighting effects and gesture to move an audience.

Ria was a woman of taste with strong opinions about her craft, but she was not doctrinaire in the playhouse. Backstage was a kind of factory floor, and there she was a hardworking master craftsman. She wanted to know what worked on the stage before an audience, and she performed everything she did for her audience. She tirelessly rehearsed every trick and device at her disposal — words, music, motion, color, line, form and personality — to make them laugh and cry, to overcome them with awe, reverence, and joy. The theatre was, at least in large part, a magic trick, and she saw it as her responsibility to be something of a magician.

There was a note of poetic justice or dramatic irony in Ria's first assignment at the Abbey. George Shiels' play, *The Caretakers*, was to begin the year 1948, and the cast included old friends Harry Brogan and Mick Dolan. She had begun her professional career as an actress at the Abbey in Shiels' *The Retriever*, and always referred to him as "the Molière of Ireland."[4] He was a great favorite with Abbey playgoers, and though Ria thought the play not one of his best, the script gave evidence of his usual and careful theatrically "workmanlike efficiency, and was enriched by his unquenchable sense of humour." George Shiels never attended performances of his plays. He was an invalid confined to his home in a wheelchair, the result of an injury sustained in a Canadian railway accident that crippled him for life. When Ria visited him, she discovered that he was the town advisor on legal questions. His chief task, however, was to write letters for his friends. From this frequent discourse with the world outside his small sitting room in the northern Irish village of Carnlough, he was able to create his characters and plots.

One critic has written that the "best of his later plays are tightly knit, convincingly realistic diagnoses of his country's morality."[5] *The Caretaker* exposed the undercurrents of placid village life created by an eccentric old lady's hidden cache of money. It is a "bright comedy about mean, grasping ruthless characters," justifying Ria's coupling the name of Shiels with the great French comic genius.

As was her usual custom, she visited with the playwright before beginning work on his play. When she arrived at Carnlough, she found that "he was lovingly cared for by a sister who quite obviously adored him, and I remember her standing near his chair when, after beckoning me from behind his parlour window as I walked away from him down the drive, I returned, and he presented me with a beautiful rose from his garden. I kept that rose until it withered and died, but I don't think his reputation will die. I believe his work will receive the honour due to it from a younger generation." T. C. Murray, a longtime friend by correspondence, sent Shiels firsthand accounts of the opening of his plays, and his report on the first night of *The Caretaker* must have been a happy one for both men.

On February 17, the *Irish Times* reviewer congratulated Ria "on her production, and on her apparent effort to revive the old Abbey practice of producing plays in the dialect in which they were written." the *Irish Independent* noted that Harry Brogan "as the avaricious, covertly slanderous old man, put a macabre quality into his mean cunning, and Michael J. Dolan put whimsicality into his roguery in his efforts to acquire a patch of land not legally his." One critic observed that Brogan's broad treatment of his part "convulsed the house with almost every line," but he preferred the "subtler study" of M. J. Dolan. Lennox Robinson had called Shiels "the Thomas Moore of the Irish Theatre," and thought that his plays had the warm-hearted simplicity of Moore's poetry. Clearly, Dolan's interpretation was more in tune with the comic tone of the play. If Ria had only seen it coming, she might have prevented the confrontation that followed upon Brogan's singular ability to provoke laughter. For the moment, the play settled down to a long run before full houses, and she had earned the right to be satisfied with her beginning as the artistic director of the National Theatre of Ireland.

Because of the comfortably long run of Shiels' play, Ria had time to direct her attention to the younger members of the company. Many of them were her star pupils brought with her from the Gaiety Acting School. Phyllis Ryan, in her autobiography, noted that "the Abbey company was again growing in strength. Nobody had thought that it could survive the premature death of F. J. McCormick in 1947. But now the company was being revitalised by actors infused with the old dedication such as Geoff and Edward Golden, Maire Ni Dhomhnaill, Philip O'Flynn, Angela Newman, Bill Foley and many more."[6] Doreen Madden, Ita O'Mahoney, Ronnie Masterson and Ronnie Walsh were all in their twenties, and they hadn't much stage experience. "She really had to teach us our jobs," said Masterson. "Ria was boss."[7] Other young members of the company who showed great promise were Joan O'Hara, and the newcomer fresh from the seminary, Ray MacAnally. Masterson remembered that Ria used to take them in the afternoon for class. "She always did Yeats' *Countess Cathleen* and Synge's *Playboy*. She was very keen on voice," and that "mysterious thing called beat." She seemed particularly interested that her charges hear the special "rhythms of Synge."

Private lessons were available at the home of the voice teacher Elizabeth Graves. Blythe encouraged the actors to avail themselves of this kind of special instruction by paying half the fees. Masterson, who later became the wife of Ray MacAnally, recalled that Ray was always looking for costumes and special make-up, including false bridgework to alter the shape of his mouth, and wigs to disguise his youth. Blythe paid half of the costs for MacAnally's wigs, and he was allowed to keep them after the run of the show. Dancing and fencing lessons were offered in the same arrangement, while "Ria worked purely on performance techniques." Masterson called her a "terribly dedicated" and "great — tremendous teacher." Ria took an interest in the careers of young people. "She was extremely encouraging."

Blythe's leadership was "benevolent paternalism." At one point he expressed concern that all the young women might get pregnant at the same time. That might, indeed, have created a casting problem. In any case, Masterson remembered fondly the family atmosphere. "It was our home. [There was] always somebody there to talk to." Of course, this was before actors were forbidden to do anything but perform. In 1948, and throughout Mooney's years as artistic director, young people were expected to work on costumes, props, and other technical chores connected with play production. "If you weren't in the play," recalled Masterson, "you watched rehearsals and in the evening you prompted."

Ria may have given a sympathetic ear to actors' technical problems or their fledgling attempts at learning stage deportment, but she never socialized after rehearsals. She was encouraging but never familiar. "She had confidence, not ego. She did very good work," and she expected the same degree of professionalism from the company, old and young alike. It, therefore, came as a shock to her when, after *The Caretakers* had been running for some weeks, she began to notice a slight deterioration in the production. She decided to "put it down to the natural boredom of Repertory players who have not been used to plays running so smoothly over a lengthy period."[8]

Ria's second effort was a script concerned with the troubles in the north of Ireland. John Coulter's *The Drums Are Out*, set in Belfast in the early 1920s, is about a conscientious sergeant in the Royal Ulster Constabulary, the RUC (the mainly Protestant police force of Northern Ireland), whose daughter has Sinn Fein sympathies. To complicate matters for her long-suffering father, the girl marries an IRA soldier wanted for the shooting of an RUC constable. The first scene of the third act contains an exciting moment when, disguised as Black and Tans, the IRA liberate their mate.

In spite of the melodramatic circumstances of the plot, and a cast one critic called "uniformly good," the play failed to find an audience. Ria's attention to voice was recognized by the *Irish Times* critic, who praised Brogan for "winning the popular fancy in a part that proves the idiom of the Falls-Shankill districts can be moulded close enough to the quality of O'Casey comedy." While the writer thought that young O'Flynn gave evidence in Shiels' play that he "may develop well," he gave gentle "counsel [to] the constable [the same O'Flynn] to have a hair cut." The *Irish Independent* thought the play "harmless popular fare" which offered "little opportunity to the actors." Brian O'Higgins and Eileen Crowe "worked quite successfully with very thin material." Both reviewers made reference to the threatening drums of the title: one criticized them as too much like "chamber music," and the other found "the drumming excellent."

"Blythe looked at the bookings," said Masterson, "and decided if it [the play] would come off on Saturday." *The Drums Are Out* went out too soon. Ria was forced to hustle a couple of revivals into place, while she prepared for the next new play, *The Lucky Finger*, by Lennox Robinson. These revivals, because they were new to most of the young cast members, were not as easy as they might have been to get up. Nonetheless, Ria felt that she and her troupe "had settled down to our work with respect for each other, and above all, for the theatre to which we had the honour to belong."

One of these quick fixes was of Synge's *Playboy*.[9] On August 16, Ria was scolded by one member of the press, who lamented that "the present production drives its [*The Playboy*'s] beauties from my mind." He missed McCormick and Cusack, and so did Ria Mooney. "Please Miss Mooney," he cried, "let us hear them [the beautiful word sequences] as they should be heard." How could she sacrifice the beauty of Synge's language to "a naturalistic approach?" It was, of course, a rhetorical question, and Ria, in any case, could make no reply. She was too busy with a final week of rehearsals for *The Lucky Finger*.

Ria thought the new script "was lacking in [Robinson's] former craftsmanship, so it took all I knew to mold it into shape. I needed the co-operation of a trustworthy cast to put it over." Apparently the chemistry between director and company proved satisfactory to everyone.

The reviews made good advertising copy. "As good a comedy as Mr. Robinson has ever given us, soundly produced by Ria Mooney," trumpeted the *Irish Times*. "Lennox Robinson has written and Ria Mooney has produced a play for twenty-two Abbey Theatre actors that has wit barbed, wit corrosive, wit kindly and wit satiric," cheered the *Irish Independent*. Eileen Crowe received laurels for her masterpiece of underplaying, and May Craig's "brilliantly malicious interpretation" delighted the reviewer. The long list of performers indicates the difficulties the director faced. Brid Lynch, a native speaker from Kerry who proved to be as effective in English as in Irish, was singled out for praise along with Ita O'Mahoney for her pert perkiness, cheek and good nature in her little role. Geoff Golden, Bill Foley, Michael Ó hAonghusa, Ray MacAnally, Maire O'Donnell and Ronnie Masterson were congratulated for their evening's efforts.

Special note was made of Carl Bonn's setting. He "did so well in the last act that anyone who has been to a dance in a small-town town hall could almost feel and see the dewdrops of condensation on the distempered walls." Masterson remembered that Ria "was pretty well precise" in her blocking of the actors' movements. To co-ordinate 22 actors in the short rehearsal period allotted to the production, to direct them where and when to move on and off the small Abbey stage, would take a confident and decisive stage manager. Evidently, Ria performed the charge with ease and efficiency.

Once again, as a result of the success at the box office of *The Lucky Finger*, Ria had time to resume her acting lessons with the company while she prepared for the next production. Rehearsals were from eleven in the morning until one in the afternoon. Actors had the afternoon free to memorize lines, cue each other, search for costumes, or rest until the evening's performance. Since it was impossible to predict how long or how short the run of a new play might be, the preparations might be intensified by the need to substitute a revival of a past success. Such stopgap methods were more easily effected if the company was one of long standing. In such a case, actors knew the play, the blocking, and their characterizations had been tested before an audience, so, as a result, their tasks were more easily accomplished.

That this schedule was not all work and no play is evident from the following story related by Ronnie Masterson. She played a nun in *The Lucky Finger* and Geoffrey Golden, another young actor new to the company, played a policeman. Golden and his good friend Denis O'Dea, who was no longer with the company, were serious gamblers. Masterson occasionally placed a bet, selecting a hat pin as her weapon of choice. After her luck had won her a couple of races, Golden jokingly asked for her pick of the day. Later, she was thrilled to hear her horse had won the big race. That evening she looked for her colleague before the show to ask if he had taken her tip and placed his bet on the winner.

The curtain went up before she could locate him, and, as the narrow stage space made it impossible for her to cross behind the back scrim once the lights were on, she gave up her quest until after the performance. "In the old Abbey," she said, "if you exited one side of the stage, you had to go out into the side lane and through a wicket gate to get to the other side" of the theatre. During one of her passages that night, she saw a policeman behind the playhouse. "When I met him in the lane, I went up to him, threw my arms around him, and I said: 'did you do it?' And then, I saw — I'm terribly sorry. I didn't know you were a real policeman," she exclaimed. "And the policeman said: 'I thought you were a real nun!'"

Everybody knew, of course, that the streets and lanes behind the theatre were the haunts of ladies of the evening.

From Ria's point of view, there was, perhaps, too much fun going on

A group of Abbey stalwarts enjoying a greenroom break. (G. A. Duncan.)

behind the scenes. An Irish-American friend who loved the Abbey and visited the playhouse whenever he returned to Ireland, made a special point of taking in *The Lucky Finger* to see the work of the new director of plays. When they met after the show, he seemed upset and unwilling to talk about what he had witnessed. Let us listen to Ria's version of the event.

"I begged him to tell me why, and when I had heard his reasons, I at once marched him back-stage, and straight up to the greenroom. When we got there, I flung open the door, and through the haze of tobacco smoke, I saw a group of men — some of them strangers— seated around the central table smoking and playing cards. I stood in the doorway and told my visitor that he could now go back and tell his audience what was being allowed to happen to Ireland's Abbey Theatre. I then slammed the door and left with my visitor. I was told afterwards that the men in the greenroom just laughed and went on playing cards."[10] While the reader might or might not share Ria's outrage at the event, it is difficult not to admire the theatrical telling of the tale. One would like to know the name and reputation of the visitor, as well as the names of the Abbey culprits.

At any rate, there can be little doubt that such distractions were sometimes present behind the scenes at the Abbey. Masterson said that "some of the lads had been up all night … they used to play poker in the green-room. There was a day when they would miss cues the odd time." She recalled that an event like the story related by Ria in her memoirs occurred when they were preparing to make a short tour of Iceland. "I remember her walking into the greenroom," said Masterson, and saying "how could I possibly take this group to Iceland?"

The character of Ria Mooney becomes clearer as we consider the circumstances of such episodes. This one is reminiscent of her conflict with the London Irish Company of O'Casey's *Red Roses for Me*. Another director, more attuned to backstage camaraderie, might have soft-pedaled each incident, trying to coax the players into curbing their sociability. Most artists are attracted to the playhouse precisely because it affords human contact in the creative process. Playmaking as an art form is less lonely, more convivial than painting or writing poetry or the novel; it is collaborative rather than the product of a single imagination. The obvious drawback rests in the fact that, if everyone isn't pulling their oar in unison, the motion of the ship may be rough and the boat may even capsize.

Ria was dedicated and serious, and those who knew her said she could be opinionated and impatient. "Ria had great dignity," said Val Merkens Kennedy. "People thought she was very uppity. She was very outspoken, very firm in her views about everything. She was quite dogmatic. But she had to be."[11] Yet, one wonders, was there no other way, no better way to persuade the few members guilty of dereliction of duty that they owed it to themselves and to their colleagues in the enterprise to concentrate for the three hours of the evening's performance on their part in the play? Was it necessary to publicly expose the culprits in so humiliating a fashion, leaving them no way to save face? Even if they reformed their behavior, resentment for the reformer would linger, creating friction and hostility.

There is much evidence that Ria had social ambitions, as well as a wide acquaintance outside Dublin. Even in Dublin, though, she made her society outside the playhouse, keeping a distance between herself as director and the company of players. "She used to gather a party to go to the theatre, and I was very often of them," said Kennedy. "She would take say three or four, … she would gather a few friends, and maybe you might have dinner before or after as her guest. Ria never gave dinner parties at home. She always brought people to a restaurant." Obviously a very private, even secretive person, Ria throughout her life kept even her nontheatrical friends separate from her family. Kennedy tells us she had a sister who lived next door to her, but she doesn't appear to have been invited into Ria's family circle. Mary Manning was never asked to visit her at home, and, in her memoirs, Ria only refers to her father and sister in reference to a theatrical connection.

MacLiammóir's preface to her memoirs gives clear evidence of respect for her theatrical talents and application, but there isn't a hint of affection or camaraderie for his subject. It is, of course, important in any craft to have high standards, and all seem to have agreed that Ria's were of the highest. Unfortunately, those who tell the story of their time tend to eulogize those they liked. Ria is never blamed or criticized, but she is often ignored or patronized by those who have given us the history of that time and place.

Storms seemed to be gathering on the Abbey horizon, and Ria's tempestuous attitude and dramatic righteousness had something to do with getting the wind up backstage. At that moment, she hadn't the time to worry about any whirlwind. She had another play to get ready, and this one she knew looked like being good theatre and, perhaps, even great art. And she had the cast she wanted to do it.

M. J. Molloy was anointed by Dublin critics as Synge's successor in the folk romantic comedy. (Courtesy Ann Molloy.)

Walter Macken joined the Abbey acting company in 1948. He had already had his play *Mungo's Mansion* produced there in February of 1946. At that time, and until he joined the Abbey as an actor, he was director of plays at the Gaelic theatre in Galway. Ria saw at once that this huge Gaelic speaker from the west with the booming voice and the powerful presence was the man to play Bartley Dowd, the shillelagh fighter from Tyrawley in M. J. Molloy's new play, *The King of Friday's Men*. Molloy, a shy, retiring man from Milltown, County Galway, had laid claim in two previous Abbey outings to the folk playwright's mantle of the now revered John Millington Synge.

As a young man, Molloy, the son of a village schoolteacher, was forced to leave the seminary because of a bone disease that left one leg shorter than the other. While in hospital in Dublin, a friend took him to the Abbey, and he fell in love with the theatre. He fashioned his plays around the folk traditions he had grown up listening while visiting in homes in the rural west, and his third play, *The King of Friday's Men,* was a historical drama set in 1787 which took up the provocative theme of the droit du seigneur. Molloy described it as "the old feudal rule or custom, whereby the landed aristocrats could compel the prettiest daughters or wives of their tenant farmers to become their mistresses for a night, or for a lifetime."[12] Because Molloy's lyric dialogue was being compared to Synge's speech, it might be worth the reader's time to sample some of the language of this important play.

Caesar French has cast off his current tallywoman (mistress) because she told him "all us girls dubbed and deemed him too old for us now." At the fair dance that night, she asks Gaisceen to hide her 15 guineas dowry for her, while French's men come looking for her replacement among the village beauties.

> GAISCEEN: Evermore the Frenches led all Ireland for decency. I'll dyke it [the money] in here for a whileen.
> MAURA: What good are his guineas now when my character is broken over him?
> GAISCEEN: Why would it? Don't all know Boorla and his Press gang brought you to Caesar against your will, and your people could say no word on account they were Caesar's tenants?
> MAURA: No matter; when the decent lads are looking out for the wife they duck their eyes past any girl that has another man's brand on her.[13]

French's minions come looking for Una Brehony, a lovely young girl about to be wed to Owen Fenigan. Once married, she will be safe, for Caesar never meddles with married women. When Boorla appears at the dance, he comes directly for Una, who pleads for help.

Bartley Dowd, a famous shillelagh fighter, has come to the Pattern (Saint's festival) as a mercenary for the local army. Una tricks him into believing that she loves him, and he gallantly steps in to plead her case.

> BOORLA: 'Tis herself was picked, so no other'll do. Very apt he'll not keep her long.
> BARTLEY: Una, girl, I wouldn't wish this for many a round guinea. Still, he'll maybe not keep you passing a few days, so you should humour him. 'Tis always safest to keep to the west side of the gentry.
> UNA: Is that all you care about me? Or d'ye know what he wants me for at all?
> BARTLEY: For task work? What else?

UNA: 'Tis not. 'Tis for tallywoman.

BARTLEY: What's that? Does he want to ruin her?

BOORLA: I have six great wipers, their shillelaghs in their fists. Any man that stands against Master Caesar they'll slash him to death like a rat in a haggard.

He rescues Una from Caesar's police with bone-crushing efficiency, but the cunning landlord and his servants trick the fugitives. They secure the girl and wait for Bartley to chance an encounter in French's demesne.

Molloy isn't interested in villains and heroes alone, however. His clear vision of the brutal effects of the system upon owner and tenant alike creates a conflict between realities. Maura's chance for a marriage is countered by Una's loss of freedom. Bartley's romance is predicated upon a lie, and Maura has lied to French about his age in order to have the opportunity to ensnare the unsuspecting Bartley. Maura decides to confront Caesar with the truth, and the aristocrat's vanity is soothed.

CAESAR: You're not going with him, you're stopping here with me. I cannot marry you: my own class would shun me if I did; but neither will I marry anyone else. I'm forty-five, and at that age a man doesn't tire of a girl so quickly. I'll not tire of you; don't you fear it.

He is aware that "she has enough brains to stick" to her business "and leave the man to mind his." Almost plaintively, he asks; "Will you take your chance with me?" But she knows that "too many young handsome girls are rising up on" his property. He dismisses her, telling her as she goes: "As for this Dowd fellow, I'll avoid killing him, if I can."

The last act heaps irony upon every action, and Bartley's departure from the scene is a lyric sung with sadness and courage.

BARTLEY: 'Tisn't for good fortune God put our like in the world, but only to do odd jobs for him. ... myself to snatch a girl from the Press-gang, and to keep hunger from my sister-in-law and her orphans. We can no way complain. Himself gave His life for us of a Friday...

GAISCEEN: It appears all right y're picked amongst the King of Friday's men... But if ye are itself, He'll reward ye highly when yere life's day is over at last.

BARTLEY: 'Twill be something. If ye cross her ever, tell her send to the Joyce country any time she's in jeopardy, and, if Bartley is living, he'll not fail her. And let ye spare an odd prayer for myself — for a few days whatever. Misfortune that sticks too long'd wear the rocks.

The lyric language, the fierce action, the excitement of the dance, the confrontation, the battle, and the chase, combined with the melancholy reflection on a faded society, presented Ria with the opportunity she thrived upon, and the result was headlined in the *Irish Press* as the "Abbey's best for a long time. *The King of Friday's Men* fulfills the promise of M. J. Molloy's two previous works," wrote the reviewer. The *Irish Times'* critic thought that Molloy had written the "loveliest lines ... in the Irish Theatre since the death of Synge. Macken's performance has a satisfying wholeness such as has not been seen since Cusack's *Playboy* in a part of the kind," and Ronnie Masterson supplied a "good measure of tragic sympathy" as the "discarded mistress." The writer lamented the "indifferent reception accorded ...[Molloy's] fine first play, *The Old Road*," and he declared Molloy a "dramatist of rare courage and shining talent."

Praise was lavished on the picture painted of a time when the "landlord system was absolute and the tenantry little more than serfs. The evils of the system are stressed, and we see the debasing effects it has on landlord and tenant.... All of which is not to say that this is a propaganda play. Molloy is too good a dramatist for that." Macken was called "brilliant," and the rest of the cast "were on a high standard. Ria Mooney's production was sure and showed a real feeling for the heart of the matter."

The heart of the matter was in the "pity and irony of the telling, and through it all runs a wide leavening of humour. It is in his poetic and sincere feeling that the author scores most, and his play ... holds till the final curtain." Even Carl Bonn's three settings, including a dance hall and the French mansion's center hall were applauded. Ria had managed to produce three successful productions of three distinguished Abbey playwrights, and she was given credit in each case for her effective marshaling of the repertory company's resources. The final play of 1948, *The King of Friday's Men*, was considered a work of theatrical art in the best Abbey tradition and M. J. Molloy hailed as Synge's successor.

If there was a caveat, it was buried in the rave *Irish Times* review. The reviewer didn't "know whether to blame the actors or the audience for what I regarded as an over emphasis of the broader comic aspects of the parts in the wrong places." It was a small but prophetic observation of trouble to come.

Shortly after Christmas, *The King of Friday's Men* was replaced by the annual Gaelic Pantomime. It was the work of the young Gaelic-speaking director, Tomás MacAnna. While most of the Abbey's critics disapproved of Blythe, thinking him incapable of recognizing and using artistic talent when he found it, Hugh Hunt thought his choice of MacAnna as director of Gaelic productions showed he was "a shrewd judge of artistic ability, even if he sometimes abused it. Of MacAnna's first production for the Abbey, a Gaelic translation of Chekhov's *The Proposal* (16 September 1947), Blythe wrote, 'We have struck a man who will be a tower of strength in the theatre.'"[14] Blythe's discovery of MacAnna convinced Hunt that this otherwise theatrically deprived accountant dressed up in borrowed dramatic garb seemed to hint, in this case at least, at hidden powers of playhouse discernment.

Reflecting on that time in her career as the Abbey artistic director, Ria came to the conclusion that her "engagement in the theatre was looked upon as being a 'holding' position until such time as Irish-speaking Directors could take over. I was told that the nation was at war with the English language."

As it happened, Blythe created MacAnna's job and guided his career until he assumed the position Ria held. Aside from his long experience, nearly 20 years directing Gaelic programs at the Abbey, MacAnna's background consisted of some scenic design for the Dundalk amateur theatre. "His [Blythe's] well-known dedication to the Irish language and the influence this was having on Abbey policy had meant the creation of a new position in the theatre, that of Gaelic producer, and this was the position he offered me," wrote MacAnna. "That was in June 1947. I produced all the plays in Irish, mostly one-acts presented after, not before, the main attraction; and of course the Christmas pantomimes, eighteen in all between the Abbey and the Queen's. My work was completely in contrast to that of Ria Mooney: where she found herself producing play after play in the same naturalistic style, I was romping through Gheon, Jalabert, Benevente, Molière and Chekhov in styles ranging all the way from late Guthrie to music-hall."[15]

The thought of MacAnna's tall, gangly, publicly morose figure romping anywhere is risible. Nonetheless, although neither MacAnna nor Mooney ever pointed a finger at the other, it is clear from this dialogue created from materials separately stated long after the fact that Blythe manipulated the directorial situation to his own advantage. Ria wanted "to spend more money on the presentation" of the work of new writers. "The type of presentation I had been aiming at in my earlier efforts," she noted without comment, "was to be seen only in plays produced in Irish.... But since I was not an Irish speaker, I was cut off from this source of expression." Lest it be thought that MacAnna had no designs on Ria's position, let us remember that he said he fretted "somewhat at not being given the odd English production."

However that may be, Ria was too busy to have been aware of Blythe's agenda. She was engrossed in a new play from the pen of short story writer Bryan MacMahon. *The Bugle in the Blood* concerns itself with the son of the Trimble family jailed for political activity and dying on a hunger strike. Unlike the "naturalistic style" so derogatorily referred to by MacAnna, MacMahon's script featured songs, poems, plus a juxtaposition of comedy and tragedy that ended with a somber funeral, drunken antics, and an effective stage fight.

The playwright was Master of the Listowel school and had already received recognition as a short story writer. He was interested in Ireland's folk traditions, particularly those attached to the life of the "tinkers," the island's traveling people.

This complicated production could not be rushed, so, when the pantomime's houses dwindled toward the end of January, Ria was forced to throw a couple of revivals onto the boards to create the time needed for the new production. On February 1, 1949, Brinsley MacNamara's *The Grand House in the City* replaced the pantomime. This 12-year-old play took some trouble to mount, because the company regulars had not appeared in the first production. Brian O'Higgins and Walter Macken took the leads, and Harry Brogan gave a "good reading of lines about ruined houses," while Brid Lynch was recognized as having performed with her "accustomed skill."[16]

On the first of March, Robinson's spoof of Russian acting in a west of Ireland summer resort, *Drama at Inish*, was given an "undistinguished production." Newcomer Jack McGowran was praised for supplying a "bucketful of neat comedy," but the critic saw the merit of the play "in spite of, rather than because of, the acting."[17] Finally, on Tuesday, March 15, 1949, *The Bugle in the Blood* made its first sound.

The Irish Times declared that the "Abbey may congratulate itself on staging a new playwright who has grafted a rich originality of observation onto the tradition of O'Casey." As for the acting, the applause for the entire company was enthusiastic. "Brian O'Higgins' Joseph Trimble and Walter Macken's Circus Jack kindled a new flame of hope for the survival of Abbey acting," while Brid Lynch brought "a restrained and controlled economy of tragic underacting more moving than I have seen in the Abbey for a very long time," said the *Irish Times*.

The *Irish Press* was equally impressed by the production. After observing the effectiveness of the leading players, the critic noted "Jack MacGowran's subtle shadings" and Michael J. Dolan's old neighbor, who "was suitably garrulous and soft-hearted by turns." The *Irish Press* found that MacMahon had "a rich flair for local colour. He is an acquisition to the Abbey. His first attempt … is remarkably good."

The play, perhaps because of its subject matter, failed to attract large audiences. Dublin and all Ireland were making preparations throughout March for the formal declaration of the Republic. It was just possible that people didn't want to be reminded at that moment of the civil strife that had racked the country in those tragic days that followed the signing of the Treaty. Michael Collins had been, no doubt, right in thinking that the Treaty was the best settlement that could have been had at that moment. The formal declaration merely ratified what had been practiced by the Free State from the beginning. Perhaps, it wasn't the time to look too closely into the events that shaped the celebration of April 17, 1949.

Meanwhile, always on the lookout for good dramatic material, Ria came up with a winner to open on the night of April the 18th. *All Souls' Night*, by Joseph Tomelty, is set in a small northern fishing village. This story repeats Synge's theme of "the elemental clash with the sea." The conflict is between the ambitious son, who wants to spend the family's small savings on a bigger boat, and his mother, whom grinding poverty and the constant threat of the sea have reduced to miserliness.

The Irish Press called the play "vigorous, gripping and strong in its drama. It has an exciting plot, is couched in Abbey terms—and by that I mean in the best traditions of the Abbey's repertoire." Tomelty, an actor and former manager of the Ulster Group Theatre of Belfast, used the theatrical device of the return of the dead to their home on All Souls' Night. It was the kind of moment, a theatrical "escape from dull reality," in which Ria immediately sensed the dramatic power. It did not go unnoticed by the critics. "Ria Mooney's casting and production are probably the best she has done since her return to the Abbey," said the *Irish Times*. Mac-Anally "got into the skin" of his character and the company deserved "with their producer, almost as many congratulations as the dramatist for a most interesting new production."

The *Irish Press* thought the "acting and production were also in the best Abbey traditions of all-round capability. Though the team work was outstanding one could not help remarking what towers of strength are Harry Brogan and M. J. Dolan. Marie Kean's grim mother was perhaps a little too tight-lipped in the beginning. Raymond MacAnally is developing rapidly as an actor of power. Very nice balanced acting came from Joan O'Hara, and I liked Wally Macken's easiness. Vere Dudgeon's setting were completely in atmosphere."

All Souls' Night proved popular at the box office, and was followed by only one more original script during 1949. On October 4, Ralph Kennedy's *Ask for Me Tomorrow* touched on the impact of World War II on a middle-class Irish family. The play has an unusual setting of the bank house in an Irish provincial town, and the plot charts the "crumble of character behind the solid facade of respectability and the plate glass social front." The moral devaluation of the central character is the result of the loss of the sterling standard occasioned by the recent war. The play was praised, "in spite of a tendency to wordiness."

"The Abbey Players, with their peculiar ease and sureness of touch, made this a credible play of Irish country life," observed the *Irish Press*. Dolan, Macken and MacAnally, as well as Brid Lynch, Crowe, and Doreen Madden, "a young actress with a beautiful speaking voice," all received individual praise. Once again, Vere Dudgeon's sets were noted with approval.

After two years at the head of the National Theatre, Ria could be satisfied that she had made a good beginning. The company was beginning to distinguish itself, and the new additions, MacAnally, Macken, MacGowran, O'Hara and Marie Kean were given the same good notices as Brogan, Dolan, O'Higgins, and Crowe. Furthermore, the new designer, Vere Dudgeon, was managing to infuse some new life into the Abbey's stage spectacle. Ria had staged four plays in succession with a wide variety of settings, from French's elegant big house central hall, to the impoverished cottage of a Northern fishing village. MacMahon's political play had given her the opportunity to employ her love of lighting and costume enhancement of character, and Dudgeon's bank office served to symbolize the entire theme of the play. These can hardly be described, as MacAnna and many others were to do much later, as plays set in "the same naturalistic style."

Nonetheless, she could not help but notice Blythe's increasingly enthusiastic support for what were, in the end, tag-on Gaelic afterthoughts to the principal entertainment of the evening. One act plays in Irish kept hardly 50 members of the audience after the final curtain fell on the English-speaking production. Still, they made accessible to theatregoers who spoke or understood the native language the plays of European playwrights much on the minds and the lips of trendsetters. It was curious that many of these critics of the Abbey repertoire abhorred Blythe's Gaelic policy while approving of his choice of MacAnna and the foreign plays that he translated into Irish.

There was one aspect of company performance that continued to nettle. Ria had not succeeded in totally erasing the rowdy backstage behavior of some of the players, or the tendency of actors like the popular Harry Brogan to exploit every possible comic moment in his part no matter what effect it had upon the play as a whole. Furthermore, she had to admit, however ruefully, that his audience appeared to like it that way.

CHAPTER SEVEN

"We Must Keep Faith with the Public"

Ria Mooney began the second half of the 20th century with her theatrical talents engaged on multiple fronts. The Abbey was reviving many of its former successes, as a playhouse with national pretensions must. The acting company was improving in experience, training, and maturity, and the siren song of more lucrative motion picture contracts was, for the moment, not a distraction. The company remained constant and strong. Vere Dudgeon's set design was receiving good notices and the last plays of stalwarts like Lennox Robinson and George Shiels had been mounted to good effect. Most encouraging of all, perhaps, was M. J. Molloy's latest work, *The King of Friday's Men*, which established the Galway man as John Millington Synge's successor. Finally, new plays by Bryan MacMahon, Joseph Tomelty, and Ralph Kennedy offered hope for the future of Irish playwriting.

Times were changing, though, and, while Ria's relationship with Blythe remained cordial, it reflected strains prevalent in Irish society. Blythe's Irish linguistic nationalism may have been ascendant at the Abbey, but it was losing ground in Irish society. The educated Anglo-Irish class had always resented what they conceived to be an intellectually and culturally impoverished middle-class fixation with the Irish language, and they struggled against it, in the city at least, with some success.[1] During the 1940s, they had managed to paint the revivalists as irrational dogmatists, and teachers themselves began to question the effectiveness of the Gaelicization policy in English-speaking areas. Furthermore, the teaching of religion was mostly in the home language of the student. Clearly, the Church was unwilling to sacrifice religious understanding to government policy.

At the same time, it was becoming increasingly evident that the Irish rural world was in decline.[2] If Ria noticed the growth in population of her beloved Dublin, she never mentioned it in her memoirs. Nonetheless, as the second half of the century got under way, "over one-fifth of the population of the twenty-six counties [was] living in Dublin and its immediate neighbor, Dun Laoghaire." Dublin's denizens jumped in number by 100,000 in a decade, and "this change of the social profile was due less to the growth of the towns and cities than to rural depopulation." Satirist Myles na gCopaleen published a send-up of books that exploited the rural west. The author mocked the miserable life of such places and characterized his book as "an enormous jeer at the Gaelic morons with their bicycle-clips and handball medals...."[3] While the writer, a well known Dublin character, protested his devotion to the Irish language, his books made the government's language policy seem ridiculous.

Sean O'Faolain described the cultural vision of the heroic west as mere escapism. "The Romantic illusion, fostered by the Celtic Twilight, that the West of Ireland, with its red petticoats and bawneens, is for some reason more Irish than Guinness' Brewery or Dwyer's Sunbeam-Wolsey factory, has no longer any basis whatever."[4] To label the work of Yeats, Synge, Lady Gregory, and Denis Johnston as "romantic Illusion" seems foolhardy, even when coming from so talented a writer as Sean O'Faolain. Perhaps, O'Faolain, a realist himself, was staking out the ground for an artistic battle to be fought against the new lyricists of the west. Maybe it was not the Anglo-Irish he was aiming at, but their designated descendants, Molloy and MacMahon. Thus did the city folk assert that their country cousins in the west had become culturally irrelevant.

However, what makes this emigration even more interesting is that those deserting the countryside were the children of the revolutionary war heroes on whose behalf the conflict had been waged. Many of them spoke Irish. They were the beneficiaries of government programs of education. Were they deserting the land out of disenchantment with life in the countryside, or, quite simply, "in order to secure a reasonable standard of living"?[5]

Whatever the truth of the matter might be, Ria's dealings with Ernest Blythe were clearly affected by the changing social conditions. She was a Dubliner at heart with an intimate acquaintance with and affection for Anglo-Irish literature and its creators. She had no Irish, though she doesn't seem to have had any animus toward the language and its government promoters. She was appointed to her position at the Abbey because she was a sophisticated practitioner of the playhouse craft. Ria's friend and the editor of her autobiography, Val Mulkerns, was convinced that "her

standards were entirely theatrical and of the highest."[6] She was an entertainer who wanted to please her audience. That audience was impercep-
tibly changing, and she must change with it. Blythe, on the other hand,
was a nationalist politician and patriot with an extensive background in
finance and a passion for the Irish language. He appears to have been sin-
cerely persuaded that Ireland could not sustain its national identity speaking what was to him essentially a foreign tongue. His knowledge of the
theatre was gained in his association with the Abbey. For him, as for so
many others, the national identity was wrapped up in the Irish language,
and the Abbey, as a national theatre, must use its native tongue.

Economics, the Irish language, and depopulation of the countryside
created a new climate in Dublin, and it was in that climate that the struggle for the Abbey's policy was to be conducted.

Many proclaimed, Hugh Hunt the most prominent among them,
that the "Old Lady of Abbey Street" was suffering from an illness that had
no known cure.[7] Meanwhile, Anglo-Irish Dublin kept up the drumbeat
for international sophistication, criticizing Abbey plays as dreary, local
comedies and melodramas reproduced in the same old, familiar, naturalistic style. Ria's first presentation of 1950, Seamus Byrne's *Design for a
Headstone*, seemed calculated to give the lie to all such criticism.

The author was born in Dublin on December 27, 1904.[8] A solicitor
by profession, he became involved with and was jailed for his activities
with the new IRA in 1940. He staged a hunger strike of 21 days, and was
released after serving nine months of a two-year term.

The action of his play takes place in Mountjoy Prison sometime before
1950. The play's theme is the Church at odds with Republicanism. Political prisoners jailed for IRA activity are about to lose their military status and be tried and treated as ordinary criminals. In an attempt to
dramatize their plight, Republican leader Conor Egan goes on a hunger
strike. As his physical condition deteriorates, he is confronted by a prison
chaplain, who argues that the strike is a form of suicide. The priest, therefore, must refuse absolution to the dying leader. Hogan notes that "the
priest is not treated with kid gloves, but even roundly abused by one of
the prisoners."[9] Byrne offers no solution to the dilemma, but Hogan
thought the final insight "is rather a revelation of how Jesuitically oppor-
tunistic the Church is in its primary interest of saving souls."

The play opened on April 8, 1950, to a tepid critical reception. The
Irish Press thought that the author "tries to do too much. This three act
production leaves no clear-cut character images, throws out no line to
imprint the memory."[10] The *Irish Independent* found that "all the old questions are asked: all still remain unanswered."

On the sixth night, however, the play gained some notoriety, when angry members of the IRA protested that some of the views expressed by one of the prisoners were Marxist, while the religious organization, Maria Duce, contended that the play was a smear on the Catholic priesthood. The playhouse peace was disturbed by a delightful din of protest, an attempted attack on the playwright, and some young men crowding the aisles and shouting refutations of lines from the play.

In her memoirs, Ria remembered *Design for a Headstone* as "a fine controversial play." She was disappointed when, on that night of disturbance, the all-male cast seemed reluctant to go on the stage, and said they "thought it was time for me to intervene." Her version of the event is worth recording in its entirety.

"I stood before them and asked them if they were men at all? I spoke of being a very young actress playing my first big part in 1926, when I experienced the riot over Rosie Redmond in O'Casey's play *The Plough and the Stars*. I reminded them that I had lumps of coal and copper coins thrown at me, and filthy abuse shouted at me, but that, true to Abbey tradition, I had remained on the stage. If a young girl had the courage to do this, how was it that the men of the present Abbey company were too afraid to go on? There was silence after I had spoken; then they trooped quietly out of the greenroom. The play went on, and there were no further incidents."[11]

This locker-room speech has a fighting Irish ring to it, and must have seemed silly and insulting to the assembled acting company, provided it was given as she remembered it. While it is the recollection of an incident that occurred 20 years before the report, it reveals that Ria still saw the Abbey through the eyes of a young girl. The heightened nature of the confrontation is undermined by the weak ending of the story. "The play went on, and there were no further incidents." What she fails to report in her autobiography is that, when it appeared that a scandal might restore the Abbey's good name, the police arrived and the demonstration faded away. From the commotion, wrote Hugh Hunt, "it might seem for a brief moment that the Abbey was back among the heady arguments over *The Playboy* and *The Plough and the Stars*."[12] It is ironic that even this champion of progress should be found alongside Ria Mooney looking with nostalgic longing toward a distant past. Times were changing, and the Dublin theatrical world was changing with them. This play, however confrontational it intended to be, failed to excite its audiences as had the plays of O'Casey and Synge. Perhaps Hunt and his Anglo-Irish friends had succeeded in taking the shock out of attacking the Church. If that was the case, they could no longer expect audiences to react to such attacks.

If the reviewers registered disappointment with the play, they found much to praise in the production. The *Irish Press* critic applauded Walter Macken's Ructions, a "Voltaire and Marx-quoting prisoner whose theological arguments with the priest [Bill Foley] ... were good performances." These provided some added fire "when the flint of Marxism rasps against the steel of Catholicism." Brian O'Higgins played the comic codger Jakey, but the consensus was that the humor was forced rather than genuine. The *Irish Times* critic remarked that "it will not be the fault of the audiences if Mr. O'Higgins is not required to dole out this most desirable commodity in buckets...."

The *Press* observed that Ria Mooney "did wonders with grouping to handle a cast of thirty, often with fourteen on the small Abbey stage at the same time." In addition, Vere Dudgeon was praised for creating the prison atmosphere using suggestion rather than real iron-barred windows.

Design for a Headstone continued until the June vacation, after which the Abbey reopened in July with two short plays, Shaw's *Village Wooing*, and O'Casey's *Shadow of a Gunman*. On August 10, 1950, Jack P. Cunningham's prize-winning play, *Mountain Flood*, stirred up new controversy. An Abbey competition had been set up to encourage potential playwrights with the promise of an Abbey production as reward for the winner. The *Irish Times* found that the play "holds a mirror not up to nature but other Abbey plays." It was written, he declared, for an Abbey audience that "invariably laughs in all the wrong places." He lamented its cheap melodramatic form, which he blamed on the success of such plays as *The Righteous Are Bold*, and *The Rugged Path*.

Set in the wilds of Mayo in the year 1900, the plot concerns the sons of Old Black Jameseen Brennan, and the other members of the "Faction." They live in squalor, "spending their nights making poteen and their days drinking it; quarreling and fighting and not stopping at murder when it is necessary to their ends."[13] Dublin critics scorned the melodrama and refused to approve of such unsavory mountainy folk. But the acting company, apart from some overplaying, received due credit for their handling of the material. Ria seems to have enjoyed the romp, for it was remarked that she "might have toned down her production considerably."[14]

The third new play of the year, which made its debut on October 2, was Donal Giltinan's episodic piece set in Cork City, entitled *The Goldfish in the Sun*. The thin plot tells of an old sailor who returns in search of an earlier love, and two young people dreaming of escape from an ugly slum. Ria's production was said to be "expertly handled" with "great dexterity," but it was Vere Dudgeon's settings that came in for special praise. "A particular tribute must be paid to Vere Dudgeon," said the *Irish Independent*, "for a setting which captured the spaciousness and atmosphere of the quays along the Lee, and which must have made every Corkman present feel nostalgic."

As the year came to an end, Ria could look back on her work with some satisfaction. While there had been only three new plays, they had all been popular with audiences, and two had caused some heated discussion. She admitted in her memoirs that "my memory does not serve me very well," but, she went on, "I think that the actor who was to have spoken the words from Voltaire [in *Design for a Headstone*], somehow skirted around them."[15] Walter Macken, as Ructions, was responsible for those lines. If he skirted them, as she seems to imply he did, one of her best players was ignoring her direction and taking matters into his own hands. If that was the case, it would appear that her imperious manner was causing her to lose contact even with the newer members of her troupe.

The year 1951 was welcomed by the Abbey's latest Gaelic pantomime, *Una agus Jimin,* while English counterparts reigned throughout Dublin's playhouses. Popular Jimmy O'Dea was packing them in at the Gaiety with *Happy as Can Be*, while Edwards and MacLiammóir were *Home for Christmas* at the Gate, and *Aladdin's Lamp* burned at the Queen's.[16] When attendance began to flag toward the end of January, Ria concentrated rehearsal time on the first new play of the year, Maurice Meldon's big house drama, *House Under Green Shadows*.

Ria was impressed by the 25-year-old civil servant, and "many canny Dubliners," said Robert Hogan, "already regarded him as 'the most exciting new voice in the Irish theatre.'"[17] Set in Tullakeevan, the play's central theme is embodied in an "old house crumbling away while the people in it [are] imprisoned, like the house, by the rain-bred weeds of decay."[18] The reviewers were reluctant to condemn the play, but they had to report that the author was a man of promise rather than competence. The *Irish Times* duly recorded that M. J. Dolan gave a "magnificent performance," and Marie Kean evidenced a "flair for comedy as the housekeeper," but the critic chided Ria's "use of a real actor in the apparition scene, instead of his voice only." Vere Dudgeon's settings were said to have struck just the right note of characteristic stuffiness.

The Abbey's schedule allowed little time for regret, and Ria found herself reviving previous Abbey successes to gain time for rehearsing the next new play. First out of the block was Lennox Robinson's *The Far Off Hills*. On April 30, 1951, the *Irish Times* proclaimed Lennox Robinson "the finest writer of parlour comedy that the country has produced," and the present Abbey troupe has "a very happy flair of handling his work." The

senior members gave effortlessly easy performances, and the junior ones
were "well up to their elders' standards in a production by Ria Mooney
that crackles along with a laugh in every line."

Two weeks later, on May 14, the company revisited Sean O'Casey's
The Plough and the Stars. The same critic turned his attention toward the
audience that seemed, he thought, to "need to titter" at every line. The
production played until the June vacation began, and was to resume its
run the first week in July.

Ria took her holiday that year in Paris, her first visit since before
World War II.[19] Although her French was poor, she made several pil-
grimages to important French theatrical shrines. The Comédie Française,
led by the famous Louis Jouvet, seemed affected to her eye and ear, and
their vocal tricks annoyed her. She almost passed up Paul Claudel's *Le
Soulier de Satin*, because she was told it was five hours long. She decided
to go anyway, and, "after the first half-hour, I forgot how long it was going
to take, and after another, I was ready for it to go for ever!" She admired
director Barrault's scenic use of hundreds of yards of folded velvet cloth,
but she found the realistic sets were not so good. Nonetheless, she enjoyed
her vacation and, "refreshed ... and full of new ideas, I returned to
Dublin."

The Plough and the Stars resumed its run and was doing quite well
(Ria later referred to it as her best O'Casey production), with William
O'Gorman as Fluther, Marie Kean as Bessie, May Craig in her original part
as Jinnie Gogan, and Eric Gorman as Uncle Peter. Ria thought Gorman
was perfect as Peter, and May Craig, though she was getting on in years,
was still an effective Jinnie Gogan. Ria was privately pleased to be forced
to step into Craig's part, as the senior actress was allowed time off to play
in a film being made in the west of Ireland. Since she had played the part
many times with the older company, and there wasn't time to rehearse anyone else, Ria was the logical choice to assume the role. The sequence of
events that followed was as heartbreaking as it was dramatic.

On the morning of July 18, 1951, Ria's father awakened her early.[20]
"It's the Abbey," he said. She finished the sentence for him: "I know it has
burnt down." It had happened shortly after midnight, but he had refused
to waken her. "I told him then of my premonition."

At this point in her memoirs, Ria informs the reader that she never
intended to remain at the Abbey for more than four years. She was sure
she would be sacked before then. On the other hand, she remembered a
politician telling her that "he had been taught never to make the mistake
of sacking anyone. 'It is better to make it impossible for them to remain.
They will then leave voluntarily, which is the better way.'" Obviously, in

hindsight, Ria interpreted Blythe's behavior toward her in that light. "The black cloud of which I was still aware," she tells us, "seemed to have grown thicker as it concentrated around the Theatre." What black cloud? The thought that she might be dismissed or forced out of her position as artistic director? Five pages earlier in her writing she cheerfully remarks that after her June vacation in Paris visiting their national theatre, she was "refreshed ... and full of new ideas...."

By the time she came to put pen to paper to describe her theatrical career, Ria, possibly in a state of depression, seemed to have adopted the general view of the Abbey's years in exile. "The Abbey did not die"; wrote Hugh Hunt, "but the years of its exile radically altered its character and reduced its standing as a leading European theatre. The fire destroyed more than a building, it destroyed an atmosphere, a sense of dedication to an ideal, however tarnished it had become through the passing years."[21]

In any case, when she arrived at the theatre later that morning, she came upon a small group of players standing morosely among scorched seats gazing at the spaces in the burnt-out roof. She thought she heard one of them say, "Get away, you witch! You have been foretelling this for a long time!" She wasn't sure but he might have used the pejorative word which begins with the letter "b."[22]

Two Dubliners were said to have discovered the flames at 1 A.M. and five sections of Dublin's fire brigade were summoned to put out the fire. Within the hour, however, the backstage was destroyed, the stage badly damaged, the auditorium roof gone, and all the scenery, furniture props, and much of the wardrobe and prompt scripts were devoured by flame and water.

Next day, in the *Irish Times*, Lennox Robinson, having surveyed the ruins, mournfully intoned the old playhouse's *Nunc Dimittis*. "The theatre took the matter into its own hands," he said, "waited until the house was empty, and deliberately set itself on fire. It went up in flames and in glory, reflecting the glory of its players and its playwrights." It did not go unnoticed that the last scene of *The Plough and the Stars* concludes with "the fires of Dublin's Easter Week ... seen through Bessie Burgess's attic window."

Standing there amidst the charred remains, Ria had a selfish thought. Now that all the stock scenery had been destroyed, she would get the new designs she had always wanted for the repertoire of standard plays she was attempting to establish. Despite all the signs and portents, she was thinking about her future at the Abbey.

At this point, she was summoned into the managing director's office. Already gathered there awaiting her arrival were Blythe, the secretary, Eric

The morning after the fire, Abbey members survey the damage on stage. (University of Delaware Library Special Collections.)

Gorman, and in the shadows, seated near the far wall, the stage carpenter, Seaghan Barlow. Blythe began the conversation by announcing there was some talk of a performance that night in the Peacock Theatre. Ria says she scorned the suggestion, citing the inexperience of a young company playing in a strange, much smaller space, with neither scenery, props, nor costumes for the production. Later, in her memoirs and for the movie news cameras, Ria dramatically related the response her reaction elicited from the modest stage carpenter, Barlow.

"Suddenly, a voice spoke from the shadows: 'The Abbey Theatre has never closed its doors except during Easter Week 1916. We must keep faith with the public. Even if we are to recite on an otherwise empty stage tonight, we must give a performance!'" Ria heard Barlow's words as "a voice from the past; from one of those who had begotten our Theatre. Like a chastened child, I rose to do his bidding."[23]

What followed might have been scripted for one of those Hollywood films about a country barn being turned into an opulent playhouse. Clothes materialized from a supportive public, Barlow pieced together four sets, props appeared like magic, and, at eight o'clock, Seaghan Barlow struck the Abbey gong, which had been saved from the fire, and the young Abbey company rose to the occasion. The only prop that had to be replaced was a large double perambulator, which would not fit upon the tiny Peacock stage. In its place, Ria "wheeled on a doll's go'car belonging to my small niece, Ria. I swear the emotional reaction from that packed audience became audible."

After the final curtain, a relative of Lady Gregory's appeared like a specter out of the playhouse past with "a magnum of champagne to drink to the memory of those who had gone."[24] That performance would have been a great triumph, Ria and her tiny band of gallant players snatching victory from disaster, if, on that night, the final curtain descended upon the Ria Mooney story. There was, however, a morning after the fire. The struggle was to endure for 12 more years.

Once the excitement of "going on with the show" had passed, the cold light of theatrical reality shed its rays upon the empty Peacock stage and auditorium. The view would have disheartened the most determined of players. It was shabby and small and at the top of a narrow set of stairs. The audience, so supportive in their hour of need, would not long accept such Spartan conditions. Much of their repertoire wouldn't fit on the tiny stage, and the auditorium was not large enough to support the numbers needed to pay the players' already parsimonious salaries. They had just completed their vacations, so there wouldn't be any grace time in which to plan and execute some interim arrangement. Something had to be done, and done quickly. But what were they to do, and where were they to do it?

On the day after the fire, July 19, 1951, Cathal O'Shannon, writing in the *Irish Times*, gave the company encouragement in their moment of crisis. "While the Abbey has always had the warm loyalty of its audience," he wrote, "it has been taken for granted too often of late years that in the old days attendance was good. Far from it, indeed; for in the early years— and, indeed, until the nationalist resurgence from 1917 onwards— half empty houses, often more than half-empty, were customary. In the beginning, performances were generally for three nights a week only, and at times occupants of both stalls and pit were not much more numerous than the players on the stage." O'Shannon's vision of the Abbey past is in marked contrast to the roseate picture of "the glory days" conjured up by both Ria and Hugh Hunt some 20 years after the fire. In time, the popular view that Abbey theatrical tradition and performance had perished in the fire would poison the playhouse atmosphere and color even the performers' views of the value of the work they accomplished under impossible circumstances.

At that moment, Lord Moyne, of Guinness and Sons, came to the

From top left: Lord Moyne, Lord and Lady Longford, and Ria at the theatre — "running with the hare, and hunting with the hounds." (G. A. Duncan.)

rescue with an offer of Rupert Guinness Hall. Ria was gratified that the Guinness gift included electricity and the salaries of all connected with the firm who were working temporarily for the troupe. Ever the society matron, Ria couldn't help but note "this fine gesture" in her memoirs, hardly mentioning the heavy lifting the company had to do in order to move into the new space. Others observed with amusement Ria's desire to be seen in the company of titled society. She was sensitive to such criticism, and she responded to it in her autobiography. Once, "when I told Lennox Robinson ... that I had met a Countess, he accused me with a smile of 'running with the hare, and hunting with the hounds.' This is something one must never do in Ireland — or anywhere else I suppose — even if one does not quite believe in either hare or hounds."[25] It wasn't really a question of belief. Social class was easily discernible to anyone who had suffered from it. If she was free of such prejudices, why did she so strenuously segregate her private and public lives? Ultimately, though, no matter how generous Lord Moyne's gesture may have been, the acting company still had to bear the brunt of the consequences of the fire. It is disappointing that, in her memoirs, she hardly refers to their contribution at all.

The Plough and the Stars continued to run at the Peacock until the company was ready to open Louis D'Alton's last play, *The Devil a Saint Would Be*. The Abbey accepted the play shortly before the author's death, which was said to have deprived the theatre of a writer who "might have kept its great traditions alive."[26] The play's earlier opening had to be postponed on account of the fire, but once the players had settled into Rupert Guinness Hall, it was decided to open as soon as possible. On September 10, 1951, then, the second new play of the interrupted Abbey season reached the stage.

This impudent play charts the conversations of an old Kerry woman with an Irish saint who instructs her to dispose of all her earthly possessions. When this action results in her niece's simple husband turning into a schemer, two tinkers getting drunk with her pension money, and a policeman nearly losing his sanity trying to fill out the government relief forms, it occurs to all that she is mad.

The critics praised D'Alton for posing "stimulating questions through the medium of everyday business activity."[27] The *Irish Press* remarked that "once again the Abbey players looked like a rejuvenated lot. Ria Mooney set a cracker pace in the production and introduced such colourful touches that made the premiere quite unique." The critics agreed that it was Brid Lynch's play and it stamped her as "a really fine actress," but there was also abundant applause for Harry Brogan, Phillip O'Flynn, and Ita O'Mahoney. The *Irish Independent* singled out Ray MacAnally for special notice. "Ray MacAnally, as Guard Herlihy, makes a lovely piece of fooling of the scene in which he helps the unwilling Stacey to fill up her old age pension form, and teaches her the difference between breaking the law illegally and legally." Ria was given credit for an excellent production and Vere Dudgeon's settings were said to "strike a novel note."

There was, however, little time in which to rejoice. Sometime in August, Blythe had met with Louis Elliman, theatrical magnate and owner of the Gaiety, proposing the Abbey become his tenant at the Queen's Theatre.[28] Elliman set a rental fee of 227 pounds a week, and, on August 24, a five-year lease was entered into by the two parties. The company must once again pick up its tattered finery and move to the decaying playhouse situated across the river from its old Abbey Street premises. Why a five-year lease was accepted, when it was proposed that the Abbey be rebuilt in two years, is never explained. The announcement was made that the troupe would have its premiere at the new location on September 24, 1951.

Expectations were that the Queen's would be but a temporary home for the Abbey company. Earlier, in 1948, a fund had been established to be spent on a competition for a design of a new Abbey playhouse.²⁹ There was general agreement among those concerned with theatrical affairs that the cramped and aging quarters on Abbey Street were old-fashioned and inadequate as a home for the internationally respected national company. Moreover, the rising costs of production compared with the tiny government subsidy and the small Abbey auditorium made it evident that the current building could not continue to support the theatre's production schedule.

For similar reasons, Edwards and MacLiammóir had searched for several years after the war for new premises. They specifically had an eye on the possibility of buying the nearly 800-seat Queen's Theatre, which, according to their biographer, was "a charming but ill-maintained building of 1823 in the city centre, which was the home of melodrama and variety."³⁰ The Boys particularly admired the building's Celtic Revival plasterwork, which had been installed during a turn of the century refurbishment. The backstage accommodation was small, but the stage was excellent and had the added production advantage of a fly-gallery. The purchase price was 30,000 pounds, of which the Boys were able to provide only 2,000. Eventually, as a result of their failure to raise much financial support from the community, they abandoned the project.

In light of this evidence of the playhouse's desirability, it is interesting to read Hunt's description of the place. "The building itself was in poor repair: it was draughty; its walls were in need of paint; its carpets and upholstery were shabby; the stage lighting was many years out of date; plaster was falling from the ceiling, and patches of damp disfigured the approach to the dress circle. It possessed no workshop or wardrobe store; its dressing-room accommodation was inadequate, and the sight-lines from the sides of the circles were bad."³¹

Hunt admitted that "the Abbey itself was scarcely eligible for top league rating," but for him the Queen's greatest fault was that it lacked the intimacy of the old Abbey. He believed that it was that intimacy between actor and audience that had "shaped the character and acting style of the old theatre." The Queen's had twice as many seats as the old Abbey, but that the number of seats reduced the intimacy of the relationship between players and patrons is an open question. Kathleen Barrington, who played for almost a decade at the Queen's before moving into the current Abbey playhouse, never thought it too big or impersonal. "It was a nice — a very nice — theatre to play in. O. K., it was shabby, decrepit, backstage accommodations were pitiful, but it was probably a nicer theatre to play in than the old Abbey. The modern Abbey needs more energy and projection than the old Queen's [did]."[32] In any case, the need for a larger seating capacity would have created — in fact did create — the same circumstances in a rebuilt Abbey.

The players began moving into the new facility immediately. Ria suggested they celebrate the opening of their new location with a production of O'Casey's *The Silver Tassie*.[33] It was a mistake. Rehearsals were plagued by builders' scaffolding on the stage and in the auditorium, and the workmen's voices raised in conversation didn't help the actors' concentration. Since the task of sprucing up the place had to be accomplished within a month, the players had to work through the chaos. It would have been wiser, no doubt, to transfer the current D'Alton success to the Queen's, but, by the time that Ria realized her mistake, it was too late. "I carried on with the best heart I could muster," she remembered, "but I ... wanted to go out and run...."

On the 25th of September, the *Irish Times* agreed with Ria that *The Silver Tassie* was "a wrong choice of play for the changeover." Without previous knowledge of the rehearsal conditions, the reviewer found only "one or two minor irritations [in] Ria Mooney's good production." However, the "producer and designer will have to bring their groupings nearer center-stage if every member of the future Queen's audiences is to see what goes on."

The last two months had passed in a maze of smoldering ruins, evenings performing a large play on a tiny stage, moving the remains of props, furniture, and costumes first to Rupert Guinness Hall and then on to the Queen's, where the smell of fresh paint and the clutter and clatter of busy workmen suffused the atmosphere of distracted rehearsals. These were, indeed, the times that tried men's souls, and it was Ria's task to urge her charges under each new challenge to walk once more "into the breach dear friends." It must have seemed a never-ending effort to merely stave off impending disaster, and there didn't seem to be any relief in sight.

Furthermore, signs on the Abbey theatrical horizon might have caused her some anxiety even before the catastrophic fire. It was obvious that the audiences were changing. Several Dublin reviewers had noted the demand for comedy where they thought none was needed or intended. This "tittering," as one critic labeled it, often in the wrong places, and O'Higgins's forced humor in *Design for a Headstone*, along with audience demands that he "dole out this most desirable commodity in buckets," indicated that the Abbey patron profile was not the old intimate, familiar, family gathering it had been.

This audience came to the play to be entertained, and they showed their disdain for using the playhouse as a center for political, religious, or academic discussion in the case of the *Headstone* uprising. These demonstrations were obviously a tempest in a teapot. Ria's remembrance of the uproar created by *The Plough and the Stars* clouded her apprehension of the actual climate in Dublin at the time of its production. The Civil War was still being fought in many pubs and kitchens in 1927, and many of its heroes walked the streets and nursed grudges against their opponents to the edge of eternity. Eamon de Valera's self-supporting rural economy was, as he himself had been in 1948, set aside. Most of his revolutionary comrades had gone to their reward, and the new generation had only the stories of their parents to remember them by. The young seemed more interested in jobs than reliving the wars of the past.

The actors must have found Ria's greenroom speech the same kind of exercise in nostalgia. That she had the courage of her convictions was never in doubt, but the players might be pardoned if they saw no comparison between 1927 and 1951. It is hard to believe that a man of the physical stature of Walter Macken was afraid of the noise and fuss coming from the auditorium. It is much more likely that he found it an intrusion on the real purposes of the place. As actor and playwright, he was there to tell a story, to read out the play's meaning, not to conduct a public debate about religion and politics. If he excised certain provocative lines in order to get through the performance, he was not doing anything that actors haven't done since time immemorial. Ria suggested cutting *Red Roses for Me* to Sean O'Casey for similar reasons; some of the dialogue seemed to her to detract from the story and merely served to alienate audiences.

She had another less pressing but, for all that, no less threatening problem to deal with. The Queen's was a fine replacement for the old Abbey, and, if it wasn't in good condition, it was no worse than their burned playhouse. Nonetheless, as Cathal O'Shannon noted in the *Irish Times*, there was a developing picture of "the good old days" at the Abbey that threatened to make anything done in the present playhouse pale by comparison. The town critics who remembered those glory days refused to see that the world had changed, and, in any case, their memories were not entirely accurate. Their constant criticism of the present situation was disheartening to the players and served to further undermine the already shaky condition of the National Theatre.

Of course, Ria might look at the bright side of things. Plans for a new playhouse could no longer be put off indefinitely, as an extended stay at the Queen's was unthinkable. First, because rental fees nearly doubled the cost of production and consumed the annual government subsidy. Second, it would be impossible with that financial burden to spare any funds for maintenance of the building, not to mention improvements backstage. Third, the property was in a desirable part of Dublin, and plans for its removal and replacement with a more profitable piece of real estate would no doubt eventually leave the Abbey without a home.

It would be her task to keep the place open until that new facility was constructed. It wouldn't be easy. If they failed to enlarge their audience, the number of unoccupied seats might make the place look empty. While the theatre was in the center of Dublin, it wasn't located on the fabled Abbey grounds. It might be hard to attract the fashionable crowd that kept the city talking about the theatre. Besides, she still had to contend with the advocates of the Irish language, and they promised to keep on sapping the financial and personnel resources of the main stage work. She couldn't expect any help or understanding from them. She would have to go it alone.

Since she never fraternized with the players in the company, and, as her relationship with Blythe was strictly professional (she often referred to him outside of the playhouse as the "gentle monster"), she stood isolated on the National Theatre stage, without anyone to offer her the solace of companionship, at the helm of a drifting theatrical barque on a dangerous sea. That picture might have pleased her sense of the romance of the theatre; it could not have assuaged her fear and anxiety.

Nearly 20 years later, she was to ruefully comment in her memoirs: "Having inherited my father's robust constitution, which kept him mentally and physically alert up to a week before he died at the age of ninety-five, I carried on at the Abbey in spite of having no help at all."[34]

CHAPTER EIGHT

"A Capital of Hopeless Promise"

Opening the new playhouse with *The Silver Tassie* was Ria Mooney's artistic nod to the Dublin arts community, but their numbers could not sustain the financial cost of performing it for more than a week. While Dublin playgoers came out in large numbers to see revivals of O'Casey's trilogy about the "Troubles," only the trendsetters had any affection for the rest of the O'Casey canon. Since the Abbey, with the large Queen's rental fee added to its production budget, would be relying more than ever on box-office receipts to pay its bills, Blythe ordered a change of program immediately. So Louis D'Alton's *The Devil a Saint Would Be* reappeared before the public on October 8, 1951, and held the stage until Ann Daly's *Window on the Square* was ready to open two weeks later.

In retrospect, although this new play was not critically well-received, it clearly seems to have touched upon Ireland's provincial dilemma.[1] The plot charts the 22-year marriage of a village beauty, who, under the thumb of her snobbish mother, ensnares a Dublin architect of promise, and ties him to the narrow world that can be seen through the frame of their drawing room window on the square of Dromeen in County Cork. The lives wasted in this forgotten backwater isolated from the challenges and chances of the big city seem prophetic images of the Irish cultural picture in the '50s. Indeed, even such highly touted artistic names as Patrick Kavanagh, Brian O'Nolan, and Brendan Behan, who lived in the metropolis of Dublin, were condemned to penury in their own land, or finally forced to employ eccentricity, showmanship, and bravado in order to attract the attention of the English and American public.[2] Such public characterizations remarkably resembled the artistically disdained figure of the "stage Irishman." This melancholy adaptation to international demands doomed the trio to a drink-sodden final curtain.

This *Window on the Square* had a view of all Ireland. The author appears to have believed that an Irishman's only hope is to escape to London, as the artistically minded daughter of the provincial socialites is forced to do at the play's conclusion. In other words, it wasn't simply the lack of creature comforts or a reasonable standard of living that created the current exodus to foreign shores. Poets, playwrights, and novelists felt artistically constricted on their tiny cultural island. *Envoy*, a new magazine that attracted young writers, turned its attention away from problems of national concern and increasingly became self-consciously European in outlook.[3] The journal adopted as its cultural icon, ex-patriot James Joyce, who, ironically enough, spent his entire imaginative life within Dublin's confines. Unfortunately, emigration appeared to be the only option open to those who had this perception of Ireland as a place burdened with intolerable cultural provincialism. Young poets like Brendan Kennelly looked upon that eventuality with bitter poignancy. In his poem "Westland Row"(the name of a Dublin railway station for the boat to England), he wrote:

> Brown bag bulging with faded nothings;
> A ticket for three pounds one and six
> To Euston, London via Holyhead
> Young faces limp, misunderstanding
> What the first gay promptings meant—
> A pass into a brilliant wilderness,
> A capital of hopeless promise.

Was emigration a mere synonym for exile? Ria had tried it 25 years before, and her present place at the head of the National Theatre was the result of her recent rejection of that alternative. Who could blame her if, after surveying conditions around her, she now regretted that decision. Though they were a stone's throw across the Liffey from their old Abbey location, the Dublin river now seemed a cultural divide as wide and as deep as the Atlantic Ocean.

Perhaps there wasn't any good solution to the problem. Maybe once you have departed from your native place, as Thomas Wolfe suggested in the title of his novel, you can't go home again.

Window on the Square was replaced after only one week with O'Casey's *Shadow of a Gunman*, which played with Shaw's *Village Wooing* as a curtain-raiser. This program gave the company a breather until they were ready to open Seamus Byrne's new play, *Innocent Bystander*. The *Irish Press* review began with a reflection of an apparently new Dublin attitude critical toward the National Theatre.[4] "Seamus Byrne's new play," wrote the critic, "which was given its premiere at the Abbey [in the Queen's last night], has a tone and quality which give a definite lift to present-day standards in that long-suffering institution, but one must be careful not to assess its value by comparison with the merely mediocre." The *Press* liked the first two acts, but criticized the last act, while the *Irish Independent* took exactly the opposite view. Perhaps, with more comment than was intended, the *Irish Times* didn't even bother to take any notice of the opening of a new play at the Queen's.

The story tells of a country solicitor's embezzlement of his clients' money in order to save his father's honor. Byrne's play suffered, the reviewers said, from a surfeit of ideas and a loss of a sense of direction. Harry Brogan and M. J. Dolan were accused of being "in their Abbey element," and Angela Newman's Delia the maid was "the Abbey of the caricatures and skits."[5] All in all, having the title Abbey attached to one's name seems to have become a distinct liability. Dubliners need not worry excessively, for there were other more elevated entertainments to be had in the city. Weren't "Big Bill Campbell and his singing cowboys" at the Olympia, where a packed house gave them a warm reception?[6] Byrne's first play, *Design for a Headstone*, had created something of a sensation, and the playwright's future was given serious appraisal. Now he was dismissed out of hand. Such summary critical judgment did not augur well for the future of the Abbey at the Queen's.

On December 3, 1951, *The New Gossoon* replaced *Innocent Bystander* and ran until the new Irish pantomime, *Reamonn agus Niamh Og*, began the holiday season. It had been a disastrous year. Of the four new plays, only D'Alton's *The Devil a Saint Would Be* had met with any approval. The destruction of the playhouse whose name had become synonymous with the national theatre had thrown the organization into confusion. After heroic efforts to live up to the Thespian adage, the show must go on, the stark reality of the tiny Peacock's limitations was replaced by a blur of scene shifting from there to Rupert Guinness Hall, and then on to the hastily cleaned up Queen's. Both new plays produced under these new circumstances had failed, and the already tired, harassed, and depressed company had been forced to rehearse and replace these failures with the work of two Abbey stalwarts, O'Casey and Shiels. The Abbey pantomime was the responsibility of Tomás MacAnna. Ria would have a month or so to collect her thoughts and get ready to direct in the new year a dispirited company in new plays not yet chosen for production amongst hostile critics and amid unfamiliar playhouse surroundings.

On January 21, 1952, the Abbey began its new year with a revival of dependable George Shiels' *Grogan and the Ferret*. Three weeks later, the much-scorned melodrama about possession by the devil, *The Righteous Are Bold*, once again proved its popularity with Dublin audiences. While the *Irish Times* thought it lost a little on second seeing, the critic had to admit that "it still retains moments of compelling theatre."[7] Marie Kean attracted attention as Nellie the Post. The *Irish Times* critic grumbled that she was able to get the "broadest of comedy out of the mumbo-jumbo." He was, of course, deriding the pagan superstitions of the benighted west islanders. The final derisive reference, obviously aimed at the climactic third act exorcism scene, noted that "Ria Mooney's direction exacts every ounce of sensationalism from the story." Readers were left to draw their own conclusions as to whether or not that was the right theatrical thing to do.

Brinsley MacNamara's *Look at the Heffernans* followed a month later on March 11, and Louis D'Alton's early success, *The Money Doesn't Matter*, played through the month of April. May continued the rash of revivals with St. John Ervine's comedy, *Friends and Relations*, and O'Casey's *Juno and the Paycock*. The only new piece was the curtain raiser to O'Casey's drama, written by Conal O'Riordan, entitled *An Imaginary Conversation*. The Abbey took its annual holiday during the month of June, and O'Casey's *Juno* resumed its run the first week in July, until replaced by Molloy's *The King of Friday's Men*.

The first six months of 1952 demonstrated the power of the Abbey repertoire by producing seven revivals of past successes from the pens of six of the theatre's own playwrights. It was an impressive demonstration of the quality and popularity of its repertoire. But why had they not included one new full-length play in the list? Was Ria cautiously discovering the new playhouse's production strengths and limitations, or was it simply that they hadn't received a manuscript worth producing?

Enter Walter Macken. The actor who, as Bartley Dowd in *The King of Friday's Men*, came to the rescue of the pretty damsel in distress, now exchanged his actor's cap for a playwright's shade and effectively bailed out Ria's distressed troupe of weary performers. *Home Is the Hero* not only served notice that a new Irish literary voice had arrived on the scene just in time to save the Abbey's staggering reputation, it also produced the longest run in the history of the Abbey. As it turned out, however, Dublin's cultural community appeared to disdain anything that smacked of theatrical effectiveness, and Macken's play, although it ran until Christmas, was almost completely ignored by the leading newspaper critics.

The play is set in the county council house in Galway, where the

O'Reilly family awaits the return of their father Paddo who has been away for five years.[8] Poverty has stalked the family in his absence: his wife, Daylia, has taken to drink, daughter Josie is consorting with the town ne'er do well, and son Willie, handicapped by a lame leg, is about to make the most sinful of alliances. Dovetail, one of Paddo's drinking pals, is planning a big bonfire welcome for the prodigal's return, and Daylia is excited to distraction by the waiting.

> DAYLIA: It's like the time when we were coortin'. I used to work in the big house in Taylor's Hill. I never thought the hour'd be up until he'd be outside the gate waitin' for me. Heart-scaldin' it's been all those years without him. Nobody'll ever know what it has meant to me, to be without him so long, and not a penny piece comin' into the house except bloody charity.

Lily, the girl next door, joins Willie to welcome Paddo home. Delicately, she asks him if he was always lame. He was born whole, but, in order to tell his story, he must inquire whether she has any memory of his father.

> LILY: I do. He was a nice man. We used always wait for him in the street on a Friday night when he got paid. He always dished out a bag of sweets. I thought he was a giant. He was always great life, wasn't he?
> WILLIE: He was. Great laugh, great songs, great stories. He'd make you sit up. He was like holding a charge of electricity. He had a way with babies. He used to hurl them into the air and catch them lightly in his arms as they came down. He did that to me when I was a baby, but he didn't catch me once on the way down. It was pay night. He had a few drinks taken. That's what happened to my leg.
> LILY: Do you resent Paddo, Willie?
> WILLIE: No, Lily, I don't. (He looks at her. There is a tense silence in the air). Do you resent Paddo, Lily?
> LILY: Do I resent Paddo?
> WILLIE: After all, he did kill your father, didn't he?

Macken craftily reveals the complexity of his hero while keeping him from the scene until the end of the first act. The audience is held in tense anticipation, waiting to discover how will this larger-than-life figure deal with the crumbling world he is about to find. Paddo enters through the back door. He is there before anyone sees him.

He dismisses Dovetail's celebration curtly: "What kind of fool do you take me for? What kind of a spectacle do you want to make of me? Amn't I shamed enough without you having to make more of it?" He makes Daylia pour away some stout she has purchased for his return, throws Dovetail out of his house, and sits for his tea. "Mabbe none of ye want to sit at the same table with a criminal," he says as the curtain descends.

The first act exposition is accomplished with fascinating character revelations of the central figure, using the same delayed entrance device employed by Molière to introduce his *Tartuffe*. Willie's love affair with the daughter of the man his father killed is reminiscent of Corneille's *The Cid*. The entire action of the play takes place in the time it takes to play it. Clearly, Macken had some classic models in mind when he sat down to construct his play.

In the second act, Paddo warns his son away from Lily, makes an inept, self-pitying apology to Lily's mother who has come to make peace over the slaying of her husband, throws Josie's lover, Manchester, out of the house, and goes after her with his belt as the curtain falls. Macken's action, crammed with violent confrontations, is not for the delicate or weak of heart. His Paddo is larger than life, straightforward yet complex, a guilt-ridden manipulator, and a charming egoist.

Robert Hogan, who seems to have written his criticism of *Home Is*

In *Home Is the Hero*, Brian O'Higgins' Paddo threatens Bill Foley's Manchester with a chair as Paddo's daughter, Josie, played by Ita O'Mahoney, tries to keep her boyfriend from striking her father. (G. A. Duncan.)

the Hero without having seen it onstage, found the play a "curiously cold, almost ill-tempered play, although technically it is an adroit example of the best Abbey realism."[9] Neither the *Irish Press*, the *Irish Independent*, nor the *Irish Times* carried a review of the production. Of course, the *Times* was on vacation when it opened. When the paper reappeared on newsstands at the end of August, the play was already in its fifth sell-out week.

"Walter Macken is one of the most successful modern Irish writers," writes Hogan, "and one of the best. His plays are little known outside Ireland, but his fiction has found a fairly wide, Book-of-the-Month Club, upper-middle-brow audience."[10] Aye, there's the rub. The smart set acknowledges they are melodramatically effective, but, perhaps, too accessible to be art. "Still," Hogan grudgingly admits, "even though his stories lack the qualities likely to get them discussed in the *Hudson Review* or *Modern Fiction Studies*, they are fine work, and no less fine for being both traditional and easily readable."

As artistic director of the National Theatre, Ria found herself in an ambiguous position. She had an extraordinary theatrical hit on her hands, playing to delighted and packed houses, but she found that her friends in the cultural community refused to take any notice of the work. The play and the production were not even damned by faint praise; they were simply ignored. Walter Macken was an Irish speaker from Galway, already a celebrated Dublin actor and budding writer of fiction, and his new play was attracting huge audiences willing to pay hard-earned money in a time of economic depression for the pleasure of seeing his play. Ria wanted to please paying customers, but she also longed to belong to Dublin's cultural elite. Whatever the family comforts of life at home with her father, her sisters and their children, her social world was made up of writers, painters, art dealers, architects, and even nobility such as the Longfords. She must have recognized the implied snub in their silence.

Added to this journalistic rejection was the fact that so long a run effectively kept the elite from attending Abbey openings. *Home Is the Hero* was so popular that the theatre, with the additional rental expenses and the deficits it had incurred in the past fire-interrupted season, couldn't afford to take it off and risk a new play's financial failure.

As the long run dragged on, Dublin's critics began carping about Blythe's accountant's attitude toward the artistic life of his theatre.[11] Now, it was said, the Abbey was no different from a commercial playhouse. It played strictly for money without regard for artistic merit or its subsidized responsibility to present new Irish playwrights. The minuscule amount of the subsidy, most of which was reserved for Gaelic productions, was never mentioned. Neither did the critics give any consideration to the impossible situation the Abbey had been forced to deal with as a result of the disastrous fire that had destroyed their home.

It is not difficult to imagine the effect such criticisms had upon the company morale. Furthermore, while a long run might be rewarding for those in the production, it had the effect of leaving much of the repertory company of nearly 30 actors cooling their heels in the wings. They weren't working at all in English. Their only employment was in the Gaelic afterpieces that played to the first three rows of the Queen's. The Abbey company under the direction of Tomás MacAnna played Lady Gregory's *The Rising of the Moon*, and George Shiels' *The Passing Day* in Irish into a gaping, nearly empty auditorium, and, during the rest of the evening, sat around and complained about their enforced idleness. It was, it seemed, an unhappy time for all concerned.

On January 26, 1953, the Abbey at the Queen's opened the New Year with M. J. Molloy's *The Wood of the Whispering*.[12] The plot revolves around a Galway rogue named Sanbatch, a proud descendant of a line of big house herdsmen who has watched the steady depopulation of his world since the Free State was established. This imaginative and eloquent matchmaker, guarding his own freedom with a shotgun at the entrance to the empty big house, attempts to arrange a marriage between the Woodcutter come to despoil the demesne's ancient forest land and Kitty Wallace, the only eligible girl in the county. The play gets its name from the place where township romances were traditionally pursued. It is that woodland that is about to be demolished for profit.

The *Irish Times* called the play "a poor man's *Cherry Orchard* written in the atmosphere of Chekhov and in the language of Synge." The critic found Molloy's peasants "charged with tragedy, rather than comedy, in the story he tells of their wasted lives." The *Irish Press* lamented the opening night audience's "guffaws and applause" at almost every exit. "At times," the reviewer wrote, "the play suffered the indignity of falling down to the level of a variety theatre burlesque of the Abbey itself. The audience appeared to insist that here they had the choicest selection of stage Irish westerners and they were going to enjoy every moment of their company." The stage types appeared to be nothing more than caricatures to the offended *Irish Independent* reviewer. "It is an exaggeration of Irish naiveté," he observed, for a young girl to ask "if people in England really eat their boiled eggs with a spoon instead of with a knife."

Such ferocious criticism would have intimidated more self-conscious patrons. The critics seemed angry that their readers were ignoring them. Of course, it is true that the play is a sad, almost meditative comedy, but it also features an enormous load of playfulness and physical fooling, including two 80-year-old twin brothers who see themselves as irresistible ladykillers, an accidental shotgun explosion, Sanbatch's coffin box in which he hides from the law, the teasing of the two "ole fellas" by flirtatious Kitty Wallace, and the proposed construction of a still for brewing poteen. Why these pundits think that audiences should be inhibited in their enjoyment of these "keystone cop" sequences, just because the overall theme is of emigration and depopulation of the west, they never explained. Charlie Chaplin was the saddest of funny men, and nobody criticized him for such incongruity.

The atmosphere of *The Wood of the Whispering* is lambent with the indomitable and unquenchable gaiety of these poverty stricken remnants of a society facing extinction. They carry on with poetic inventiveness and a playful good humor that manifests their tragic nobility in the face of incomprehensible circumstances—circumstances which, nevertheless, cannot overwhelm their passionate love for life.

In his preface to the published edition of his play, M. J. Molloy lamented the conditions that gave birth to the setting of his play. "For forty years Ireland has been free," he wrote, "and for forty years it has wandered in the desert under the leadership of men who freed their nation, but who could never free their own souls and minds from the ill-effects of having been born in slavery."[13] He compares the return of the Jews to Israel to make fertile a scorched desert to the stunted growth of a free Ireland. "In 1910 the Great Blasket island had one hundred and fifty people and a well filled school. Forty years later the population was a handful, there was only one child, so they called their island Tir Na Sean, the Land of the Old." That poetic title might be applied to all of the west of Ireland. "But of this fact our suburban depopulation enthusiasts know nothing. But country people know all about it, and they know the background of this play, the comedy of the eccentric old bachelors, and the tragedy, too."

Although the critics seemed obsessed by the opening-night audience reactions, they found much to praise in the work of the acting company. Philip O'Flynn, Harry Brogan, and M. J. Dolan were "in their element of unrestrained comedy,"[14] and Ray MacAnally "acts pleasantly in the part of the young bachelor" woodcutter.[15] Maire O'Donnell, "as the barmaid, Kitty Wallace, is lively and charming enough to make him [the woodcutter] change his mind." The *Times* reviewer praised "Ria Mooney's sensitive production [which] gives us some of the best team playing seen in the Abbey recently, with outstandingly good performances from Phillip Flynn as Sandbatch, and Ray Mc'Inally [*sic*]as the woodcutter."[16] Finally, Robert Hogan, in his book-length consideration of the period, *After the*

Irish Renaissance, wrote: "It is a play with memorable parts for actors; anyone who has seen the Abbey actor Philip O'Flynn giving Sanbatch's moving curtain speech could hardly forget it. *The Wood of the Whispering* could easily become lost in the more flamboyant experiments of the modern drama, but in its quiet way it is rare and beautiful."

The Wood of the Whispering continued for three healthy weeks before giving way to a revival of T. C. Murray's *Autumn Fire,* which was succeeded a week later by D'Alton's *Lover's Meeting.* The company began the month of May by alternating each evening Shiels' *The Passing Day* with Synge's *Playboy.* After two weeks, B. G. MacCarthy's *The Whip Hand* was produced and later performed on Radio Éireann in an attempt to bring the Abbey to the people.[17] The last week in May saw *The Righteous Are Bold* back for a two week stint, while the Company geared up for the theatre's second new work of the year, Louis D'Alton's second posthumously produced play, entitled *This Other Eden.*

The *Irish Times* called it a "good, rip-roaring rollicking indictment of certain flaws and certain smugnesses in Ireland today, produced at a fine pace by Ria Mooney, and with such bitterness as may be in it most palpably coated with the sugar of the broadest of comedy."[18] The critic compared it favorably with Shaw's *John Bull's Other Island,* except for its "intellectual analytic power."

The plot satirizes the actions of a moralist who has gathered together a farcical group of hypocrites to erect a memorial to a dead commandant "who might have been without fear, but was not, alas, without blame." The *Irish Independent* thought that "many of the subtleties are lost in laughter, and the general effect is of a rough sketch of a play rather than a polished piece of stage craft." The *Irish Press,* on the other hand, found it far and away "the best thing that came from this prolific writer's pen and, once again, it is right to stress that his early death was a serious loss to Irish drama." Harry Brogan, Brian O'Higgins, Bill Foley, Geoffrey Golden, Maire O'Donnell, and guest artist, Christopher Casson, were given credit for a fine production. The *Press* critic's only caveat came disguised as praise. "As far as the Abbey audience allowed them, the players did a princely job with the script, but the loud laughs which greeted every witty line and the prolonged applause which accompanied almost every exit, proved very irritating." It was almost as if these men on the aisle were about to propose etiquette lessons for anyone attending the National Theatre.

If *This Other Eden* failed to receive unstinting approval from the Dublin dailies, the queues at the box office demonstrated that word of mouth was still a powerful advertisement in the small city. After suspending theatrical activity for the annual vacation, the Abbey reopened in July to full houses that promised to keep the play on the stage until Christmas. Grumbling immediately surfaced regarding the perceived commercial greed controlling national theatre activity. Perhaps, to protect Blythe from such criticism, or, because Ria wanted to keep the rest of the players occupied, the theatre decided to present on Saturday night, September 5, 1953, and for succeeding Saturday nights only as long as *This Other Eden* should continue its run, M. J. Molloy's new one-act play, *The Paddy Pedlar*, to be played with O'Casey's first play, *The Shadow of a Gunman*.

The script had been given its first production in 1952 by the Ballina Players.[19] It did not prevent the Queen's from selling out the large house to an audience eager to be seen at an Abbey first night.[20] The *Irish Press* committed a double *faux pas* by criticizing the play for not being something it never set out to be, while, at the same time, giving away the plot's important mystery. "It is a pity," wrote the scribe, "that one of our best living dramatists does not devote his keen intellect and poetic talent to some of the great problems of Ireland to-day instead of dissipating it on old themes like that of the 'Pedlar.' I could take very little interest in his faintly symbolic story of the pedlar who carried his dead mother on his back in order to fulfil her dying wish to be buried with her husband hundreds of miles away in 'Lord Leitrim's country.'"

Put in that way, the play loses its lyric as well as its dramatic impact. The central incident of the piece concerns a peasant named Ooshla, a man whose own dissipation has ruined him, driving him to steal from the rich. A wandering pedlar with a mysterious sack that he guards with devotion arrives at his door, seeking rest for the night. Set in the 1840s during the time of the Potato Famine, the action includes a threatened long knife fight, a flirtation between Ooshla's niece and her impoverished intended, and an eloquent quarrel about the social conditions that drive a good man to roguery.

"Ria Mooney's production," remarked the *Irish Press* critic, "gave it [*The Paddy Pedlar*] every chance, but the play has not got what it takes." The *Irish Independent* said the "play has wit, it has pathos, it has humanity, and the rich poetry of the Western vernacular which, however, jars occasionally by its suggestion of a folklorist's phrase book." Still, the critic noticed that "Vere Dudgeon's setting of an 1840 kitchen in Co. Mayo is distinguished by a perfection of detail and beautiful lighting."

If these critics refused to be impressed by either the production or the play, the *Irish Times* continued faithful to its opinion that Molloy wore the lyric mantle of Fitzmaurice and Synge. This play "endorses the widely-held opinion that Molloy is the best Irish writer of lyrical fantasy since

Synge and Fitzmaurice, and the best poetic folk dramatist that we have today." He gives to the Irish stage people of the west of Ireland, burdened "with primitive poverty and savagery," who faced "love, life, and death with a classical simplicity and a redeeming humour that was close to nobility." The *Times* critic made the bold statement that *The Paddy Pedlar* was "probably the finest one act play since *Riders to the Sea*."

This Other Eden continued popular with Dublin audiences and held the stage until it was time for the Christmas pantomime, this year entitled *Blaithin agus Mac an Ri*. The long engagements of the plays of D'Alton and Macken had set the Abbey finances on steady ground. They had also reduced the number of original scripts the theatre produced each year. The critical attitude of the daily press seemed to imply that Abbey actors were making too blatant an appeal for the approval of the lower-class members of the audience. Ria was directing her charges toward the obvious, the melodramatic, even into caricatures rather than characterizations. Irish society, even when attending them, began criticizing Abbey first nights as rather déclassé affairs.

The seating capacity of Queen's rendered the homey opening night atmosphere of the old Abbey a thing of the past. Dublin's beau monde now composed but a small part of the audience on these occasions. Perhaps that is the reason why these premieres became less fashionable as the years passed. Critics certainly were making a point of disassociating themselves from the behavior of first-night Abbey audiences. They were unwilling to pan Molloy's play outright, but they were not above complaining that he was pandering to the Queen's clientele.

The long runs gave Abbey actors a chance to relax. Some took advantage of the time to perfect their own stage personae. Harry Brogan, in particular, had a gift for pleasing the Queen's audiences. He was "a great man for presenting himself. He was a master," said Derry Power, a young man with the company during the midfifties, "of getting off and getting on to maximum effect." Power wasn't disapproving of such technique. "I mean, you learned from working with him. And the audience expected it."[21]

Other actors, Brian O'Higgins among them, found the only way to pass the time during long periods of inactivity was to go to a pub. He had been with the Abbey for over a decade and had a reputation as a very good actor. When his drinking became evident on stage, Ria was forced to relegate him to minor roles. Power remembered that "there was an element at the Abbey who drank. I mean you couldn't go and see a play on a Friday night." Friday was, of course, pay day.

Ria was also taking the blame for aspects of production over which she had little or no control. The part of Juno O'Boyle was considered to be the property of Eileen Crowe. As time passed, she appeared to many as too old for Juno, but, since she had great energy, Ria had no excuse for replacing her. "She had a kind of middle class Dublin thing," mused Power. "When she played Juno, she wouldn't wear a dirty apron."

Then there were the conditions of the revivals.

Repertory companies have little trouble getting up a production of a play they have done recently, especially when the actors who played in the original production are still with the troupe. The difficulty arises when the first cast is only partially present and new members, unfamiliar with the play or the first production, must take major roles. The result is that in revivals, actors are required to perform the parts they are cast in as closely as possible to the way they were originally played. Under such conditions, the veteran members of the cast still must adjust to their new partners in the dance, and the new members are constantly being reminded, often annoyingly, how things were done in the first, successful production. Sometimes Ria was reduced by company circumstances to totally inappropriate casting. Power remembered playing a 60-year-old man at the age of 19. Someone had fallen ill and there wasn't anyone else available to take the part. Although he got along well with Ria, Power nonetheless felt that, under the prevailing rehearsal conditions, "she certainly didn't encourage young people to be creative."

Revivals were often criticized in the press when actors tried new interpretations. Since she was trying to create a repertoire of Abbey successes, it was expected that she would preserve the traditional interpretations. Such an attitude had little to recommend itself to the young anxious to express their own individuality. Ria found herself in the impossible position of trying to reconcile contradictory aims. The critics wanted to see old plays done as they remembered them. On the other hand, the company, especially the younger members who had a reputation to make, wanted to discover new, more contemporary meanings in the parts they were assigned.

As 1953 drew to a close, Ria's window on Ireland's theatrical square presented a bleak landscape to even the untrained eye. The building plans for the new theatre were hopelessly mired in political wrangling.[22] The initial designs placed the Gate and the Abbey under the same roof. The architects were told to scrap that project and give the board a plan for a proscenium-arch playhouse to seat 650, with a small, experimental stage to accommodate 150 in the same edifice. The corporation refused to permit one theatre to be built on top of the other, so these latest drawings were consigned to the trash heap.

The new building, because it required more ground space, demanded the acquisition of an adjoining pub, the Abbey Bar. The proprietor held up the clearing of the land by demanding eight times the value of his property. Meanwhile, Blythe said that, even if the theatre played to 50 percent of its capacity, it would lose nearly 75 pounds a week. The fire insurance compensation was slowly being eaten up, and no other subsidy appeared to be on the horizon.

More threatening than all these adverse conditions was the attitude of members of the production team. Tomás MacAnna, who should have known better, referred to the "grim, grey similarity between most of the plays that went on at the Queen's."[23] Hunt restated this silly observation by declaring the general prejudice of his social milieu that, "in the eyes of many of its former friends, the Abbey had sold its birthright for a mess of pottage."[24] No matter what miracles Ria performed, she obviously could never satisfy her critics. "Well might the ancestral shades of the founders," wrote Hunt, "cast a cold eye on the fate of a theatre that, fifty years previously, they had created with such high ideals. The dusty old home of melodrama (the Queen's) was indeed wreaking its revenge on the high idealists who had set out to destroy its popular fare. Not only had the Abbey grown estranged from its oldest and best friends, but more grievously it had failed to win the respect of a younger generation who had deserted to other theatres."

Hugh Hunt was no dilettante. He knew that Abbey production standards were as high as ever, and that the professionals producing the plays could not be faulted. He took aim instead at the board of directors, and, predictably, fired at the same old convenient target, the man everyone loved to hate, Ernest Blythe. Hunt and company campaigned for greater responsibility to be placed in the hands of the professional employees. The management tradition established by Yeats, Synge, and Lady Gregory "was suitable so long as they were the authors of most of the plays, but was scarcely justifiable when control was in the hands of an ex–Minister for Finance."[25] Aside from the fact that such comments were bad theatrical history, as Cathal O'Shannon had reported in the *Times* at the time of the fire, they attributed idealism only to themselves, and avoided mentioning the wonderful work Ria and her troupe had been performing for the past five seasons. Hunt completely ignores Molloy's *Wood of the Whispering*, *The King of Friday's Men*, and *The Paddy Pedlar*. He damns with faint praise Macken's *Home Is the Hero*, and D'Alton's *This Other Eden*. Mere popular successes, don't you know. Tomelty's *All Soul's Night*, and MacMahon's *Bugle in the Blood* might never have seen the light of the Abbey stage for all Hunt remembers of those years. The stir created by

Byrne's *Design for a Headstone* seems never to have happened, and *The Devil a Saint Would Be* has been completely forgotten.

Such an interpretation of Ria's first five years as artistic director of the Abbey seems like a considered effort to erase the achievements of the entire Abbey acting company, its playwrights, and the woman who, under impossible theatrical circumstances, managed to garner rave reviews from the daily newspaper critics who witnessed and reported on Abbey opening nights during those years from 1948 to 1953. Their testimony, given at the moment and without the prejudice of hindsight or special pleading, is factual evidence that the standards of production and the quality of the playwriting were every bit as highly critically regarded then, as they had been during any period in the history of the National Theatre.

Hunt tells us that Blythe was not entirely to blame. He was out of his element. After all was said and done, it would have taken someone of the theatrical stature of Jerzy Grotowski, Joan Littlewood, or Peter Brook to transform the Queen's into "a centre for artistic life." Clearly, the advocates of new artistic control at the Abbey had little regard for the Abbey's tradition. The world knew of Ireland's theatre because of her playwrights and players, not because of her directors. The Abbey had been, from its inception, a playwright's theatre. While each generation had produced fine actors, from the Fays, Willie and Frank, and Dudley Digges to Barry Fitzgerald and Siobhan McKenna, some of her best, for example, F. J. McCormick never left Dublin and were never a factor on the English-speaking theatrical scene. The playwrights, on the other hand, didn't have to go anywhere. Their plays were performed in London and New York and around the English-speaking world by local companies. Yeats, Synge, and Lady Gregory were never financially successful in the commercial theatres, but they found their way into textbooks as required reading in many if not most English and American universities. Lennox Robinson, Sean O'Casey, Paul Vincent Carroll, and George Shiels were popular with theatre audiences both at home and abroad.

The educated Anglo-Irish minority seems to have instinctively sought to regain control of the National Theatre, which had been lost with the death of Yeats. Their first task was to discredit the current repertoire. It was not a question of defaming any of the current performers or the director. They had nothing against them personally, and they avoided attacking them in their writing. They didn't even wish to discredit the playwrights. They chose as their target one man, Ernest Blythe. He was vulnerable because they despised his hated Irish language policy and looked down upon his connection with finance.

Nonetheless, Ria and her company were found guilty by association.

Never mind that Ria Mooney had demonstrated her love for Yeats and Clarke by giving her services free of charge to the founding and directing of the Dublin Lyric Theatre. It didn't matter that she had opened the Abbey at the Queen's with *The Silver Tassie*, a play that, in spite of Yeats' disapproval and refusal to produce it, had become a theatrical rallying cry for the trendsetters. It was never mentioned that she had insisted that the entire acting company be paid professionals, and her designer, Vere Dudgeon, receive the same recognition as the stage director. She won no credit for re-establishing a repertoire of past Abbey successes, and, thus, helped to preserve the traditions of the playhouse. Finally, no one seemed to care that she had to accomplish all these tasks while dealing with two changes of venue, a disastrous fire, a changing playhouse clientele, in a depressed economy, with two hour a day rehearsals over three week periods, with a young, talented, developing group of actors mixed in with veterans who were fixtures in the theatre and would not easily submit to direction from any quarter.

While Ria was depressed by the theatrical climate in Dublin, she could never bring herself to blame her society friends. In her memoirs she wrote: "It often seemed to me in the years at the Queen's, that the change from the old Abbey was exemplified in the type of play that was being written for the new theatre, and, for the most part, for its new audience. There were honourable exceptions, of course, but many of the plays were so monotonously alike that I honestly can't remember even the names of many of them."[26]

Her play production record during those first five years at the helm of the Abbey is an impressive one, notwithstanding her recollection of it. However, as M. J. Molloy's *King of Friday's Men* remarks, as he stands "in the doorway, squares his shoulders resolutely, frees his shillelagh for action, and prepares for the future, — 'And let ye spare an odd prayer for myself — for a few days whatever. Misfortune that sticks too long'd wear the rocks.'"[27] Ria Mooney was a strong and determined woman of considerable theatrical talent, but even she might one day be worn down by the world around her.

CHAPTER NINE
"More Like Warfare Than Reasoned Discourse"

In April 1953, Ria Mooney celebrated her 50th birthday. She was in good physical and mental health with apparently undiminished vigor and gave no indication that she had any intention of giving up her position as Abbey artistic director. Pictures of her taken at that time at work in the theatre give the impression of a woman of good humor and easy concentration.[1] When not covered by the familiar kerchief, her thick greying hair framed a round, only slightly lined face dominated by unplucked eyebrows over dark searching eyes. In repose, seated in the Peacock listening to Ernest Blythe, her face seems soft, her eyes attentively focused on the speaker, lips sympathetically pursed, lengthening her chin line and giving her the look of a kindly, distinguished, attractive, middle-aged, middle-class matron. By way of contrast, in a photo of her standing in the first row of the orchestra looking up toward actors on the stage before her, she appears commanding, script extended in one raised hand, her body tensed, direct in her attention, like a classroom instructor clarifying a point to her listeners.

Ria's appearance in the RTE-TV special, *Between the Canals*, gives evidence that she spoke without vocal affectation and with impeccable English diction in a clear unaccented feminine baritone. Her bearing was upright and her movement contained and graceful, disguising her small stature. Her voice and physical presence projected composed self-assurance, dignity, and polite interest. Mulkerns described her as "being lively in company and telling very funny stories. She was very humorous in that sense. I think she could not very easily accept jokes against herself."[2] Since she kept herself from any social contact with the company, Ria might have been sensitive to any familiarity that could be interpreted as favoritism. "She had some reservations," observes Mulkerns, "she felt the lack of degrees. She also had no Irish whatever." Such insecurity often gives way to aggressiveness. "As she got older," Mulkerns noticed, "she could be quite cranky, even with her friends. Ria lost her temper sometimes quite quickly. She did tend to be authoritarian, but, then, she needed to be." At the theatre, working with young, untrained actors on short rehearsal schedules, and constantly forced to monitor the time available before an opening, this distant, correct, commanding disposition would be indispensable. After rehearsals, her inability to ever let any personal warmth enter into her relations with her troupe might have caused some resentment.

"She was always impressive," recalls Ronnie Masterson. "She was small, but she had presence, enormous presence."[3] Ruminating on Ria's behavior, Aideen O'Kelly described her as "a most complicated lady—a fascinating woman."[4] Blythe may have had the last word about hiring or rejecting anyone who hadn't the Irish language, but Ria had the final say about, and responsibility for, all matters pertaining to the production of the plays.

If Ria's birthday occasioned little celebration in Abbey circles, all of theatrical Dublin took note of the creation of the Pike Theatre in 1953. Alan Simpson, a retired military engineer, established his playhouse activities at a tiny place in Herbert Lane that seated only 56.[5] Despite its size and newness, over the next four years, this small theatre generated the same kind of scandalous fuss that first made the Abbey's international reputation. Soon after this new production company appeared on the Dublin theatrical scene, another upstart creation of young and ambitious performers, the Globe, appeared in the nearby resort town, Dun Laoghaire. This fledgling troupe numbered among its enthusiastic members Godfrey Quigley, Milo O'Shea, Jack MacGowran, Michael O'Herlihy, Donal Donnelly, Norman Rodway, and T. P. McKenna. Most, though not all, of these performers were unacceptable to the Abbey because they spoke no Irish. Unable to find work in their national theatre, they decided to open their own playhouse. Their attitudes toward the Abbey, and the financial conditions under which they labored, gives us an excellent perspective on the Dublin theatrical landscape in the midfifties.

T. P. McKenna, who later made a fine reputation on the London stage, vividly re-creates the atmosphere of the time in fascinating detail. "There was a ferocious bitterness among actors about the Abbey," he recalled, "because it was subsidized theatre and the other companies were out in the cold. Many actors were antagonistic because they had been rejected

Ria Mooney and Ernest Blythe discussing playhouse problems shortly after the disastrous Abbey fire.

by the Abbey for their lack of Irish or for some other reason given by the management."[6] Making a living at the Pike and the Globe was a chancy thing. McKenna remembered the hectic schedule he kept in an effort to pay the rent. The Globe was presenting a season at the Gaiety and, at the same time, the Pike was offering late-night revues. "I joined Milo in *The Seven Year Itch* with Godfrey directing. Milo had a car, and after the final curtain we would dash from the Gaiety along Baggot Street to the Pike and whip in for an eleven-thirty curtain up. At the same time we were rehearsing by day for a season of plays which Anew McMaster was preparing. So I worked from half-past ten in the morning until half-past one the next morning."[7] His efforts earned him about six pounds a week!

When the Globe acquired space in Dun Laoghaire, it had room for 190 people. Quigley staged two artistic productions there without attracting much business. Norman Rodway remembered that they decided to try just one more time before throwing in the towel. "We presented an old farce called *See How They Run* and it ran for six weeks." Milo O'Shea, who was being compared to the Gaiety's pantomime comic favorite, Jimmy O'Dea, was not pleased with his budding notoriety. "We found [at the Globe] that the more serious plays which Norman and Godfrey wanted to do were inclined to lose money. So every second or third play would be a comedy and I would go into it. I fought tooth and nail for serious parts."[8]

The Dublin critics used Stratford's Peter Hall as a theatrical benchmark when referring to current production practice. Hall ran the Shakespeare Memorial Theatre into a 50,000 pound debt.[9] When accused of bankrupting the playhouse, he replied: "Ah, but look at our standard!" They gave him another grant. McKenna and his friends knew there wasn't a hope of such a reaction in Ireland. Norman Rodway bitterly recalled that "when the Globe Company in Dublin finally disbanded we needed something like two and a half thousand pounds to keep us going, and we couldn't get it."

Clearly, the new generation of Irish actors taking the stage was unlikely to accept much longer the economic production conditions their predecessors, living with the memory of 30 years of economic isolation and deprivation, accepted as inevitable. Meanwhile, actors unable to gain entry into the Abbey company vented their spleen against anything connected with the National Theatre. Vincent Dowling, a rising young talent who joined the Abbey in 1953, declared that "the people inside the Abbey felt they were besieged, and the people outside were the besiegers." Ria, charged with mounting the repertoire, was caught in the middle. It is ironic that her first big success of the year became the battle cry of the besieging hordes of disgruntled actors and sophisticated critics that were beginning to gather outside the Abbey's Pearse Street gates.

The first play of the New Year, John O'Donovan's *The Half Millionaire*, opened on January 25, 1954. Faint praise leaked from the acid pens of the aisle-sitters. "The lamentably low standards of present day playwriting in Ireland," observed the *Irish Press*, "should nevertheless prove entirely acceptable to the new type of playgoer who has come to patronize this theatre since the changeover from Abbey Street." The critic noted that the audience roared at the proceedings, which were to his mind on "the level of cheapest music hall." The *Irish Independent* writer agreed it was unfair for a newspaper critic to judge a play about a newspaper, but it didn't prevent him from heaping scorn on "a precociously moronic caseroom apprentice [Vincent Dowling] who is not really very funny to anyone who knows caserooms." This pundit thought that the play's "political satire involving bog-trotting politicians should be threadbare now even by current Abbey standards."

Embedded in this snide reporting was the rueful admission that Ria had assembled "one of the best casts in recent years at the Abbey," and Harry Brogan, M. J. Dolan, Philip O'Flynn, Geoffrey and Eddie Golden,

Brid Lynch, Doireen Madden, Bill Foley, and Ray MacAnally all received excellent notices. "Ria Mooney put great life into her production and Vere Dudgeon set a striking newspaper office scene," said the *Irish Press*, adding it was "a very promising play by a new writer which should certainly bring the queues to Pearse St."[10] Really!

The production lasted barely two weeks and was replaced first by Teresa Deevy's *Katie Roche*, and a week later by old reliable *The Righteous Are Bold*, while Ria hustled John Malone's new play, *John Courtney*, into presentable shape — presentable by the Abbey's current standards anyway. The play tied for first in the previous year's Abbey competition and left one critic "wondering whether Irish dramatic talent has ceased to exist or young writers with ideas are simply not submitting their work for these contests."[11] The story of a domineering father who tries to remake his children in his own image appeared to the critics to be a tired reworking of an old theme. In spite of these caveats, Ria was credited with having given a "smooth and lively production," and Eddie Golden and his half-brother Geoffrey, along with Vincent Dowling, Michael Hennessy, Ronnie Walsh, Philip O'Flynn, Maire O'Donnell, May Craig, and Angela Newman were praised for "excellent acting."[12] The production folded after two weeks and *The Paddy Pedlar*, playing with *The Shadow of a Gunman*, replaced it on February 9, 1954. The following week was taken up with more Abbey exorcisms, and, after two weeks of bold righteousness, *The Devil a Saint Would Be* once more worked his unholy magic on the stage of the Queen's Theatre. By opening night of John McCann's *Twenty Years a-Wooing*, on March 29, 1954, Ria had mounted seven plays on the Queen's stage in but three months.

"A three act comedy of virile quality and engaging humour," proclaimed the *Irish Press*. "A rough slice of Dublin middle-class life tossed to the audience in one vast chuckle," chimed in the *Irish Independent*. The trivial plot (one critic admitted that in a more critical mood it might be called trite) concerns a middle-aged man who cannot marry his girl because his father has died and he must support the family.[13] Alderman McCann, the playwright who was a former Lord Mayor of Dublin and member of the Dail, was praised for "deft characterization, dialogue that has the rich spontaneity of living Dublin speech," and "a well-knit" story line that has the "quality and power of appeal which puts it in a class apart in recent Abbey productions."[14] There was delightful acting from Philip O'Flynn, Eileen Crowe, Bill Foley, Vincent Dowling, Harry Brogan, Joe Lynch, Joan O'Hara, Michael Hennessy and Ronnie Walsh. Finally, "after the author, highest marks must go to Ria Mooney whose production must be one of her very best, both in its pace and imagination."[15]

What is most incredible about this opening night is the casual reference in the reviews that the new play was being performed in tandem with Synge's *In the Shadow of the Glen*. Geoffrey Golden, Brid Lynch, Micheál Ó hAonghusa and Philip O'Flynn were applauded for their sensitive acting, the *Irish Independent* calling the evening "a beautifully balanced programme." No one could blame the lady if, after reading the reviews of *Twenty Years a-Wooing*, she breathed a loud sigh of relief. Ria had staged nine plays and it was only the end of March. However, although she had survived a developing crisis, and the box office was doing a booming business, the theatre's adversaries continued their siege.

The Abbey's critics conducted their warfare on three fronts. First, they accused the Abbey of choosing plays for commercial attraction rather than for artistic merit. Second, they argued that such plays encouraged actors to play for laughs and playwrights to write for the "new audience." This audience, unlike the old Abbey patrons, had little theatrical sophistication, and, what was perhaps most unforgivable, had middle-class, sentimental values. They did not want life upon the stage to reflect reality — life the way it is — they wanted the theatre to give them life the way they would like it to be. Third, this pandering to audience popularity created a world limited to the same, middle class, boring, setting.

Hugh Hunt, for example, dismissed McCann's play with the observation that it "proved highly popular."[16] Hogan noted that the playwright was a "staunch supporter of such bourgeois verities as Honesty is the Best Policy, Love Conquers All, and Business is Business."[17] He quotes a 30-year-old article by Dorothy Macardle to illustrate the dangers of the repertory system. Such a system resorts to "the revival of those plays which they could perform with most facility."[18] The lady does not mention the importance of popularity in the choice of plays to revive, but the implication is clear. What is popular is easy to perform. "Their range became restricted; their excursions from the cottage interior rarely led them farther than to a tenement room, a lodging-house bedroom or a 'parlour' in 'the suburban grove,' and the dramatists followed suit." The quality of a play apparently depended, according to her value system, upon where the action takes place, not upon the quality of the action itself. Furthermore, Macardle complained that plays were not only written for the Abbey Theatre, but for the players and even the Abbey prop room. It is odd that she chose to criticize Abbey playwrights for tailoring their scripts to suit particular actors. One wonders what she would make of the plays of Shakespeare and Molière written, as they were, for their own acting companies. In any event, this kind of criticism became, as the years passed, orthodoxy when referring to the Abbey at the Queen's.

Vincent Dowling, a thoughtful, experienced man of the theatre and a charming raconteur, illustrated this formula in a delightful story about what might be any Abbey revival.[19] "Ria might say: Oh, get the jacket that Philip O'Flynn wore last in so and so." When he got to the costume shop, the elderly lady on guard there wouldn't let him have a hat or coat if the famous Barry Fitzgerald, or popular F. J. McCormick had worn it. And she'd never sew a button on a man's trousers fly. And that was costume design! Blythe didn't want anything that wasn't a three wall set ... cast of about ten, that was the guideline for choosing plays."

In all such criticism rests the assumption that mere entertainment drives out art. However, if entertainment is another word for getting pleasure from an evening spent in the playhouse, then even the advocates of sublime art receive entertainment from their contemplation of a play. So inexact a word as *entertainment* must, therefore, be dropped from the argument, and the word *popular* inserted in its place. Simply stated, if crowds assembled to appreciate a play, it was obviously popular. Since the National Theatre needed money, actors must seek audience approval or popularity, and playwrights looking to get their work produced, must tailor their talents to Abbey audiences or be left out in the cold. It followed, then, if one was rejected by the Abbey, one was talented and artistic.

The problem with this formula is that, even with the best intentions, art theatres, like the Globe and the Pike, were constrained by financial problems, and the Globe compensated for its monetary deficits by producing popular farces like *See How They Run* and *The Seven Year Itch*. Neither play can be considered anything but good farce.

Cyril Cusack, who toured as a child with his stepfather Breffni O'Rourke and, between 1932 and 1945, appeared in 65 plays at the Abbey, had strong opinions about the purpose of playing.[20] He thought that melodrama "had been ridiculed and put out of court by intellectual and literary coteries." So much the worst for the coteries. For Cusack, it would always find its way back into the popular theatre. "It is good theatre; theatre theatrical, not theatre of the intellect." Cusack prophesied that such arguments would eventually take the playhouse out of the hands of playwrights and actors and place it in the hands of the critics and directors. "The theatre director has acquired more power in the last couple of decades," said Cusack," and as an actor I sometimes rebel against this; not against the director as a person, but against the exercise of Pygmalion power over the actors to the exclusion of their personalities."

As Hogan observed, "realistic comedies created an audience, whereas the lyric plays of Yeats and the grotesque comedies of Synge drove people way."[21] If the audience decides what it wants to see, one gets popular plays. If the editorial wand is given to artists, one will be rewarded with artistic theatre. In other words, any theatre supported by the box office will be forced to produce trivial work and reject much that is artistically excellent for commercial reasons. The assumption is a bold one; i.e., if a play is popular, it is commercial, and it can't be art. Of course, nobody came forward with a suggestion about how the production bills, the actors' salaries and the playhouse rent in particular, were to be paid. Furthermore, if few people wanted to pay to see the plays that critics and directors considered to be artistic, who should fund them? A case could be made that popular, entertaining plays subsidized such art.

At any rate, battered from both directions, Ria resolutely straddled the fence. She complained about the sameness of settings in the repertory, but she remembered that when she "did have a play that called for unusual setting, it was quite likely to be a failure at the box office."[22] When a play like *Twenty Years a-Wooing* ran for six months, she was told that "our regular patrons ... were dissatisfied because they had had to wait so long for a change of programme." Varying the programme with a revival every second Saturday only confused the public and ruined the run of a popular play. "Unfortunately, there weren't enough of these patrons to fill the house, so receipts for the new productions dropped to the most miserable proportions."

After the June vacation, the management, probably to assuage the contentious allegations of commercialism, took McCann's play off and opened a new play by J. M. Doody entitled *Knocknavain* on July 19, 1954. The *Irish Times* found it to be "not funny enough to get by purely as an inconsequential fantastic comedy, and, unfortunately, it has nothing else to offer." Two weeks later it was replaced by Bryan Guinness's *A Riverside Charade*, which played for an alternating week with *Twenty Years a-Wooing* and quietly disappeared. McCann's smash continued to play to full houses until the first week in November.

Ria stoutly maintained that John McCann's plays "were deservedly popular with Abbey audiences in this period. In my opinion McCann's work killed the Irish peasant play, by showing the public that there were other situations in our country to be written about besides 'courtin' in the kitchen.'"[23]

The Abbey was first and foremost a playwright's and actor's theatre, and not the preserve of directors and designers. The plays performed under her direction between 1948 and 1954 are impressive in their poetic invention, plot construction, formal variety, and theatrical craftsmanship. Abbey actors (twenty of them given excellent notices in these plays) were rapidly becoming a tight company and many of them were to make their marks on the English and American stages, as well as in the motion pictures, in the next 30 years.

Was all this less important than the paucity of costume facilities, the incorrectly assumed similarity of plot setting, and the shabby condition of a temporary playing space? Is stage spectacle really all that important to a national repertory theatre? John McCann's plays are a Dublin mirror image of Lennox Robinson's and William Boyle's country comedies. In their kitchens and sitting rooms, they differ from *The Whiteheaded Boy* or *The Far Off Hills* or *The Eloquent Dempsey* mostly in stage decoration. Robinson, Boyle, and McCann have a lot in common. They were popular, created an Abbey audience that allowed the company to hire full-time actors, all the while exhibiting sophisticated plot construction and deft comic characterization. They sustained a theatrical enterprise that could, as the occasion offered, stage works deemed to have literary merit for short periods of time to please the palate of the cultured class.

Is there any evidence that the Abbey neglected better playwrights while producing these popular comedies? Long before Blythe assumed the reins of the Abbey Theatre, and before Ria Mooney became the artistic director, Yeats himself turned down *The Silver Tassie*, and Carroll's *The White Steed* had to move to Broadway to get a production. It is well to remember that both playwrights had already had successful productions of earlier plays. In any case, there is no evidence that, during Ria's first seven years as artistic director, the Abbey had turned away plays that subsequently found success on the Irish stage.

Hogan remarked that "there is a tendency when writing of the Abbey to fall into hyperbolic condemnation. Perhaps this is so because criticism is carried on in Ireland more like warfare than like reasoned discourse."[24] Ria appears to have been a victim of this warfare. She was not being directly held responsible for the perceived decline of the National Theatre: Blythe was the culprit of choice. He made a perfect melodramatic villain, but just how did he ravage the National Theatre? He wasn't responsible for stage production standards. Ria Mooney was, and contemporary evidence clearly demonstrates that audiences and critics alike found much to applaud and enjoy at the Abbey during her Queen's reign. It didn't matter. The carping of the cultural cognoscenti and the complaints of disgruntled actors, excluded for whatever reason from the security of a partially subsidized theatre, continued unabated and was beginning to take its toll.

Meanwhile, *Twenty Years a-Wooing* held the Abbey stage through the long summer nights and into the short fall evenings. The longer it lingered, the louder the murmurs of dissatisfaction became, until John

McCann's name became a symbol for the Abbey opposition of all that was considered to be beneath the dignity of a National Theatre. Val Mulkerns said that she didn't think his plays had anything to do with the Abbey Theatre.[25]

Valentin Iremonger's cry that under the "utter incompetence of the present directorate's artistic policy, there's nothing left of that fine glory" that was the Abbey echoed throughout Dublin's salons. He left the playhouse in 1948 as a gesture of protest. If nobody took much notice of his departure then, his action was beginning to seem prophetic. That elusive thing called public opinion was beginning by degrees to believe his tirelessly repeated convictions. They were becoming common currency.

While the bitterness expressed against the Abbey had a deleterious effect upon company morale, Ria's troupe was in otherwise surprisingly good health. Among the members, there was the husband and wife team of Philip O'Flynn and Angela Newman. There was Ray MacAnally, whose own wife, Ronnie Masterson, had only relatively recently left the company. Geoffrey Golden was accompanied onstage by his half-brother Eddie and his wife Maire O'Donnell. Vincent Dowling described her as "dangerously beautiful" and a favorite of Blythe's.

Most people who witnessed their performances from the stage or the stalls thought the O'Flynns masters of their trade. Dowling called Philip O'Flynn an "almost perfect Abbey actor in the quality of his mind and

Philip O'Flynn. (University of Delaware Special Collections Library.)

Angela Newman. (University of Delaware Special Collections Library.)

Left: Ray MacAnally. (Author's Collection.) *Right:* Michael Dolan. (G. A. Duncan.)

his dedication to his work. [He was] a beautiful O'Casey actor, but I saw him play one hundred parts. From my view, Angela Newman was the best actress in her day."[26] Dowling found her "translucent." She might appear awful at rehearsal, "but she could be beautiful" at that evening's performance.

Brid Lynch, a native of Kerry and an Irish speaker, was considered by many to have been the best Pegeen Mike to grace the Abbey stage. Ray MacAnally's extraordinary energy appeared to be fueled by a tension many found difficult to deal with in rehearsal. Absorbed by problems of make-up and stage deportment, MacAnally seemed to live and breathe the theatre.[27] Marie Kean, already known throughout Ireland for her radio role as Mrs. Kennedy in *The Kennedys of Castleross*, was demonstrating comic ability to match her impressive tragic dignity as Bessie Burgess in O'Casey's *The Plough and the Stars*.

There were veteran players like May Craig, Harry Brogan, and Eileen Crowe who helped the younger players to adapt to the Abbey acting tradition. "Nobody consciously helped you," said one of the young players, but sometimes after a scene or before an entrance someone like Mick Dolan would give off-hand advice to a new member.[28] Ronnie Masterson

Aideen O'Kelley. (University of Delaware Special Collections Library.)

Maire O'Donnell. (University of Delaware Special Collections Library.)

remembered the lesson Dolan gave her husband after rehearsal one afternoon.

"What day is today?" Dolan asked.

"Tuesday," Ray replied.

"Did you notice you paused slightly? How is it that when I'm playing onstage with you at night, every line comes back like a machine gun. Don't be afraid to pause."

Masterson maintained that the technique of listening was one of the most difficult skills for an actor to master.[29]

The young performers also learned by watching and working with their seniors. "If you weren't in the play, you watched rehearsals and in the evening you prompted," said one young actress. She felt the company had a sense of vocation. Another player referred to the playhouse as "our home."[30] "We used to congregate after the show and talk a show to death," remembered Aideen O'Kelley.[31]

There wasn't any compartmentalization backstage among actors and property, costume, or stage managers. Those young players not involved in the evening's performance were expected to help get props, work on costumes, or cue lines with their colleagues studying parts for the next show. The rehearsal schedule was so confined that no one could afford to waste time. Everyone was

Left: Vincent Dowling. *Right:* Kathleen Barrington. (Both photographs, University of Delaware Special Collections Library.)

expected to do their homework and to be prepared to profit from direction the first time it was given.

Dowling remembered an incident that demonstrates Ria's appreciation of discipline among her charges. One day, "she found me looking at the notice board, and she said: 'Oh, what are you doing here? You're not called.' And I said: 'I'm just checking on the notice board in case there was a call.' And she talked about that for a long time, that someone actually came in without having been called."[32]

Ria was herself always thoroughly prepared for her task.[33] "She knew where the focus of attention was going to be," recalled Kathleen Barrington, and "she knew when the focus changed.

Brian O'Higgins. (G. A. Duncan.)

Brid Lynch, considered to have been one of the best Pegeen Mikes in *Playboy of the Western World*, was a fluent Irish speaker from Cahirciveen. (G. A. Duncan.)

She had a sharp mind. Everything was worked out, [she] had all the pictures in her head, so she knew what she wanted to create. We just took it for granted that everybody could do it." She also had a sense of comedy. "She saw what worked, in a technical way—what made people laugh, now she mightn't particularly laugh at it herself. 'If you break your line on that one, turn on that one, you are going to get the laugh.' [And she was] always right." Joe Lynch loved to tell stories about Ria's methods. He referred to a move as Mooney-esque. "Move down left to let somebody come in up center."[34] Some actors thought she was mechanical, while others felt that her precision

and crispness made the tedious blocking of a play much easier to take.

Several players said she believed she talked directly to Yeats' shade. Once she told Brian O'Higgins that he was "missing the beat. Yeats told me its all in the beat." O'Higgins was said to have replied sotto voce, "Yeah, well it drove me asleep." To which she responded, "That's what it's meant to do."[35]

Ria had very little sympathy with actors who drank excessively. Every year the Abbey opened the Wexford Opera Festival at the

Marie Kean. (G. A. Duncan.)

lovely 18th century Theatre Royal. Once, when the players arrived at the playhouse for a run-through, it appeared that some of the troupe were absent without leave. Ria asked several actors if they knew where their missing colleagues were, and, when she got no help from the company, she called it shameful and a disgrace to the Abbey. "I will go out and I will go round every pub in Wexford and I will pull them out of it." That night, the company was given a peek into her relationship with Blythe. When her complaint was passed on to him, he responded for all present to hear: "Ah, she's suffering from menopause, you don't want to mind that."[36]

Eileen Crowe. (University of Delaware Special Collections Library.)

Micheál Ó hAonghusa. (University of Delaware Special Collections Library.)

If she thought little of a person's talent or discipline, or had another reason for being annoyed with them, Ria's own disposition could be quite formidable. One actress stated that "she systematically savaged me. Anyone that was pretty, she laid into."[37] Another novice recalled her placing a spectacle case on the back of his neck to force him to keep his head up. She told him he was short enough without walking around with his head down. After leaving the Abbey, and with a couple of jars in him, he met her at a party. Somehow he summoned up the nerve to confront her about her insensitivity. "You needed it at the time," she told him.[38]

Left: Seathrun O'Golli. *Right:* Harry Brogan. (Both photographs, University of Delaware Special Collections Library.)

On the other hand, Dowling thought she was capable of great critical subtlety. "One morning after some play that I'd done extremely well in, she said to me: 'My niece, who really likes you Vincent, said what a pity Vincent has such a high pitched voice.' And I was totally taken aback and disarmed by the fact that she said that this niece who liked me said that. From that day on, I started to work on my voice, which has been for thirty years my living."[39]

Backstage at the Queen's had the atmosphere of a close-knit family. Jealousy, acrimony, competition for recognition, and the tension of constantly preparing for an opening night had its effect upon all concerned. There were moments of amusement and fondness as well. Aideen O'Kelley remembered John McCann's brother, Father Leo, coming to see every show and standing in the wings down stage left. "He was the bane of our lives," she recalled fondly, "sitting there with his high collar, because priests in those days, can you imagine, were not allowed to go to the theatre. He sat backstage with his little curate trying to crane over his neck to get a peek in. The two of them were there for every show. He was a sweet man."[40]

Life at the National Theatre, as with life in all close families, had its

Left: Patrick Layde. (University of Delaware Special Collections Library.) *Right:* T. P. McKenna. (G. A. Duncan.)

ups and downs. For the moment, however, box-office receipts were good, financial ruin had been averted, and there was plenty of time to rehearse the next new play of the season.

On November 8, 1954, Joseph Tomelty's *Is the Priest at Home* was heralded as the second popular production of the year. Critics agreed that the Abbey players had made a success of Tomelty's satire and the play should have a good run. Nonetheless, the *Irish Press* lamented the fact that the play had been first produced by the Belfast Group Theatre, otherwise "this superior comedy would undoubtedly have been a bright feather in the not over-adorned Dublin theatre cap."

The *Irish Independent,* taking the opposite view, thought that the production "was a daring undertaking for the Abbey players following the presentation a few months ago of the same play at the same theatre by the Belfast Group Theatre, speaking in the native accents of the Northern village in which the play is set. It has succeeded brilliantly, with a perfectly chosen cast, and fast production to sharpen the comedy." Ria's interpretation heightened the theatricality, making this seem "more a play and less the grim documentary of village life which to me, as a Northerner, it appeared in the Belfast Group's finely realistic presentation." "Credit goes

Left: Michael O'Brien. *Right:* Paedar Lamb. (Both photographs, University of Delaware Special Collections Library.)

to Ria Mooney," wrote the *Irish Press* critic, "for a strikingly intelligent approach to a difficult subject."

Intelligence and difficult subject matter did not seem to be the ingredients that stirred the imagination of literary Dublin. It craved something sensational to shock unsophisticated Dublin out of its provincial complacency, preferably something libelous to stir up heated arguments and, perhaps, even social action. Alan Simpson, the director of the tiny Pike Theatre, gave them just what was needed to satisfy their rebellious longings. The play was Brendan Behan's *The Quare Fellow*, and it opened at the 56-seat theatre in September 1954.

The play did not suit the postage stamp stage upon which it had to be played. The script called for a cast of 21 and presented all kinds of technical problems, besides the trouble of finding, never mind paying for, so many performers. Behan had already received rejection slips from the Abbey and, more to the point, from the Boys. Simpson maintained "it was not Hilton's sort of play and obviously they were not going to do it," but he recognized the controversial value of the anticapital punishment theme, and he persuaded Behan to give him the play. The producer now sought a larger venue for his production, but the Gaiety Theatre said they had no available dates, and the Olympia was "suspicious of Brendan because his

Left: May Craig. *Right:* Bill Foley. (Both photographs, University of Delaware Special Collections Library.)

brother had once worked there and sold the Daily Worker in the gallery when he should have been operating the spotlight."[41] There was nothing for it but to put it on at the Pike.

Simpson knew his Dublin audience. The production created just the stir he had been hoping for. "The play was hailed by various Dublin critics as the best since O'Casey. Its potential was obvious to me. It was rather a shocking play for a Dublin which wasn't very sophisticated at the time, and I had been slightly afraid when I put it on that it might be libelous; indeed, somebody might have seen fit to take an action if it had received its first production in a large theatre. But obviously there was no point in taking an action against either Brendan or the Pike because neither had any money."[42] In spite of press approval and literary Dublin's imprimatur, and even with a full house, which included persons standing, "we took about a hundred pounds a week." Within the month, this *succès d'estime* impoverished their bank account and forced them to close the play.

Simpson regretfully noted that Joan Littlewood's production of *The Quare Fellow* at the Comedy Theatre in London's West End, "established Brendan as an important playwright."[43] Maybe, but it didn't hurt any that, soon after the play opened in London, "Brendan made his famous television appearance with Malcolm Muggeridge. He was stoned. This turned him, so far as the English were concerned, into a celebrity overnight."

Simpson later admitted that Behan's "bad language on television at a time when television was still rather pompous had almost as much to do with his popularity as his actual writing. By degrees Brendan came to realize that he was expected to behave outrageously." Dion Boucicault could not have fashioned a more typical "stage Irishman."

Ria was at the distinct disadvantage of operating the National Theatre. If scandal was not a thing to be avoided, a libel suit certainly was. Although the Boys, who specialized in scandalous notoriety, turned the manuscript down, only the Abbey was blamed for ignoring this wunderkind of the contemporary Irish theatre. The significance of this event may not have immediately dawned upon Ria Mooney. The daily press approved of her last two productions, and they showered superlatives upon the Abbey acting company. The theatre's precarious financial health was, for the moment, satisfactory, and she had the promise of two new scripts from the hands of such established playwrights as Walter Macken and M. J. Molloy. Nonetheless, a prophetic voice might have warned her that the Abbey's detractors had finally acquired the weapon they had sought for so long. The Pike playhouse was to be the little gun from which they hoped to fire the fatal bullet that would slay Ernest Blythe and, if necessary, his National Theatre cohort. The first missile was Behan's *The Quare Fellow*, but Simpson had, in reserve, another more avant-garde projectile.

There can be little doubt that Alan Simpson saw himself as the giant killer. Without any government subsidy, and operating a tiny playhouse, he had little hope of becoming a significant Dublin theatrical power without challenging Blythe's control of the Abbey Theatre. Ria Mooney was not his target. In fact, Simpson may even have counted her among his sympathizers. She had kept one foot in the artistic camp, while effectively mounting the Abbey repertoire. She had a reputation for interpreting Yeats and Synge, was a close professional associate of Denis Johnston, was a friend of longstanding of the Boys, and had been an original member of the Dublin Lyric Theatre. Unfortunately, she was working under Blythe's management. It did not seem to matter that she was constantly at odds with Blythe. Her good work was helping to sustain him in his position. Simpson and his friends would try not to hurt her. They had their eyes on the prize — the Abbey — and they would have to take action against anyone who stood in their way. The most Ria might hope for from them under the circumstances was that they would make her their artistic prisoner.

CHAPTER TEN

"Have I No Power to Stop This?"

Is the Priest at Home? proved so popular that the first time pantomime business dropped off it was rushed back upon the Abbey stage. It resumed its run on January 10, and continued until the end of April 1955. The reason for its popularity is evident in reading the script. It seemed to have been tailor-made for the Abbey company. Harry Brogan, as Jimmy McLaughlin the parish clerk, known locally as "the curate," was a crowd pleaser as "one of the best comedy characters, in the true sense, seen in the Irish theatre in recent years. Philip O'Flynn is a sympathetic new curate whose life in Marlfield, with its rumours, its malice, its bigotry, its petty politics and rivalries, is a contradiction of the glib theory that Ireland is priest ridden."[1]

Indeed, in the final act, after much comic harassment, and some excellent character acting opportunities for the acting troupe, the frustrated priest asks his "curate" for advice.

> MALAN: What can I do? Have I no power to stop this? The priest must have power in the land. I've heard of it, I've read about it, I...
> JIMMY: Maybe the priest thinks he has. The outside world thinks telling the world that the priests and bishops run the place. I tell you this, Father, some of these writing lads should write a book telling us just how many times the Irish proved their bishops wrong and went ahead to do things their own way.[2]

Jimmy's diagnosis of the Irish moral condition, for all of his forgiving, good-natured way of putting it, would require strong medicine to effect a cure. "Take some other lad, the father of an unmarried woman's

160

child, they'll shake their heads and call him a blackguard. Take McQuillan that's running around after getting five or six women into trouble. They laugh at him, shake their heads knowingly, regard [him as] a 'bit of a lad...' and enjoy telling you that he couldn't be trusted with a corpse."

Marie Kean's grocer's wife was applauded as a "prim model of malicious propriety," while Angela Newman and Geoffrey Golden as the battling Ballafers, and Ray MacAnally as the soccer coach and Catholic actionist played their satiric parts to perfection. Vincent Dowling as "Karl Marx" O'Grady and Eileen Crowe as the priest's housekeeper rounded out the hilarious, small-town, gossiping crowd that everyone in the audience recognized as their next door neighbors.[3]

Although Tomelty's play packed them in at the Queen's, it failed to impress the art critics. Its satiric attack upon their usual attribution of bigotry to a priest-ridden Ireland put nary a dent in their complacency. Within two short years, they would resume their accusations of clerical interference in Ireland's cultural life to great effect. For the moment, however, they were forced by loud laughter to hold their peace.

The extended run of *Is the Priest at Home?* gave Ria the time to savor the invitation her company had received to visit the International Theatre Festival at the Sarah Bernhardt Theatre in Paris. They were to perform *The Plough and the Stars*, but, because Vere Dudgeon had left them, they had no scene designer.[4] Ria was instructed to make out a ground plan and get someone to paint the sets for the production, but she demurred, reminding the management that they would be representing Ireland in the most art conscious country in the world. This appeal to patriotism seemed to move Blythe, and, after much haggling, she was permitted to ask Michael O'Herlihy to design and paint the sets. She also insisted that they needed more than the usual three weeks of two-hour rehearsals to get ready. A compromise was reached and the production allowed to open and play at the Abbey from the 25th of April, replacing Tomelty's smash hit. They were panned by all but one Dublin paper, but the two weeks of performances gave them time to become comfortable in their new settings and attuned to the play's rhythm and pace.

In her memoirs, Ria makes rye comment on their experience in Paris. "Michael O'Herlihy's sets, which had passed with little comment in his native city, brought the French audience to their feet in applause as the curtain rose for each act. We received excellent notices from the critics. At the end of the Festival, the Opera de Peking from China was awarded First Place, Bertolt Brecht with his Berliner Ensemble from East Germany came Second, and *The Plough and the Stars*, Third." Was there a note of irony in her final remark upon the event. "We hadn't done so badly, considering the circumstances in which we had to work. We returned to the Queen's after a few weeks' holidays, to give the same play, with the same production, to the same cool audience as before...." Ria might cling to the biblical reminder that no man is a prophet in his own country, but, under the circumstances, it would have been small comfort.

John McCann's second play, *Blood Is Thicker Than Water*, began its long summer run on Tuesday, July 25, 1955. It was praised as a "wholesome and vigorous comedy, which carries the genuine tang of Dublin humour." The plot concerns the problem of thousands of city people moving to suburban housing estates, deserting old family businesses. The *Irish Independent* complained that "Mr. McCann insists ... that things must always work out to a happy, fairy-tale conclusion." The acting was called "first rate," Ria's work was found to be "competent," and Michael Herlihy's sets "pleasing." The *Irish Times* simply ignored the event.

The leisure McCann's long-running play provided the Abbey Company was put to good use in preparing for M. J. Molloy's rollicking farce, *The Will and the Way*, which premiered on September 5, 1955. The *Irish Press* observed, with refreshing candor, "the sharp difference existing between good theatre and good drama." The full house could not have laughed louder or longer at "the magnificent slapstick comedy, but, while this is written and handled with masterly restraint by Mr. Molloy, it tends to distract interest to such an extent that the main theme gradually becomes merely an off-shoot."

The plot revolves around a young man forced by his uncle's death to assume control of an amusement hall in the west of Ireland. He finds himself in a personal dilemma caused by the terms of his uncle's will and his love for a lovely local girl. This sets up an amateur dramatic society's rehearsal of an old-fashioned melodrama, which "the Abbey Players acted with gusty exhilaration." The *Irish Press* critic, however, lamented that "the pace of Ria Mooney's production was slowed by the constant laughter and will have to be quickened considerably."

The *Irish Times* seemed annoyed that the play was a "broad comedy that crossed over the borders into farce," because the reviewer thought that "Mr. Molloy deserves a reputable place in the hierarchy of serious Abbey dramatists." Even so, he admired the skill of the acting company, and ruefully admitted that he would be "tempted back to the Queen's Theatre, if only to enjoy at least once again Edward Golden's superb sketch of the Connaughtman's Hector de la Mare." The reference was to Lennox Robinson's send-up of Irish actors imitating arty Russian acting methods. He praised Ria for her skillful use of O'Herlihy's setting, which helped to overcome difficult production problems.

Both scribes seemed troubled that Molloy's play was only good theatre. One insisted that to be reputable you must be serious, and the other, while he admired the playwright's restrained handling of magnificent slapstick, kept searching for a deeper meaning to the evening's proceedings. These writers obviously joined in the uproarious laughter, but they couldn't help blaming the audience for enjoying themselves too much. Ria was congratulated for solving difficult production problems, but she was warned she must do something about the audience interrupting the actors with all that excess laughter. The "sharp difference between good theatre and good drama" seems to have created grounds for divorce between the two apparently irreconcilable playhouse mates.

As *The Will and the Way* was creating gales of laughter at the Queen's, Samuel Beckett's *Waiting for Godot* preoccupied the attention of literary Dublin. Its first English production opened in London in August 1955. Peter Bull described the first night: "Waves of hostility came whirling over the footlights, and the mass exodus, which was to form such a feature of the run of the piece, started quite soon after the curtain had risen...." Beckett's biographer, Deirdre Bair, tells us that the entire "popular press dismissed it as rubbish."[5] There is that word "popular" again.

It was Kenneth Tynan who made a trip to the Arts Theatre Club a fashionable necessity. He wrote, "It will be conversational necessity for many years to have seen *Waiting for Godot.*" Alan Simpson's Pike production opened in September, and "the reviews were generally more favorable ... partly because the reviews of Hobson and Tynan had been available ... and the initial shock had simmered down to a curiosity eagerly shared by the Irish theatergoing audience."[6]

Simpson found Beckett was cagey about publicity and spent considerable effort in dodging newspapermen. "He attracts culture vultures as a jampot attracts wasps," observed the director.[7] The best Simpson could say about the Dublin run of *Godot* was that Irish audiences "were less puzzled" by the play than audiences in other countries. The playwright disapproved of Simpson's attempt to exploit his play's "Irish aspect," and he told him so. Born and raised in Ireland, Beckett wrote his plays in French, and "he saw Godot as a universal play...."

Ria does not mention Beckett in her memoirs. In the midthirties, she had asked him for a poem to be read during a radio broadcast, but he failed to select one. "He was sure she felt he had affronted her and went out of his way to avoid her for the rest of his stay in Ireland."[8] Whatever her feelings about Beckett, she must have been aware that the Pike Theatre was replacing the Abbey as the fashionable place for "culture vultures" to be seen. It was reminiscent of the effect that MacLiammóir and Edwards had

created with their production of *The Old Lady Says "No!"* a quarter century before at the tiny Peacock Theatre.

Beckett's play ran into February, while Molloy's farce was replaced
after barely two months at the Abbey. Of course, the 56-seat Pike playhouse would need to play ten performances to equal one night at the
Queen's with its 600-seat capacity. In any case, *The Will and the Way* was
succeeded on October 24, 1955, by Pauline Maguire's *The Last Move,* which
was almost completely ignored by the critics. They had treated Walter
Macken's *Home Is the Hero* in the same cavalier manner. They weren't
about to make that mistake with his new play, *Twilight of a Warrior,* however, which opened on November 21.

It was the first new Abbey play not directed by Ria since her assumption of the duties of artistic director in 1948. During that time, she had
staged 25 original scripts in addition to the myriad revivals of former
Abbey successes. Was she sick, or merely tired and requesting some help
with her responsibilities? "For years," she tells her reader, "I had gone on
doing the best I could always hoping for the assistance that never came."
Unfortunately, she does not tell us exactly when the burden began to weigh
her down. "I have tried to write something of the nightmare that was that
period of my final years in our National Theatre, but I find it a little too
painful to go into more detail. Those who understand how professional
theatres are run might not believe me, and those who know the theatre
only as members of an audience, might think, 'The lady doth protest too
much!'"[9]

Whatever her differences with Blythe, and however much she longed
for release, something made her hang on to her position at the Abbey long
after the work itself had begun to pall. In the early stages, Ria had been
absorbed by her task of developing an acting company, building a
respectable repertoire of past Abbey successes, studying new manuscripts,
and casting and staging them. During that time, she had been compelled
to adjust to the dislocation caused by the fire and the transfer to a playhouse with an entirely different character from the original theatre. The
crisis had been overcome and replaced by the hope of new and better
premises at the old location on Abbey Street. After four years of planning
and haggling, it was obvious now that the troupe would be at the Queen's
indefinitely.

When she finally took the time to evaluate her position at the theatre, she must have perceived that she was no longer much of an acting
presence in her own playhouse. Beyond substituting for actors on leave
or too sick to perform, she had confined herself to her duties as a director. Had these youngsters ever seen her perform? Had Dublin audiences

forgotten that she had been one the city's first ladies of the stage? Her memoirs are silent about the cause and timing of her decision to begin to ease out of the director's chair and back into an actor's harness. At any rate, her first taste of relief came with *Twilight of a Warrior.*

Eddie Golden, a player noted for his intelligence, was chosen to spell Ria for the production of Macken's play. He was greeted by the same chill assessment all Abbey efforts received. The *Irish Press* said that the "very much over-sustained note of tragedy is inclined to pall on an audience, especially one conditioned over so long a period to flighty, superficial comedy."[10] The company was lauded for "serving up some of the finest acting in years," and Golden was credited with an "intelligent, sensitive production with magnificent sets by Michael O'Herlihy." The *Irish Independent* complained about the theatrical curtain lines that were "either purple-dramatic or just cheaply obvious."[11]

On January 23, 1956, Ria was back in the director's chair for the opening of a young playwright's first professional production. Hugh Leonard's *The Big Birthday* was roughly greeted by the aisle-sitters, but the 28-year-old lad was given some encouragement in the end. The *Irish Times* critic suggested at least one-half hour could be cut with no loss to the evening, and the *Irish Independent* found it "too wordy and too repetitive to classify as good farce." The *Irish Press* thought the young playwright showed "more than ordinary promise, and if he profits from the lessons of this very competent presentation of his play he should take his place with the most successful writers of comedy in the Irish Theatre." Ria and Michael O'Herlihy were given the usual nods of approval.

The play endured for a respectable three weeks and was replaced by *The Shadow of a Gunman* and Shaw's *Village Wooing* with Ria playing featured roles in both of the evening's pieces. The *Irish Times* noted laconically that "the audience found a laugh in every line."[12] It is a mark of Ria's stamina that, while she was playing in these two plays, she continued rehearsing Francis Macmanus's *Judgement of James O'Neill*, which opened ten days later.

This script featured a runaway daughter, the Archangel Gabriel, a dream sequence where the tyrant and brutal father meets the portionless girl he abandoned, and it is set in a graveyard. The *Irish Independent* said the evening "balanced reality and fantasy on a razor edge clever production by Ria Mooney, an atmospheric graveyard setting by Michael O'Herlihy and sympathetic acting by a strong cast of Abbey Players," making it "seem almost an exercise in theatre harmony."[13] Shaw's *The Shewing Up of Blanco Posnet* was played as an afterpiece and the *Independent* critic thought it "a rollicking production." The *Irish Press*, on the other hand, said that "Ria Mooney, who produced *James O'Neill* with skill and sympathy, directed *Blanco Posnet* with most perfect and exquisite mis-understanding."[14]

Notwithstanding the harmonious production, the play lasted but two weeks. Ria was forced to quickly serve up *Is the Priest at Home?* on March 5, 1956. *This Other Eden* took over at the end of March, followed by a week of *Twenty Years a-Wooing*, and then *Juno* occupied the stage until the playhouse closed for its annual June vacation. In her ninth year as artistic director, Ria found that repeating her past successes, sometimes with new actors in key roles, was a tedious business at best. She began to display impatience at rehearsals— witness the spectacles case incident with Derry Power, a young actor who had recently joined the company. In February, Michael O'Herlihy left the company for good, and, as Ria started preparations for the annual McCann comedy, she was told Tomás MacAnna had been appointed Abbey set designer. Long an independent director of the Irish repertoire, now MacAnna was beginning to move into Ria's domain. Blythe announced that, in the fall, MacAnna's new play in English, *Winter Wedding*, would be directed by the returning Frank Dermody.

Dermody had left the company in 1948, and Ria had accepted the offer to fill the vacant position. The diminutive director had worked for the past decade in the English motion picture industry, returning to Dublin because of a severe case of homesickness. He was Blythe's man. The manager had discovered him in the late thirties as a soldier producing entertainment in the Irish Army. Blythe got him a furlough in order to learn the theatrical business with Hilton Edwards at the Gate.[15] When Dermody had served his national service, he joined his patron, mounting the first production in Irish at the Abbey. It was a disquieting development for those who thought the Abbey ought to give up its emphasis on the Irish language and employ its resources improving the English repertoire.

John McCann's third play, *Early and Often*, is a political comedy with election trickery and ingenious machinations tied up with a love affair and some social commentary. It opened on July 16, 1956. The *Irish Press* noted that "last night's distinguished capacity audience made very clear" that the play could not "fail to delight its patrons with its glorious Dublin humour ceaselessly bubbling through every lively scene...." Of course, it was to be regretted that Mr. McCann "persists in the bad habit of resorting continuously to the purely hackneyed line in phrase." The company was given a backhanded compliment when the critic remarked that "needless to say the Abbey players just wallowed in the lively material." Ria's direction had "pace and precision against a fine set by Tomás MacAnna."

Ria's stage technique was hardly challenged by the material of *Early and Often*. It was made of cloth cut to the measurements of the strong ensemble she had nurtured over the last decade. As soon as the premier was accomplished, her attention was focused on the next production which she had persuaded Blythe to allow her to produce, Denis Johnston's *Strange Occurrence on Ireland's Eye*, the subtitle of which was "a play about a murder trial."

She knew the story from its first incarnation as a radio drama entitled *Blind Man's Bluff*. Johnston, who had been absent from Ireland for nearly 20 years and was teaching in New England, was encouraged to adapt the plot to Abbey dimensions. The script is part detective story and part commentary on the procedural tricks used in Irish courtrooms. What distinguishes the play, aside from its clever plot revelations through delightfully eccentric characters, is the shocking revelation that the only witness who might help the convicted man is his former mistress, for whom he has procured money to abort her pregnancy.

Since his 1929 *succès de scandale* with *The Old Lady Says "No!"* Johnston had been the favorite playwright of cultured Dublin society. Ria had faith in his artistic pedigree. The Abbey was sure to receive the respectful attention of Dublin coteries with this production. She had to wait until the end of summer to get a reaction to her work, because *Early and Often* did sufficient business to keep it afloat for five weeks.

The Ireland's Eye of the title is an island in Dublin Bay, the setting for the alleged murder. On the evening of August 20, 1956, the eyes of the Dublin elite were focused on the event taking place on the Abbey stage. Artistic respectability might yet be rescued from the upstarts at the Pike. Ria was rewarded by the buzz that infused Dublin social conversation about the plot based upon actual happenings of over 100 hundred years before. One critic said the play "proved that you cannot go wrong in the theatre with a trial, especially a murder trial."[16] Another exulted: "Comedy, suspense, satire, caustic wit and philosophic argument — all the ingredients of the intellectual thriller, mixed by a master hand, are in Denis Johnston's *Strange Occurrence on Ireland's Eye*." There was admiration for the author's skill in convincing his audience of the suspect's guilt, only to reverse the process "in a third act of dramatic surprises."[17]

Everyone applauded the huge cast which, even to the minor roles, gave expert performances. Ria was cheered for having "overcome many of the difficulties of presentation which is of cinematic breadth." Tomás MacAnna's black-and-white settings were found excellent. It was left to the Sunday pictorial section of the *Irish Times* to prick the balloon. Ken Gray, a featured columnist, felt it was a "pity it was not fresh material."[18]

The Pike was playing Ionesco's *The Bald Soprano*, and the Globe advertised Isherwood's decadent Berlin drama, *I Am a Camera*, but neither had the controversial resonance of a *Waiting for Godot*. For the moment, the Abbey appeared to have reclaimed the artistic high ground. The seven-week run of *Strange Occurrence* proved that good drama could coexist with good theatre. Meanwhile, Ria was rehearsing her own production of Brendan Behan's *The Quare Fellow*.

On October 8, the eagerly awaited Abbey premier had "as intellectually distinguished an audience as Dublin can offer." It was obvious that the Abbey board — particularly its éminence grise Ernest Blythe — which had rejected the script, were being forced to eat crow in public. However, the Dublin critics were themselves a bit resentful of the playwright's London notoriety. "Like the Prodigal Son in reverse," wrote the *Irish Press* reviewer, "Mr. Brendan Behan, modestly munching his West End husks, presented us with his fatted calf at the Abbey last night." It has been said that nothing fails in Dublin like success. If the opening-night audience hoped their man would repeat "those TV skylarkings that turned [him] into a London legend overnight," they were disappointed. A sober Behan was brief and modest when summoned onstage to make a curtain speech.

The Quare Fellow is a mood piece about an imminent prison hanging and its effect upon all concerned. "A crack team of Abbey veterans headed the all-male cast," while Ria's work was judged to be only competent, even "unimaginative."[19] The *Irish Independent* was disappointed that "as an indictment of capital punishment, its oblique attack has none of the compelling force or hot fire of the convinced gospeller." At least he could approve of "the highly effective settings of Tomás MacAnna."

MacAnna's big chance, his play *Winter Wedding*, was delayed by the six week run of *The Quare Fellow*. No one was heard to criticize the management for exploiting the commercial possibilities of Behan's work of art. MacAnna's play opened on November 26, to mixed reviews, an indication of the acrimony that was building against Blythe's leadership. The *Irish Press* was delighted that *Winter Wedding* "has lifted appreciably the general standard of creative writing for the theatre of recent years. It earns that tribute for the unusually virile content of its drama, the appeal and colour of its characters and, most of all, for the quality of Mr. MacAnna's writing." The critic was sick of the "rough-edged comedy with which Abbey authors generally have been preoccupied for some time." The "splendid acting" was duly noted, but the "major share of the credit must go to guest producer Frank Dermody, whose firm handling of the many crowded scenes was an object lesson in good production. Mr. MacAnna's own settings were outstanding."

In contrast to this partisan review, the *Irish Independent* found the plot hopelessly melodramatic. "He [MacAnna] drags in two strolling players to clown through ripe melodrama — a high price to pay for a good last line — and he sends his smugglers out on the most dangerous mission of their lives, singing in the manner of 'horse opera.'" The reviewer agreed that the acting was good, but he thought Ray MacAnally's MacDara had to pierce "through much of the prunable material to reach the author's intention." Frank Dermody's direction was "excellently-paced if uninspired in a well adapted setting by Tomás MacAnna." The production was followed in late December by the annual Irish pantomime *An Cruiscin Lan*.

Ria began 1957 with Hugh Leonard's *A Leap in the Dark,* which prophetically raised the question of armed raids in the six counties by the outlawed IRA. The *Irish Press* observed with approval that Leonard, underneath patriotic facades, "frequently finds heroics; protestations of 'principle' often hide vanity, and much that is cheap and fraudulent may lurk behind loud talk of truth and justice."[20] Patrick Layde, as the pacifist who sneers at his father's war record and his 1916 service medal, was credited with a performance that put him "in the top class at the Abbey." Although the reviewers criticized the unfocused subplots and the undeveloped small character parts (the actors seemed "almost as bewildered as the audience about what they are there for"), the playwright was encouraged to learn from his mistakes.

During the holidays, MacLiammóir and Edwards had teamed up with the Gaiety's pantomime female impersonator, Jimmy O'Dea, for the Christmas season. The Boys' biographer, Christopher Fitz-Simon, tells us that "there was talk in Dublin that Edwards and MacLiammóir should not be involving themselves in such lighthearted fare, that it was 'beneath them,' and that they were wasting their talent."[21] Fitz-Simon labeled this "simply bourgeois disdain for the popular, an attitude which could not comprehend the fact that the same resources of talent and technique were called upon, whether one was playing a part in a comedy sketch of one's own authorship, or in a scene by Sheridan or Anouilh." Such constant carping about low comedy, at least in the press, seemed reserved for the Abbey. It was hardly ever joined to the names of MacLiammóir and Edwards. Everything they did could be forgiven as eccentric, including their strange appearance in a modern-dress production of Shakespeare's *Julius Caesar,* in which Marjorie McMaster, MacLiammóir's sister, said they "looked like two out-of-work bus conductors."[22]

The Boys' activities, which were constantly on the lips of fashionable Dublin, now became the focus of Ria's attention. Their leading lady, Coralie Carmichael, was dying, and she could not be depended upon to play the Dowager Empress in the Gate's March production of *Anastasia*. Edwards, who was directing, asked Ria if she could make herself free to take the role. She had no trouble telling the Abbey management that she intended to take a two-month break from her directing chores in order to freshen up her feeling for the actor's craft.

After the opening of *A Leap in the Dark*, Ria handed over the Abbey production reins to Frank Dermody and began rehearsals for Marcel Maurette's drama about the supposed survival of Tsar Nicholas II's child, Anastasia. The production opened at the Gaiety Theatre on March 26, 1957. It is interesting to compare Fitz-Simon's evaluation of Ria's performance with the report carried the next day by the *Irish Times*.

"It was many years since Ria had played with the Gate," Fitz-Simon tells us, "and she had latterly been resident producer at the Abbey Theatre, a post which had tired her greatly. She had the command, but not the regality, for the part, and she did not manage to project the feeling that there were centuries of privilege behind her. There was also a physical difficulty, very obvious on the stage: small of stature, she was cast opposite Blanaid Irvine, who had previously played Anastasia in Belfast to much acclaim; though not overly tall, Blanaid Irvine made Ria Mooney look almost comically dumpy."[23]

The *Irish Times* critic started by telling Edwards he would need "slicker playing in the first act for it to be good theatre." His advice to MacLiammóir, who had most of the first act in his hands, was to provide a more incisive characterization in the future. "This is proven in Act II," continued the reviewer, "where Ria Mooney as Dowager Empress triumphantly tightens up action and interest in her scene with the girl whom she rationally believes an impostor, but wants emotionally to claim as kinswoman. Miss Mooney and Miss Irvine retain their domination in Act III. Both play so beautifully all through, in fact, that apart from the melodramatic interest of the story ... [it] should be seen for two notable performances from two actresses who are not seen often enough."[24]

Thirty years later, Vincent Dowling retained "a powerful image of this little figure at the Gaiety, who I went to see, coming in, and she was magnificent. She was like a little giant."[25] The younger players from the Abbey went to everything playing in the other Dublin theatres. They "thought she was fantastic in it. Of course, we knew the actress she was," continued Dowling, "and we knew how good she could be." It is fair to say that Dowling must have seen her improvising for her company during rehearsals, or how else would he be able to evaluate her grasp of the actor's craft.

In any case, these diametrically opposed visions of Ria as the Grand

Duchess illustrate the antagonism existing between the Dublin cultured community and the Abbey Theatre. To begin with, physical size has little to do with noble carriage. Ria was small, but the Broadway Duchess, Eugenie Leontovich, wasn't five feet tall. Yet when MacLiammóir and Edwards joined the Gaiety panto for high salaries, Fitz-Simon leaps to the defense of the Boys, accusing their critics of disdain for the "popular." The Boys were artists, and, therefore, it was admissible for them to court popularity when they needed money. Because the National Theatre had a government subsidy, it should be free of commercial considerations. Dublin's small theatrical community knew that the Abbey subsidy was a pittance, however. When consistency is not a critical requirement, it becomes easy for a critic to level the charge of commercialism against anyone who produces a play the critic deems unworthy of artistic consideration.

Ria played the Grand Duchess until April 13, but she was back in her director's chair a week after the opening night of *Anastasia*. On April 23, Donal Giltinan's *The Flying Wheel* entered the Abbey lists in a "smooth and well paced" production by Ria Mooney. The wife of a materialistic former guerrilla fighter, desperately trying to overcome her hatred for life, kills an old man in a car accident. Her husband uses his power to cover up the incident. The *Irish Press* noted that "it has become fashionable of late for dramatists to depict present day life in Ireland as something which is essentially corrupt—in which the shining idealism of the struggle for independence has given way to rather sordid materialism." Was Blythe attempting to mute criticism of his commercial outlook by producing plays with "fashionable ideas?" In spite of a mixed reception from the critics, the Abbey company was praised for "a night that was marked by some first rate acting. In the leading roles Jeffrey Golden and Marie Kean give two performances which reveal what these good artists are capable of."

In spite of recent reviews, Ria's success was not the talk of Dublin that spring, because, on Friday, May 24, 1957, four detectives arrived at the Pike Theatre Club in Herbert Lane, Dublin, and arrested its director, Mr. Alan Simpson.[26] The cause célèbre was Tennessee Williams' melodrama, *The Rose Tattoo*. The star, Anna Manahan, was a young actress who had just returned from a tour of Egypt with the Boys. While traveling there, her husband had come down with polio and died from it. Young, alone, and frightened of the responsibility of so large a role, the relatively unknown actress nonetheless took the part and rehearsed for several weeks without pay for the chance it offered her career. "We have no censorship in the theatre in Ireland," Manahan stated, "but if somebody complains

to the police they must act on that complaint."[27] Act they did, by arrest-
ing Simpson for putting on an obscene production. The legal muddle
that resulted has never been fully explained, but it caused a sensation
that occupied the newspaper columns for weeks, and Simpson's dramatic acquittal made him a local legend. "He [the judge] strode out of the
courtroom in a magnificent final exit," Manahan recalled, "as though to
suggest that people who bring such charges should not be tolerated. The
case finished the Pike Theatre financially, but it made that little theatre
known throughout the world." Well, throughout most of Ireland, anyway.

However, it did prove that Dublin theatre was no longer the preserve
of the Abbey or the Gate theatres. They had lost the scandal touch. Such
risks were left to the impoverished small theatres. They had, after all, by
their own admission, not much to lose. The Pike was out of business, but
it remained a useful stick with which to harass the National Theatre. It
wasn't long before a successor in that role was found, and this time the
central characters were famous playwrights.

In the midst of all this fuss, Frank Dermody was assigned to direct
the next Abbey production, relieving Ria for the June vacation and much
of the summer. *Juno and the Paycock* played for the first three weeks of
July, and, on the 22nd of that month, John O'Donovan's *The Less We Are
Together* had its premier.[28] "Mr. O'Donovan makes a great effort," wrote
the *Irish Press* reviewer, "to turn our Jeremiads about the hopeless state
of everything into witty penetrating, and possibly constructive, comment." This critic, given to lamenting the laughter at the Abbey, had a
reason in this case for excusing the levity. "The parts that came closest to
downright farce seemed to be the parts that appealed most (I suppose
quite naturally) to the first-night audience: and Mr. O'Donovan's merit,
and his trouble with audiences, may be that at his best he is too cerebral,
he implies too much." The critic was also shocked that the play's opening setting was a TV studio. What had become of the mythical country
kitchen?

In September 1957, Brendan Smith proposed that a theatre festival
accompany Ireland's Tostal (the Gaelic word for "a hosting"), and sub-
mitted a list of 25 productions to the Irish Tourist Board, which was to
sponsor the program by granting the director 15,000 pounds.[29] The board
accepted the proposal and determined that a new O'Casey play, *The Drums
of Father Ned*, an adaptation of Joyce's *Ulysses*, and three mime plays by
Samuel Beckett would be the festival's centerpiece. The plays by authors
of international reputation were sure to prove a strong tourist attraction.
When the Tostal board asked Monsignor McQuaid to open the festival

with a votive Mass, they neglected to inform the Catholic Archbishop of Dublin that plays had been added to the usual military tattoo, athletic games, and folk dancing. That oversight set off a series of events that distracted Dublin's attention for the entire next year.

Under the circumstances, the archbishop thought it best not to lend his name to the theatre activity and canceled the Mass. Sean O'Casey, convinced that he was being censored, withdrew his play. The Tourist Board told the Tostal council to drop the Joyce adaptation, and Beckett withdrew his plays in protest. Irish Actor's Equity got into the fracas, condemning the abandonment of the theatre festival. In the midst of the conflict, Hilton Edwards was heard to remark: "Everyone will feel very smug and very pure here; and they will be wrong as usual.[30] Smith, who benefited greatly from the sensational publicity, was "convinced that the situation developed as it did because members of the Toastal council representing non-theatrical interests provoked a public row quite unnecessarily. They did this deliberately as a means of sabotaging the Theatre Festival."[31] O'Casey behaved irrationally throughout, and, as a parting shot, refused to allow his plays to be produced in Ireland. Since his Dublin Trilogy was a staple of the Abbey repertoire, Ria and her troupe were made to suffer for an incident in which they were innocent bystanders.[32]

The archbishop and his Church took a beating throughout the prolonged affair. O'Casey, in particular, took the opportunity to bash Catholic Ireland. Apparently, the exiled Irish playwright hadn't seen Tomelty's *Is the Priest at Home?*

Meanwhile, Niall Carroll, a newspaper theatre critic and the brother of Paul Vincent Carroll, had his first play, *The Wanton Tide,* produced by the Abbey on October 21, 1957. The *Irish Press* declared that "the author is served by the pick of the Abbey players and by Miss Ria Mooney's intelligent and incisive direction," and the *Irish Independent* noted that the curtain raiser, Lennox Robinson's vintage one act, *Never the Time and the Place,* was "well worth seeing." His readers failed to take his advice, for, on November 11, Ria rushed George Shiels' country comedy, *Professor Tim,* onto the boards. Meanwhile, she was preparing John McCann's latest comedy, *Give Me a Bed of Roses,* for its proposed premier set for November 25, 1957.

This tale revisits the Kelly family, who were the stalwarts of his first stunning success. The newest edition was praised for presenting "a day in the life of the Kelly family, told with wit and tenderness, an expression of the author's knowledge of and affection for his native city." It "is as much a part of Dublin as O'Connell Street and Nelson Pillar." It wasn't long before a bomb made Nelson's Pillar a thing of the past, and if the Abbey's artistic critics had anything to say about it, soon the plays of John McCann would be removed from the Dublin theatrical landscape. Dublin audiences ignored the cultural censors and kept *Give Me a Bed of Roses* on the Abbey bill for 11 weeks.

In her autobiography, Ria never commented upon the radical change in the Dublin theatre world in the late fifties. The row that placed first the Pike and then the Dublin Theatre Festival in the newspaper headlines and on everyone's lips is never mentioned. As a young actress, she had been at the center of such artistic fights, and her lecture to her Abbey team before the curtain of *Design for a Headstone* demonstrates her pride in such activity. It must have been painful to be a mere spectator in this most cherished of Dublin playhouse sports. Her memoirs are filled with references to Yeats, Synge, and the Dublin Lyric Theatre she helped organize with Austin Clarke. Her work with these poets, and her own affair with F.R. Higgins, were among her most treasured memories.

Did she have any affinity for the plays that were now making headlines as the new wave of art theatre? Did the crude language and vulgar references, the socially shocking details of the Pike's repertoire, excite her theatrical imagination? Did she long to be a part of the festival fuss? For whatever reason, Ria Mooney remained silent about this new wave of playwrights being heralded as the creators of the culture of the future.

More important, perhaps, to her professional future was the discovery that she had become an outsider within her own company. The Abbey Players were beginning to organize in order to challenge Blythe's rule, and, while she had her own strong disagreements with him, she was, as far at the company was concerned, a part of management. The politics of the acting troupe, as with the behind the scenes manipulations of Blythe, were a closed book to her. No one felt the need to consult her about either.

Her acting stint with the Gate company in *Anastasia* not only garnered good notices for her, it also gave her back the feeling of camaraderie with her colleagues she had so zealously shut out as artistic director of the Abbey. Dermody's return together with MacAnna's promotion to scene designer, and the production of his play in English, were an indication that Blythe was probably trying to isolate her in the organization.

She must do something or she would find herself an old woman without a job in a theatrical world that had forgotten her. She had created a fine troupe of performers who played with great skill the new plays being written for the National Theatre. Next year's offerings numbered among them new plays by Macken, D'Alton, Johnston, and Molloy. What other

English-speaking repertory theatre could boast so strong a season of plays with so accomplished a company of actors?

She was tired, but she wanted to direct the next season. Even if she had enough money to retire upon, she would be nobody in Dublin theatre without her position at the Abbey. It seemed that Ria Mooney was all alone on the Dublin stage. The contradictions that appeared at the very beginning of her career had come back to haunt her.

Was there a contradiction between artistic merit and popular appeal? Popularity translated into box-office receipts with which to pay production costs. The current bitterness aimed at the Abbey was almost entirely a question of the government subsidy. Without the subsidy, all productions depended upon popularity at the box office. As long as actors subsidized the operation by accepting low wages and poor job security, there had been no separation between art and entertainment. But, if the government gave money to one group, it seemed to place all others under a measurable disadvantage.

Should actors care about playing to empty houses as long as they had the approval of those granting the money? Who exactly were these critics? When they were represented by Yeats and his devoted coterie, it was simple to know who and what one was following. How did one now recognize this select group of cognoscenti? Were they merely a group of managers who produced plays the public had no interest in patronizing?

She had once courted the society of Anglo-Irish cultural leaders. The aftermath of the World War had decimated their ranks. Comfortable in their company so long as they stressed language, Ria was now confronted with playwriting that often scorned language and stressed social, political, idealistic commitment.

Economic conditions of the Abbey at the Queen's forced Ria to adhere to the principle that the public's voice mattered. In her private world, though, she avoided the society of actors, making her society with writers, art dealers, architects, and anachronistic republican nobility like the Longfords. While they may not have at first manifested any enthusiasm for the so-called theatre of the absurd, neither did they stand up for the Abbey's repertoire. Kenneth Tynan's remark that they would be out of fashion should they miss Beckett's play forced them to take sides. Dublin society, as it always had, took its artistic cues from English critics.

The result of this change in Dublin theatrical atmosphere was that, after 11 years of service, Ria Mooney appeared to be an exile in her own artistic world. There was nothing to do but to carry on as long as possible and hope that somehow she could find a way home.

CHAPTER ELEVEN

"Long Day a Fine Night at Abbey"

Harsh, blustery March weather greeted the first new play of 1958, Walter Macken's *Look in the Looking Glass*.[1] The script charts the return to his small village of the author of a striking and successful play. Friends and neighbors decorate the village with banners of welcome, but soon discover that their hero has actually exposed them to ridicule in his play as the deceitful hypocrites he thinks they really are. The subtle conflict deals with the question of whether or not it was best to let the villagers live with their pretenses, or, by exposing their false behavior, to bring some real happiness to them, even if they can attain to it only through more and deeper suffering.

Though Macken was praised for his fine theme, and the company was applauded for its "uniformly high standard" of performance, one critic complained that the Macken "sparkle" was missing from the dialogue. Eddie Golden, Michael Hennessy, Philip O'Flynn, Eileen Crowe, Harry Brogan, Brid Lynch, Dorren Madden, Joan O'Hara, T. P. McKenna, and Michael O'Brien were all mentioned as stalwarts of a stellar Abbey acting ensemble.[2] Ria was merely mentioned as the director.

Look in the Looking Glass failed to attract an audience and was replaced after two weeks with O'Donovan's *The Less We Are Together*. Ria pushed her charges through their paces over the Easter holidays and opened Louis D'Alton's *Cafflin Johnny* on April 7, 1958. The playwright had departed from the scene some eight years before, but the Abbey had produced two of his plays posthumously with extraordinary success. Bill Foley heard about this last script from the author's widow, and he managed to persuade her to let the Abbey produce it.[3]

The reviewers thought the script might have been improved had D'Alton lived long enough to revise it. As usual, they bemoaned the fact "that a potentially strong psychological theme should be so often and so ruthlessly shattered by gusty laughter." Nonetheless, they entered into the charm and humor of the piece and found the essentials of the play as good as those in his popular work, *This Other Eden*. The *Irish Independent* took some delight in defining the obscure title word. "The Caffler—a provincial 'character' word of subtly shaded meaning—is part dreamer, part adventurer, part confidence man, wholly braggart, and wholly charming, his own worst enemy and logically by all conventional standards, a ne'er do well."[4] In other words, one of those wonderful acting creations found in the melodramas of Dion Boucicault.

Johnny Fortune—D'Alton's ironic name for his central character—returns to his mother's home after a long while away. Once within the boundaries of this small town, he discovers he has become a legend, responsible for exploits he himself says he would never think of doing when sober, and couldn't do if he was drunk. The *Irish Independent* rhapsodized about the final scene, "a moving piece of understatement, and a perfect crystallization of the often misunderstood mother-son relationship among undemonstrative people. In the light of that climax, all the unsaid things in the play fall into their pattern, the characters come into focus. It is a hazardous experiment which Brid Lynch and Ray MacAnally carry off by the sheer brilliance of what I can only describe as acted thought." The rest of the cast, including Vincent Dowling, Maire O'Donnell, Philip O'Flynn, Marie Kean, and Bill Foley were applauded for their support. The *Irish Times* noted that "Ria Mooney made the most of every scene."

Three weeks later, Niall Sheridan's *Seven Men and a Dog* appeared on the Queen's stage. The playwright was a noted poet and Dublin literary figure, and the premiere attracted the fashionable set. The *Irish Press* critic remarked that "after a writing career which has brought him through the realms of prose and poetry, and during which he touched some of the high spots of scholarship," his play "reveals qualities of authorship in this highly skilled sphere which have more than ordinary potentialities." He did admit, however reluctantly, that the fun and "pace flags lamentably in spots...."[5] The *Irish Independent* dismissed the piece as "a crude and utterly graceless burlesque of life in a rural Garda station," while Ria was credited with having made the play "as effective as the piece allows."

The main entertainment of the evening was preceded by Lennox Robinson's one-act comedy, *Crabbed Youth and Age*, which the *Irish Press* said "rippled along as merrily as ever in a sparkling revival." Ria produced both pieces in settings by Tomás MacAnna.

Ria was now in her element. Sheridan's play had artistic pretensions beyond mere playhouse appeal, and her next production was Denis Johnston's Anglo-Irish answer to O'Casey's *The Plough and the Stars*. Vincent Dowling remembered that Ria directed *The Scythe and the Sunset* "too cerebrally. It was Denis Johnston and there were all these theories." Dowling thought that "the play had a huge heart in it hidden under manners." In a long review, the *Irish Times* called the play an O'Casey pastiche in Act I, and saw Shaw's character, Bluntchli, from *Arms and the Man*, in much of Act II. This critic viewed the play as "Denis Johnston's latest iconoclastic sabotaging of both sorts of Irish martyrs," and Ria was chastised for allowing too much speech-making.[6]

The *Irish Independent* described the piece as "a lively and provocative psycho-analytical study of a representative group of men and women in the five days of the Rising of 1916." The *Irish Press* found none of O'Casey's incisive qualities in *The Scythe and the Sunset*, and, although Johnston was "too good at his trade to be led away by anything so foolish as mere sentimentalism," he lacked O'Casey's "power as a dramatist." The play is set in an O'Connell Street cafe which has been taken over by the volunteers as a casualty station. Johnston examines the might-have-beens of the rising, while O'Casey's play used the rebellion as background to his story. The critics treated the play as something special, but they obviously failed to respond to its message. The *Irish Independent* thought the "development of the drama is, perhaps, too slow, and often appears inconclusive, with tautness impaired by too many words, however much matter in them. I would except the interpolations on religion, which are superfluous to the theme and slacken the tension further by diffusing the ideological conflict."

Denis Johnston was being treated with the deference due an artist, and, if his play was lacking in dramatic power, and even offensive to some of the religious and political convictions of his audience, Dublin's elite insisted his work be given serious consideration. So the *Irish Independent*, after making an extensive list of theatrical caveats, ended by summarizing its evaluation of the production on a positive note. "Yet, all in all, this is the most vital play by an Irish author which Dublin has seen in many years, and the Abbey Players rise gallantly to it. Effective production is by Ria Mooney in a character setting by Tomás MacAnna."

Denis Johnston's brand of Anglo-Irish literary appeal had been replaced by Samuel Beckett's nihilism. Beckett came from the same alienated Anglo-Irish stock as Johnston. Frank O'Connor remembered the first time he "realized the isolation of the Anglo-Irish, which Elizabeth Bowen once compared to the isolation of an only child."[7] There were, of course, many ways of displaying petulance and alienation. Beckett, for example, had decided to take his spiritual direction and method of expression from the former Catholic, James Joyce, and, seen in that literary light, Johnston's style appeared to be a quaint cultural remembrance of things past. His play appeared to be picking over the bones of dead controversies about Anglo-Irish disenfranchisement and Catholic religious and linguistic exclusion. What relevance could such resentments have for a current avant-garde that thought them old hat? Ria thought she had a special understanding of Johnston's Anglo-Irish angst about modern Ireland, but neither was any longer living in modern Ireland. They were both of them out of touch with the intellectual temper of the times.

On August 4, 1958, Ria made her third attempt to regain the lost artistic ascendancy of the Abbey with John O'Donovan's *A Change of Mind.* Lucas Barnaby, one of the new rich, a man who has risen to the financial top in a single generation, is almost killed in a car crash, which alters his personality from sinner to saint. He puts his children to manual work, and he makes many other strange household changes, but, in the end, the tycoon returns to his charming villainy which, in the opinion of all who live with him, is far better than his temporal sanctity.

The *Irish Independent* credited the playwright with having "something more to say than most of the present generation of Abbey playwrights." The *Irish Press* praised O'Donovan for trying "to help us to laugh at ourselves and he wants to be sanative by way of ridicule. And while we are wonderful at laughing at other people, we are not so good at laughing at ourselves." The critic lamented his stooping to "the easy, cheap joke," but, "after all that high-falutin' talk one might as well admit that this comedy, with its occasional serious knife-stabs, kept the house laughing last night."

It should have been evident to Ria that she couldn't win this cultural war with the weapons at her disposal. Whether or not she recognized her untenable position, she kept on trying to win the approval of Dublin artistic society. Her next production returned to the same period as O'Casey's *The Plough and the Stars*, and, inevitably, was compared to that highwater mark in Abbey playwriting.

On September 23, 1958, The Abbey premiered James Plunkett's *The Risen People.* The story focuses on the Fitzpatrick family whose lives are threatened by the labor strike led by Jim Larkin in the dark days of 1913. The *Irish Press* found "echoes of Joxer Daly and Mrs. Tancred" in the playwriting, "but so skillfully did Mr. Plunkett handle his characters that there was little reason to fault him on that score." While this reviewer regarded the first act as "slow and unsatisfactory," he admired the innovative cinematic production technique employed by Ria to accommodate the script's constant shifting of time and place.

The *Irish Independent* noted with approval the subtle questions raised by the playwright. "How much of a man's fight for a principle is personal pride; how far is he justified in sacrificing humanity to honour as he sees it?" The play began as a radio script and was subsequently to become a popular television film. The critic lamented the fact that, in the process of transferring his play from radio to stage, Plunkett made so much of Jim Larkin, who seemed to him to be nothing more than a radio voice "uttering socialist platitudes." Still, this reviewer was much impressed by "the gallant efforts of Eddie Golden as Big Jim," and he extolled "the brilliant expressionist artifices of Ria Mooney as producer." Furthermore, he observed that "Mr. Plunkett has been well served by the impeccable acting of the Abbey Players," and "by the skillful production of Ria Mooney, and by Tomás MacAnna's evocative settings."

Plunkett's play proved popular enough to carry the troupe through to their next opening night. On December 4, the Abbey presented M. J. Molloy's latest effort, *The Right Rose Tree*, the central theme of which is that war is only romantic in perspective. Set in 1922, the story concerns a young IRA recruit who has as his worst enemy a brother-in-law and former IRA leader, now an implacable opponent of the Free State Treaty. The contemporary setting did not seem to suit Molloy's lyric talents, which were ritually remarked upon by the *Irish Press*. "Mr. W. B. Yeats," observed the writer, "in the young, glorious days of the Abbey Theatre, would have loved to have Michael J. Molloy as one of his lieutenants in the war he was waging at the time. To Mr. Yeats nothing in the theatre took precedence over what he called the majesty of the spoken word. To him things like flashy sets and other stage arrangements were merely so many mechanical aids which served only to distract attention from the dialogue." The reviewer thought that the current play advanced that "worthy cause a little further."

The *Irish Independent* critic took an altogether different view of the proceedings. He thought that at their best the characters were "little more than types," and "at their worst, they are perilously close to folkloric caricatures." Ria's production did not achieve the cohesion, according to this reviewer, that "would make the piece at all credible as theatre, and the off-stage effects of gun battle are, in the main, slightly ludicrous." On December 26, the annual Irish pantomime, *Oisin i dTir-na-nOg*, took the Abbey into the New Year.

By any theatrical standard, the Abbey had completed a banner year, yet artistic Dublin talked of nothing but the scandal of the canceled Dublin

Theatre Festival. Ria had staged seven new plays by such distinguished dramatists as Walter Macken and Louis D'Alton, and literary lights such as Niall Sheridan, Dennis Johnston, and M. J. Molloy, with the added attraction of Plunkett's sweeping patriotic melodrama about labor leader Jim Larkin. Newspaper criticism mentioned Sheridan's "more than ordinary potentialities," and praised Denis Johnston's work as "the most vital play by an Irish author which Dublin has seen in many years." John O'Donovan was also praised because he "had something more to say than the present generation of Abbey playwrights," and M. J. Molloy was numbered among the Olympian pantheon presided over by the shade of W. B. Yeats. *The Right Rose Tree* was said to have advanced the cause of poetic dialogue in Irish theatre.

Accolades for the acting company featured such phrases as "sheer brilliance" and the "impeccable acting of the Abbey Players," with their performing technique described as "acted thought." Ria's production work was admired for its "brilliant expressionist artifices," and her direction was said "to have made the most of every scene." Furthermore, the Abbey troupe was recognized for its "uniformly high standard," an observation that said much about Ria's handling of the training, casting, and general development of her team. On top of this high grade, Ria was credited with having given one of Lennox Robinson's old plays "a sparkling revival," a tribute to her concern for the Abbey's playwriting heritage.

In spite of these witnesses to her craftsmanship, the variety of the Abbey repertoire, and the polish of the acting ensemble, Ria was ignored by the society critics whose approval she appeared to covet. It must have been disconcerting to be lauded in the daily press while being condescended to, when not completely ignored, in Dublin's literary salons. Yet, in spite of this maddening rejection of her work, Ria never seems to have succumbed to self-pity. In her memoirs, she asked: "How can I honestly regret being born just after the Golden Age commenced? How can I honestly regret being born in time to know Yeats and his brother Jack and Maud Gonne and O'Casey and the Countess Markievicz and all that delirium of the brave?"[8] No matter how apparent her rejection by those in the know, Ria never publicly complained of their treatment of her. Still, in the thick of the Abbey's theatrical action, such memories must have been small consolation to the tired little lady.

On January 26, 1959, John McCann's *I Know Where I'm Going* opened the new year to glowing reviews. The *Irish Press* critic said that "his most ardent admirers, among whom this reviewer unashamedly includes himself," suffered through a "rather disjointed first act." Nonetheless, the reviewer said that this latest effort represented "far and away the best piece

Pen poised and cigarette at the ready, Ria prepares another Abbey premiere. Notice the overcoat for the chilled auditorium. (G. A. Duncan.)

of writing Mr. McCann has done." He liked the playwright's "sympathy towards the faults and failings of his fellow humans," and he found the play's denizens "the most fascinating lot one could wish to spend an evening with. One hates to part with them at the end." It was said to be Harry Brogan's night, the actor revealing "hitherto unsuspected versatility in his playing. But he got wonderful support from Philip Flynn, Angela Newman, Eddie Golden, T. P. MacKenna, Aideen O'Kelly, Brid Lynch, Michael O'Brien, Geoffrey Golden, and Michael Hennessy. Ria Mooney gave the play a smooth and easy production with fine sets by Tomás MacAnna."

After reading this rave notice, one cannot help wondering why the writer feels he must list himself "unashamedly" as one of McCann's admirers. The *Irish Independent* reviewer somewhat acidly remarked that "it looks as if it will be staying for quite a while at the Queen's Theatre, judging by the audience reaction on its first night presentation there by the Abbey Theatre Company." Well, there you are! The play was just too popular to be worth considering as art. There was no denying the playwright's gift for "easy, natural-sounding and highly amusing dialogue," but what can one say about the facile "touch of sentiment, a dash of mystery and two romances [which] form the plot with a fairy-tale ending."[9]

The popularity of *I Know Where I'm Going* bought time for Ria's next project, her return to the stage in the leading role of Eugene O'Neill's *Long Day's Journey into Night*. The three-month run of McCann's comedy gave her 12 weeks in which to create the character of Mrs. James Tyrone.

Vincent Dowling remembered Ernest Blythe's reaction when the play was first recommended to him for production. "Ah, well," he responded, "it's only four of them anyway. We can just keep them out of everything. It's harmless rubbish, but it's only taking up four of them, and it will keep them quiet."[10] The younger members of the company were trying to organize, and Dowling was in the forefront of those Blythe dubbed "the trouble-makers." If Blythe thought he could pacify these young Turks by throwing them an artistic bone, he was wrong. They kept up the pressure for the next five years. Nonetheless, whatever Blythe's reason for agreeing to allow Philip O'Flynn, Ria Mooney, T. P. McKenna, Vincent Dowling, and Kathleen Barrington to perform O'Neill's four-hour tragedy, it proved to be a stirring and significant moment in the Abbey's long history. Anyway, the manager had one consolation. Ria obviously couldn't direct and play such a large role in the same play. Blythe seized upon this circumstance to bring back Frank Dermody as a company director.

During the rehearsal period of *Long Day's Journey*, Dowling noticed for the first time that Ria was having problems with her balance. He thought it was her inner ear that was giving her trouble. As the long occupation with the play progressed, he noticed that she sometimes walked with the aid of a cane. Val Mulkerns thought that Ria injured herself by a fall from the stage while directing a rehearsal. No one seems to recall such an incident, but the progressive deterioration of her health appears to have begun at this time.

Kathleen Barrington remembered going to Ria's house in Goatstown to run lines with her,[11] and Dowling recalled being invited "for a meal or a drink and to do lines. She was very insecure about her lines." In her memoirs, Ria expressed her feeling of relief "to have something besides production alone to occupy my mind, something to stimulate me into new thinking, even though it meant weeks of unrelieved hard work."[12] She began to study the role at the same time she was rehearsing the cast for the opening of *I Know Where I'm Going*. "I had usual productions to attend to every morning from eleven to one; then for lunch, and back for rehearsals of the O'Neill play; after which I spent the hours until bed-time memorizing lines. Since Mrs. O'Neill refused to allow cuts to be made for those first Abbey productions, once I knew the lines it took me two-and-a-half hours to speak them on cue from a friend who was kind enough to drive over at night to hear me." Barrington remembered Ria's attention to physical detail, the development of her drug-addicted character's arthritic hand movements, and the slow evolution of her attire as the play progressed. She thought she was good in performance, but "marvelous in rehearsal." She did "magic stuff" while going over lines, but she was never as comfortable in performance.

During the rehearsal period, Vincent Dowling recalled that "a whole different relationship came," the relationship of an "actor and actress, not this producer who kept apart. We realized, then, especially as we got to work with her in *Long Day's Journey*, how vulnerable she was." Dowling and Barrington enjoyed those evenings in Ria's Goatstown home running lines after a drink or a snack. It is curious that neither of them can remember having met any of the members of Ria's family on those occasions.

The play opened on April 28, 1959, to such cheering headlines as "Long Day a Fine Night at Abbey,"[13] and "Excellent Acting by Abbey Players."[14] The *Irish Press* thought that the "Abbey patrons redeemed themselves in full for all the sins of their past by the hushed attention with which they received almost every syllable of the four-and-a-half hour Eugene O'Neill play." The curtain went up at the inconvenient hour of 6:30, and the critics noted that the house was packed, expectant, and attentive throughout. "The Abbey Directors," remarked the *Irish Press* writer,

"can justly claim the occasion to be a major triumph for themselves, a vin-
dication of their judgment in presenting the marathon drama and an
emphatic denial that their audiences want only to listen to the uproarious schemings of our rural matchmakers."

The *Irish Independent* critic didn't much care for the play, referring
to the evening's effort as "ploughing a fifty-acre field of rather poor soil,"
but he didn't blame the actors, "who presented it with tremendous feeling and finesse. Philip O'Flynn is perfect in the quiet desperation of the
father and Ria Mooney, using her voice beautifully, is superb in the nervous desperation and moving in the final witlessness of the mother. T. P.
McKenna and Vincent Dowling are excellent as the elder and younger
sons, respectively; the unfaltering production is by Frank Dermody."

The *Irish Press* critic admired the play's "biting—at times savage—
satire, flashing humour and high-powered drama that even after four and
a half hours one feels the wrench of parting with the characters." The
aisle-sitters, however, did agree about one thing—the strong production
given the script by the Abbey company. The *Irish Press* critic noted,
"Directed with consummate skill by Frank Dermody who kept his production on taut razor-edge balance in Tomás MacAnna's excellent setting, the play was a personal triumph for Miss Ria Mooney in the part of
Mrs. Tyrone. This was a spell-binding performance which will be long
remembered. T. P. McKenna, as the elder son; Philip Flynn, as the father,
and Vincent Dowling, as the younger son, played up to her lead magnifi-
cently, and Kathleen Barrington contributed a delightful little cameo as
an Irish maid. A real theatrical occasion which does honour to all concerned."

Incredibly, the *Irish Times* seems to have ignored the production! It
wasn't until a letter written by the director of the Arts Council, Sean
O'Faolain, appeared on May 13, that any praise was given to Ria's monu-
mental effort. That highly regarded writer thought the Abbey's O'Neill
production was the finest to date, including those of London and New
York. It was, he maintained, "acted superbly, and directed with skill."
O'Faolain lamented the fact that the Abbey "management is obliged to
stage cheap plays, over long periods, in order to put on a worthwhile play
occasionally. The Abbey Theatre is meanly undersubsidized" and should
be awarded a quarter of a million pounds a year.

Even while lauding the Abbey's conscious reach for artistic excellence, the literati can't help including their prejudices about the "uproarious schemings of rural matchmakers," and "cheap plays" staged "over
long periods, in order to put on a worthwhile play occasionally." Whatever might be said of the seven new plays produced by Ria Mooney in the

Long Day's Journey into Night: Philip O'Flynn (top) as James Tyrone, Ria Mooney as Mrs. Tyrone, and Vincent Dowling as their son Edmund. "The play was a personal triumph for Miss Ria Mooney...." (G. A. Duncan.)

preceding year, it could not be said that there was a rural comedy or a cheap play among them. Nor could it be factually stated that there was a country kitchen setting in any of them. These asides so casually thrown away by noted writers and newspaper critics had a cumulative effect on public opinion about what went on at the National Theatre. That these remarks were patently false does not matter in the least. It was the considered opinion of those who ought to know, and no accumulation of facts could serve to refute their authoritative judgments. The praise heaped upon Ria's creation of Mrs. Tyrone would soon be forgotten. All that would remain were the caveats composed by the critics.

While Dowling remembered "she was wonderful to play with," he also recalled that she had trouble with her lines. "Particularly Philip O'Flynn and myself, who had a lot to do with her, we had to take her out of line situations again and again." Dowling admired the "worn light bluish — washed away almost — little dressing gown" she wore, and how, in the last act, she "let her hair down with a little ribbon in it." The actor couldn't remember whether it was during the first run of the production, or a subsequent revival of it, that she hired Patrick Laffan, a young addition to the company, as her "personal book and cue man — her prompter." He remembered that one night "she couldn't say a line. She was all over the place. She would be stuck and we would give her a line, and she would take it back to a beginning line."

During the act break, the two actors talked about what might "happen in the fourth act, where nobody can help her." The long meandering fourth act monologue of Mrs. Tyrone is difficult enough to memorize under any circumstances, but in the shaky situation of that night, the men believed they foresaw disaster staring them and Ria in the face. At that moment, they heard a knock on the door. It was Ria. "We thought," said Dowling, " she was going to say, 'boys, thank you.'" In retrospect, he felt it was exactly what she was saying, but, at the time, her response to the earlier, unsettling incident seemed bizarre to him.

"I just wanted to tell you," she said, "that, in the fourth act, I'm not going to wear the blue ribbon. I'm going to wear one slightly different, and I hope it doesn't throw you."

Dowling, embracing that faded memory of a fond association, quietly remarked upon that sad moment: "She was so lovely in her gentleness. So vulnerable. It was the best production the Abbey ever did." It was so unlike her demeanor as a director; the gentleness and vulnerability seemed such a completely theatrical creation, that he appeared to be wondering from what depth of recall the actress brought up these qualities.

It was Ria's misfortune that, just as she had become the artistic success

of the Dublin theatrical world, a phenomenon of nature called *Sive*
appeared in the Irish dramatic firmament and dominated the Amateur
Dramatic Festival finals at Athlone.[15] The work of an unknown Kerry pub-
lican, John B. Keane, it introduced two Bodhran (drum-like gypsy instru-
ment)-playing, curse-chanting tinkers, singing a tune that resonated
throughout Ireland for the next year.

> May the snails devour his corpse,
> And the rain do harm worse;
> May the devil sweep the hairy creature soon;
> He's as greedy as a sow,
> And the crow behind the plough;
> That black man from the mountain, Seaneen Rua.

It was rumored that Keane's play was rejected by the Abbey "without a word of explanation or apology." Tomás MacAnna admitted that he
"was one of the readers of the manuscript, and I do admit that I was one
of the people who didn't like it all that much." Along the competitive route
that led to the final prize in Athlone in April, *Sive* was first evaluated by
Micheal Ó hAodha, then by broadcaster Harry Morrow, Abbey set designer
Tomás MacAnna, and, just before the Athlone finals, by Globe director,
Jim Fitzgerald. Ó hAodha, who wrote the first Irish pantomime for the
Abbey in 1945, "described the production as the finest contribution to the
amateur movement since M. J. Molloy's *The Paddy Pedlar*." Morrow said
he would be surprised if it didn't win all the drama festivals in the country, and remarked, "I do not salute the management of the Abbey who, I
am told, had the stupidity and impertinence to reject the manuscript of
this play without a word of explanation or apology. I despair!"

It remained for Tomás MacAnna to recover the Abbey's lost prestige
by joining the distinguished group of *Sive* admirers. Instead, the lanky,
morose MacAnna threw oil on the fire. He began by awarding first prize
in the Charleville festival to Tuam's production of *Thunder Rock* by Robert
Ardrey. He compounded the problem by claiming that "tonight's production of *Sive* is a rewritten version and has been rewritten in the way
suggested by the Abbey Theatre." Keane called MacAnna a liar. "Any alter-
ations in the revised version," he said, "were suggested by Micheal Ó
hAodha." The confrontation excited the news media and Keane's reputation began to grow outside of his native Kerry.

The final statement of artistic Dublin's prejudice was left to the
Globe's Jim Fitzgerald. With presumptuous professorial pedantry, he
placed Keane in the direct tradition of Abbey dramatists like MacMahon,
Macken, and Behan, all of whom represented for him the "stranglehold

of naturalism of the Abbey. Perhaps the tragedy is," he went on, "that none of these writers seems to have found a subject big enough for the immense force and vitality at their disposal. This has been, in my view, the mystery which has rendered Irish writing ineffectual generally." It seems curious that so recognized a man of the theatre as Jim Fitzgerald could call the plays of MacMahon and Behan naturalistic, but, since Keane had been rejected by the National Theatre and had not yet received a professional production, why compare him to Abbey playwrights at all?

One effect of this controversy was to undermine further the morale at the playhouse, distracting attention away from Ria's record as a director and the acclaim accorded her for her performance as Mrs. Tyrone. One wonders what might have happened if Keane's play had been given its first production at the Abbey. Surely such Dublin playhouse insiders as Fitzgerald would have scorned the commercial popularity of his work as they did every Abbey box-office success. In addition, wasn't MacAnna assuming the same attitude in his rejection of *Sive?* Here was an Abbey insider joining the Abbey's critics in condemning the very repertoire he was charged with designing! As it turned out, Keane was rudely dismissed by the Dublin arts people, but his plays remained money cows for the next 30 years.

At any rate, Keane's confrontation with MacAnna over the Abbey's attitude toward *Sive* demonstrates the set designer's growing importance at the National Theatre. At the Charleville Festival, he felt free to speak with authority about Abbey play selection and his own significant part in the process. In his comments on the Listowel production of *Sive*, MacAnna implied that Keane had improved his script as a result of Abbey criticism. In spite of that assertion — an obvious explanation for the Abbey's rejection of the play — he still gave the first prize to another play. This performance as adjudicator at Charleville seems to have been intended to give the impression that he had some significant artistic authority at the Abbey beyond his post as set designer. His reputation among the players was not so exalted. One member of the troop maintained that "Tomás was looked on as a kind of lackey of Blythe's, a kind of heavy light weight."[16] Val Mulkerns was sure that MacAnna "was not a person she [Ria] would approve of, because his talents were minimal. Blythe pushed him all the time. Ria was, in a sense, crowded out."[17] Ria later realized that Blythe was gradually inserting MacAnna, whose principal task had been the Gaelic productions and the Irish pantomime, into the main English-speaking repertoire. After ten years of carrying out Blythe's "main policy of making Irish entertaining and colourful to our audiences,"[18] MacAnna was rewarded by being promoted set designer for the theatre. A decade later,

Tomás MacAnna, Blythe's Irish-speaking director of Gaelic plays, slowly insinuated himself into Ria's position as artistic director of the Abbey. (G. A. Duncan.)

after the manager had retired from his position and his name had become a title of opprobrium, Mac-Anna put on a good face about his position as Blythe's Irish advocate. He insisted that, during those years, he had enjoyed himself hugely, although he confessed he did fret "somewhat at not being given the odd English production."[19]

In her memoirs, Ria only hints at the forces that were marshaling to ease her out of her position as artistic director. She doesn't accuse Blythe of undermining her authority, even though it was clear to those who knew her that she had a strong distaste for the man. "Ria didn't have confrontations," said Dowling, "except under extreme circumstances." Perhaps that is why the name of Tomás MacAnna never appears in her autobiography. Whether she ignored him out of contempt for his part in Blythe's plans, or because she thought him a man of marginal talents, Ria did not deign to note his presence at the playhouse. MacAnna, on the other hand, subtly insinuated that she had been an ineffective Abbey artistic director. In an interview given in 1975, he contrasted his Irish work with Ria's English-speaking productions. "Where she found herself producing play after play in the same naturalistic style, I was romping though Gheon, Jalabert, Benevente, Molière and Chekhov in styles ranging all the way from late Guthrie to music-hall."[20]

Ria's first production experience with these European playwrights was made at the time she was performing and directing at Eva Le Gallienne's Civic Theatre before MacAnna had even seen a play. The implied judgment that she had a narrow acquaintance with international theatre is evident, and, since he knew better, it appears as an intended slight to her theatrical acumen. The notion that the National Theatre produced nothing but naturalistic plays might be believed by someone who had been an occasional visitor to the Abbey at the Queen's. MacAnna knew better.

He had designed sets for productions such as Plunkett's *The Risen People*, and he must have read the reviews that congratulated Ria on her superb use of cinematic staging techniques. He must have witnessed the production of Molloy's *The King of Friday's Men*, Johnston's *Strange Occurrence on Ireland's Eye*, D'Alton's *The Devil a Saint Would Be*, and Tomelty's *All Soul's Night*, to mention but a few of the plays with unusual settings, lyric prose writing, whimsical satire, and ghostly appearances. Tomás MacAnna was an ambitious man, and Ria Mooney stood in the way of his advancement. Blythe and Dermody promoted his elevation within the management of the playhouse, while the younger members of the acting company were beginning to agitate for more rehearsal time, significant salary increases, and a chance to play in plays written outside Ireland. Ria might have sided with the players, but, unlike MacAnna, she was a loyalist. As long as she was artistic director of the National Theatre, she would promote the welfare of that playhouse without public dissent from company policy.

Long Day's Journey into Night was not expected to have a long run, and it didn't. It was replaced on May 11, 1959, by John Murphy's *The Country Boy* with Ria occupying the director's chair. The story revolves around an emigrant Mayo boy who returns to his father's farm after 15 years in New York City. The young exile has married an American girl who seems responsible for his drunken disillusionment. The *Irish Press* thought the play would find "an echo in many a heart," and the theme had "a deep ring of authenticity about it." The *Irish Independent* found the "production by Ria Mooney is more than competent in the better scenes, but does little to compensate for heavy, slow writing in the first act. Setting by Tomás MacAnna is commendably traditional."

Ria had exerted herself for six months, first with the McCann play, at the same time preparing for and subsequently performing in the O'Neill marathon, and finally, staging Murphy's touching story of an exile's longing for his youthful home. During that period, her fellow players noted some deterioration of her physical condition and the memory lapses that often accompany attacks of nervous anxiety. It was evident to all that she needed relief from her duties as director, so Ray MacAnally was given the task of staging the next scheduled new production, Tom Coffey's *Stranger Beware*.

While this mystery of a Dingle murder solved with the aid of a Father Brown–like priest received mixed reviews, the city's attention was focused on the impending Dublin Theatre Festival. The papers celebrated the return of this event, suspended the previous year by a scandalous misunderstanding that was the subject of gossip and rumor throughout the whole of 1959. Denis Johnston's *Dreaming Dust* was being produced at the Gaiety and Orson Welles was said to be putting in an appearance at a midnight matinee.[21] Milo O'Shea and Jimmy O'Dea headed a Globe Theatre production of Shaw's *The Simpleton of the Unexpected Isles*, and Sir Donald Wolfit impersonated the painter Gainsborough in a play by Cecil Beaton. The Abbey's contribution to the festival was Anne Daly's *Leave it to the Doctor*, and if Ria Mooney had anything to do with it, that fact wasn't mentioned in the press reviews. Marie Kean and Ray MacAnally were applauded for outstanding comic work in a thin script about a doctor's irresponsible romantic schemings.

Once the excitement of the Dublin Theatre Festival was exhausted and the city returned to its normal routine, the Abbey brought out J. D. Stewart's *Danger, Men Working* on October 19, 1959. The play appeared to the reviewers as a thesis about the struggle between labor and management. The *Irish Press*, however, approved of the evening on the grounds that it gave "a number of Abbey actors the finest vehicle for character studies in a long time." The *Irish Independent* thought the production suffered badly "from a lack of pace and sense of urgency at the beginning," but neither critic made any mention of a responsible director. The *Irish Times* simply ignored the Abbey's work completely.

Peter Hutchinson's *No Man Is an Island* premiered on November 9, and, while the *Irish Press* ignored Ria's contribution, the *Irish Independent* remembered there had been a director of the evening's entertainment. One reviewer praised the script's interest in Irish army life and was glad to see a thriller presented at the playhouse. Apparently, *Stranger Beware* made little impression upon this gentleman, and he discounted the IRA as an Irish military force.[22]

In Dublin's Fair City by Criostoir O Floinn was the seventh new play produced that busy year, and it added nothing to the reputation of Irish playwriting. Ria had labored mightily on the only foreign play of that season, O'Neill's *Long Day's Journey into Night*, and the effort had not diminished or altered the haggling over the National Theatre's lack of artistic purpose or distinction. The following year must have seemed a repeat of the last, with the exception that Ria did not have a new O'Neill character to create. No wonder she referred to that time as the "nightmare that was my final years at the National Theatre."

The decade of the sixties began with another McCann play entitled *It Can't Go on for Ever*, but to Ria it must have seemed like it not only could, but it probably would. New critics seemed to have taken over at the *Irish Press* and the *Irish Independent*. The *Irish Press* writer ignored altogether Ria's contribution to the production process, and the *Irish Independent* reviewer gave her instructions about direction. Bryan MacMahon's *The Song of the Anvil*, a poetic fantasy with authentic Irish music included in the fiery final scene set in a west of Ireland forge, attracted some attention, but a revival of *The Lady of Belmont* by St. John Ervine and Anthony Butler's *The Deputy's Daughter* were dismissed as "poor successor[s] to Shakespeare play[s],"[23] and scripts with "good dialogue but ... poor plot[s]."[24]

In 1960, Ria directed six new plays and the first Abbey production of *The Lady of Belmont*. As the year wore on, her friends began to notice that her zest for her production tasks had faded away. "I think," remembered Val Mulkerns, "she became quite disillusioned toward the end of her life. She probably worked too long in a hostile atmosphere at the Abbey." There was "defeatism about Ria toward the end."[25] With poor health weakening her body, the political infighting at the Abbey disturbing backstage company solidarity, and the long exile at the Queen's entering its 11th season, her determination seems to have given way to resignation. It wouldn't be long now. She had done her best to carry on the Abbey tradition, but no one seemed to care about that heritage anymore.

CHAPTER 12

Ria Mooney and
The Enemy Within

As she approached her seventh decade, Ria Mooney was besieged from every corner of the playhouse by circumstances beyond her control. Her deteriorating physical condition made her shy of appearing in public without the aid of a special prompter onstage, and the discreet use of a cane offstage. Adding to her physical woes, she found herself caught in the crossfire of a war being waged backstage. The acting company was engaged in a fierce combat with the management. Salaries were the main source of contention, but the actors also were demanding more rehearsal time for each production, as well as the opportunity to play in contemporary European plays. At the same time, these same disgruntled performers found themselves under attack from fellow actors because they were a privileged part of a subsidized operation. As if this loss of professional solidarity wasn't depressing enough, Dublin's literati joined the fray, deriding the Abbey's performing standards and the playhouse's repertoire. Hugh Hunt maintained that the Abbey had "grown estranged from its oldest and best friends," and never gained the "respect of a younger generation who had deserted to other theatres."[1] Such constant agitation severely compromised company morale and undermined Ria's theatrical authority. The playhouse atmosphere, often tense and sometimes unpleasant, seemed to point toward an actors' strike in the not too distant future. Under these conditions, is it any wonder that Ria began to look around for employment as an actress? Her attempt to create an acting ensemble and an Abbey repertoire that balanced new work with a distinguished repertoire of past successes seemed doomed to failure under the pressures created by backstage bickering and cultural backbiting.

Ria's return to the stage as an actress had brought her offers to appear on the developing Irish television, and her fear of physical failure in public must have made the relatively insular nature of broadcast production attractive to her. It also coincided with her gradual withdrawal from her position as the artistic director of the National Theatre. In the next three years, from 1961 through 1963, Ria Mooney directed but two new plays.

As if Abbey working conditions weren't sufficiently unsettling, Ria's Ireland was undergoing a social and cultural sea change described by historian David Thornley as "the end of an era."[2] The island was being invaded by European philosophical ideas brought into Dublin by English television. This modern attraction, coupled with government economic decisions that further urbanized the country and depopulated the countryside, resulted in the "death-knell of a traditional Ireland." Dublin took on the personality of any small European city, and this attempt to be cosmopolitan not only undermined Ria's effort to bring to the Irish audience plays that reflected the Irish character and Irish national issues, but it dug at the roots the "indigenous Gaelic folk culture" of the country. "What is remarkable," wrote Thornley, "almost to the point of incredibility is the passiveness with which this change has been accepted inside a single generation."

Thornley's observations reflect the historian's detached attitude, but for Ria it was a case of "future shock." The swiftly developing changes made her seem a relic of the past, a dedicated and talented theatrical practitioner, of course, but old-fashioned and frozen into theatrical techniques and conventions that gave off the delicate odor of another era. No one wished to insult her or attack her as a person, but neither did anyone consult her or defend her position at the playhouse. She was a respected remnant of the past, and, so long as her authority held sway at the Abbey, she was in the way of artistic adventure.

The 1961 season began in January with *The Evidence I Shall Give* directed by Frank Dermody, and it was followed by Tomás MacAnna's production of *All The King's Horses*. In April, John McCann's new Kelly clan comedy, *Put a Beggar on Horseback*, had MacAnna in the director's chair, and it was followed by Bryan MacMahon's *The Honey Spike* with MacAnna once again directing.

During that entire season, Ria did not direct a new play. MacAnna was assigned a new one-act play entitled *The Long Sorrow* by Thomas Coffee for September, while Ria staged the main piece of the evening, a revival of Lennox Robinson's popular comedy *The Whiteheaded Boy*.[3] The season closed with a new play entitled *Brave Banner*, but Ria was not asked to carry it. Instead, she was left to bear her own burden in dignified silence.

Ria in her seventh decade was in failing health and losing her grip on the Abbey's production reins.

The season of discontent at the National Theatre, stranded in temporary quarters for the past 12 years, crippled by backstage infighting between actors and management, and under attack by resentful outsiders excluded from its sheltering subsidy, extended inexorably into the year 1962. Amidst this playhouse desolation, Ria's personal isolation was nearly complete. MacAnna was the anointed successor being seasoned to assume control of Abbey artistic fortunes, with Dermody as an experienced substitute waiting in the wings should the pretender stumble. It is somewhat surprising, therefore, that Ria did manage to make one more memorable directorial effort. For some reason, she was given the task of staging a new young playwright's first Abbey production.

Playwright Brian Friel was educated at St. Columb's College, Derry, and St. Joseph's Training College, Belfast.[4] A schoolteacher until 1960, his success as a short-story writer encouraged him to desert the classroom and rely entirely upon his pen. His play entitled *This Doubtful Paradise* was first performed in Belfast in 1959. *The Enemy Within* opened at the Abbey on August 6, 1962.

Friel's story is a biography of St. Columba, a "full-blooded, warm-hearted individual whose call to the things of the spirit is often foiled by the weight of his fiery temperament."[5] His love of his home is locked in a struggle with his dedication to his God and his loving concern for the monastic community entrusted to his care. The *Irish Press* found that "the monastic life in its rigours, its good humour, its clash of personalities and, above all, in the childlike simplicity of its practitioners is well captured." While some of the incidents didn't appear especially dramatic and there might be an occasional weakness in the dialogue, critics praised the piece for its "genuine feeling and considerable understanding of human nature." The *Irish Independent* called the play "a compelling and thought-provoking study of Columba, the exiled Abbot of Iona," and praised the author for "giving an insight into the never ending struggle that goes on in the minds of men who set themselves the highest standards in the attainment of spirituality."[6]

Here was a play exactly suited to Ria's mood and methods. She could empathize with Columba's desire to remain with his assembled company, dedicated to the work he espoused. She could also understand his feeling of exile even while among his own people. Furthermore, at her disposal to mount this script, she had the fine company she had assembled and nurtured for the past 14 years. Ray MacAnally played the part of Columba "with depth and meaning. His Columba is a very credible saint, whose outbursts of anger are followed as quickly by sorrow." Michael Hennessy's Dochonna was praised as "one of the finest pieces of acting he has done," and Philip O'Flynn, Michael O'Brien, Geof Golden, Vincent Dowling, Pat Laffan, T. P. McKenna and Eddie Golden were called "outstanding."

The *Irish Press* critic's final words seem almost like a valedictory wave of the hand to a faithful servant fading from the scene. "Ria Mooney's vigorous direction," wrote the critic, "also helps to make this play one of the most adult and interesting the Abbey has given us recently." The story seems quintessentially Irish, and, at the same time, reflects a specifically human and, therefore, universal dilemma; i.e., the eternal conflict between what a man knows he ought to do, and his emotional desire to accommodate a conflicting impulse.

How ironic it is that Ria was being excluded from the future of the National Theatre just as she was presenting to the Dublin stage for the first time its most modern and most successful commercial playwright. Samuel Beckett may have won the loyalty of the literary and academic community, but he has never been a popular attraction in any playhouse. Brian Friel was to become the undisputed artistic hero of the trendsetters, and, at the same time, he has managed to attract large audiences to his plays. It is interesting to note that Friel's next play, *Philadelphia, Here I Come,* was not given to the Abbey but to the Boys at the Gate.

Friel's debut at the Abbey was followed by John McCann's seventh successful comedy, *A Jew Named Sammy,* and, on November 12, 1962, the Abbey finally got around to producing a John B. Keane play entitled *Hut 42.* The final production of the year was Eugene O'Neill's *Ah, Wilderness!,* about which the *Irish Press* critic wrote: "O'Neill is one of the few 'outside' dramatists of stature whose plays, because of his Irish-American background, may be performed under the existing charter of the Abbey Theatre. Surely it is time for a re-appraisal of the position, to allow plays from 'world' theatre to alternate with good-class Irish plays. At present, far too many second rate Irish plays, which should never see the light of day in a national theatre, are being presented."[7]

This observation is especially thoughtless when one considers that the last three Abbey productions had come from the pens of Brian Friel, John McCann, and John B. Keane. McCann's plays were lauded by the critic himself as authentic, warm-hearted, and well-constructed comedies of Dublin life, while Friel and Keane were to dominate Irish playhouses for the next 30 years. So much for the prophetic powers of Dublin artistic gurus.

Ria's last new play production at the National Theatre was John O'Donovan's *Copperfaced Jack*. The play opened the Abbey's new season on February 26, 1963. The plot charts the final years of John Scott, Lord Chief Justice of Ireland in 1798. Nicknamed "Copperfaced Jack" because of the amount of brandy he has consumed, the dying figure remembers his considerable vices with guilt-ridden irony at his own perversity. The *Irish Independent* praised O'Donovan's "dialogue which has a fine crispness and a jaunty wit, and is excellent."[8] Ria's production was praised for its "nice pace." The acting was considered to be "generally top rate" with Micheál Ó hAonghusa's Scott praised as a "fine effort."[9]

Robert Hogan reported that "this production caused O'Donovan some justified anguish." Apparently, the rehearsals had begun before the playwright had been informed of its impending production. Adding to this affront, the play received little or no advertising prior to its opening night and unauthorized changes were made in the author's text. "When I discovered at rehearsal that several lines had been cut by his [Blythe's] order without reference to me, and indeed in spite of his verbal undertaking not to change the text, I sprang up from my seat in the theatre and emphasized an apostrophe to the heavens with a blow of my fist on the back of an iron seat that broke it (the iron seat, not my fist)."[10]

"Several discriminating people," wrote Robert Hogan, "who saw the Abbey production have told me they thought the play quite bad. The playscript, however, strongly suggests that the production was at fault."[11] Hogan doesn't seem to have considered the possibility that his "discriminating people" may have been wrong about the play, so he draws the only other conclusion that someone reading the script and admiring its theatricality might assume. The contemporary reviews, however, indicate that the actors and the director did excellent work. Maybe Hogan's discriminating friends weren't so discriminating after all.

It is all too predictable. O'Donovan created an ironic self-portrait of a Falstaffian figure that ought to have attracted the attention of star character actors of the English-speaking theatre.[12] Instead, it was damned with faint praise because it was produced by that dreaded Blythe monster at his Abbey. No one blamed Ria Mooney for the failure. She was not even mentioned as a contributor to the performance, and Micheál Ó hAonghusa's Copperfaced Jack, praised in the daily press, was forgotten by the literary critics. Any injustice might be done to innocent bystanders so long as that villain Blythe got his comeuppance.

Ria's position at the Abbey had now become intolerable. There is no way of knowing whether or not she had agreed to the cuts in O'Donovan's script, but, since she was always direct in her dealings with actors and playwrights, it is unlikely that anyone even bothered to consult her about the excision. If she was capable of facing the O'Casey temperament and advocating a cut in his sacred text, it is unreasonable to suppose she would not have granted the same consideration to John O'Donovan. In her memoirs, she never mentions the playwright's destruction of playhouse furniture. The incident, like much of what went on in those final years, is dismissed with a weary plea for her reader's sympathy and understanding. "I have tried to write something of the nightmare that was that period of my final years in our National Theatre, but I find it a little too painful to go into more detail. Those who understand how professional theatres are run might not believe me, and those who know the theatre only as members of an audience might think, 'The lady doth protest too much!'"[13] Ria Mooney remained discreet to the very end. "It was with deep relief when, in 1963, my way at last became clear, and I was able to resign my post at the Irish National Theatre."

Hugh Hunt tells us that "in 1963, Ria Mooney, worn out by the heavy demands of a thankless and unrewarding task, suffered a break-down that led to her resignation."[14] Unfortunately, he gives no source for this assertion, and members of her company have either forgotten or refuse to disclose her mental state or physical health at the time of her departure.

Once Ria Mooney gave up her place at the National Theatre, she was almost completely ignored. "I do feel," said her editor, Val Mulkerns, "that professionally, once she resigned at the Abbey, once she no longer had the status of Artistic Director, her status plummeted. Meanwhile, her health was giving out."[15] What appeared to Vincent Dowling as a loss of balance seems to have been the beginnings of a disease of the spine. This creeping disability gradually reduced her mobility until it finally took her life.

Although she was ignored by Dublin's cultural movers and shakers, Ria never lost her interest in the well-being of the theatre in which she had spent the greater part of her distinguished career as an actress and a director. When she came to put her memories on paper, she recorded the changes that had taken place there since her retirement. She noted that her place had been taken by two men and that the government subsidy was first doubled, then trebled, and, by the time the new theatre opened in 1966, the grant had "jumped to more than £ 50,000 per annum."[16]

She observed that the new theatre, though not as large as the Queen's, had one hundred seats more than the original Abbey playhouse. She found them "infinitely more comfortable than they used to be, and the auditorium is warm and airy, with an easy view of the stage from every seat." She admired the lighting system, and seemed pleased that the public appeared to be "very proud of their new National Theatre."[17] If she was careful not to appear too critical of the new building, she was not about to surrender her powers of observation. "This new Theatre of ours," she wrote, "is comfortable, functional — and quite without character. It reminds me of every large university theatre I've seen in America; even the non–Irish repertoire is much the same too."[18] In short, to her mind, the National Theatre was just another coldly international, academic, and literary theatre.

As she came to the end of her musings, Ria couldn't resist commenting on the decline of what had been a playhouse created for the work of Irish playwrights. "Every time I go to the theatre these days it amuses me to note that the list of helpers in both Theatres — but especially the larger one — grows longer and longer. For instance, the programme for a recent production shows the following:

Artistic Adviser
Director
Assistant to Director
Designer
Music: one man
Set constructed by: two men
Set painted by: two men
Special lighting by: one man
Property Master
Stage Director
Stage Manager
Costumes made by: three women
Men's costumes tailored by: one man
Sound: one man
Adviser for this production on the moves of XVIII century
Adviser to the Designer of 18th century Ireland
Bust of Goldsmith: one man
Programme Cover designed by: one man

General Stage Manager
Chief Electrician
Hair stylists for two of the girl principals: two Professional hairdressers
Corsets: Commercial concern.

Any programme of my own productions, up to the day I left, would have shown three credits: to the Producer (i.e. Director), the Scenic Designer, and the Stage Manager."[19]

When Ria was finishing her memoirs in 1969, she could not resist noting that the government subsidy had risen to £110,000." The Abbey now appeared to be just another government boondoggle. The 28 jobs listed in the playhouse program demonstrated that the National Theatre was no longer an actor's and playwright's theatre. It seemed to have lost its unique vocation as the center of original Irish playwriting performed by Irish actors before an Irish audience.

In 1967, Ria was included in a list of 10 players who had given distinguished service to Irish National Theatre.[20] They were all accorded honorary membership in the Abbey company with the right to appear as guests from time to time on the Abbey stage. It is an impressive list, which includes Cyril Cusack, Ray MacAnally, Jack McGowran, Siobhan McKenna, T. P. McKenna, Denis O'Dea, Shelagh Richards, Arthur Shields, and, curiously enough, Micheál MacLiammóir. None of the members of that impressive group had ever guided the artistic fortunes of the Abbey. Ria's special contribution to Abbey fortunes during the theatre's long exile at the Queen's was ignored.

Memories of her during those final years of her life make melancholy reading. John Jordan, a Dublin critic, academic, and sometime actor (Ria had auditioned the college student for a small part in the burnt-out shell of the old Abbey in that fateful summer of 1951) remembered the last time he saw her. "My last memory of her is sad; infirm and ignored, seeking to gain entrance to the Olympia during the 1969 Theatre Festival."[21]

Mary Manning recalled visiting the ailing actress in her home in Dundrum, a Dublin suburb. Manning, who returned to Dublin in 1970 after raising a family in Boston, renewed her acquaintance with this touring companion of her youth. She discovered that Ria's illness had made her a recluse.[22] Ria acknowledged those conversations in her memoirs. "My friend, Mary Manning Howe, seemed to trust me to write of her — I could not be truthful and write otherwise." Manning sadly recalled those last visits. "I went to see her several times. I saw her in hospital twice." She was "very sick. She was in a depression." Val Mulkerns did not remember her friend's last sickness as one spent in lonely isolation. She remembered that Ria had friends and family around her throughout her final illness. Nonetheless, she had been at first neglected and then forgotten by the Dublin artistic world.

Ria finished her autobiography in 1969, but it did not receive publication in her lifetime. In a footnote to her memoirs, published in magazine form in the summer and fall of 1978, Val Mulkerns documented her death. "Ria Mooney died in Dublin on January 3, 1973, after a long illness."[23]

On January 4, 1973, the *Irish Times* announced her passing on its front page with a headshot of the aged actress, lines of pain etched into her smiling face, with a summary of her importance to the Irish stage. "The Dublin-born actress, who had a distinguished career at home and abroad, and was producer at the Abbey Theatre from 1948 until she retired from the post in 1963, died in Dublin yesterday. She was 69."

The one-column obituary gave an accurate account of her early appearances. The article noted that she possessed "from her earliest days a beautiful voice." Her special friendship with Sean O'Casey was observed on an autographed picture she kept among her many theatrical souvenirs. "To her he wrote on a photograph taken on-stage during rehearsal: 'Be clever, maid, and let who will be good.'" This reference appears to refer to her naive Rosie Redmond in *The Plough and the Stars*. At the same time, the obituary recognized that "her interests ranged freely beyond the theatre as was proved by her membership at the Royal Society of Antiquaries and by the many examples of the work of Irish Artists which hung in her Dublin suburban home."

The final paragraph gave witness to her most important accomplishment. "Her fifteen years as the first woman producer ever appointed at the Abbey Theatre were probably the most arduous of her career. When she came to it she was faced with the task of virtually rebuilding the theatre tradition with a group of untried young actors and actresses recruited mainly from amateur dramatic societies, and she achieved a notable success."

The next day, in *An Irishman's Diary*, a daily feature in the *Irish Times*, the columnist remarked that "as a teacher and director of the Gaiety school of acting and at the Abbey, Ria Mooney molded the techniques of many actors and actresses who have since become famous. Marie Kean is one such who has always gratefully acknowledged this debt."[24] The author observed that her years at the Abbey as producer "were tough ones," but "Ria Mooney was totally and committedly a woman of the theatre. She dedicated her life to the art of the theatre in all its aspects. I never remember her giving a performance that was less than complete. In some, notably in 'Wuthering Heights,' she was superb."

Epilogue

The passing years have not been kind to the memory of Ria Mooney. Once the new playhouse opened, the rapid changes in management and repertoire altered the National Theatre's reputation as the home of Irish playwriting. Although new writers such as Thomas Murphy, Thomas Kilroy, and Henno Magee received warm praise from Dublin's artistic elite, the repertoire now featured international literary favorites such as Jean Genet, August Strindberg, Tom Stoppard, Anton Chekhov, Bertolt Brecht, and even Günter Grass. Meanwhile, the company Ria had so painstakingly assembled and patiently trained slowly drifted away to England and America. The Abbey Theatre ceased to be a repertory company playing new Irish plays, and, consequently, any fond memory of Ria Mooney's achievement was interpreted as an implied criticism of those guiding the National Theatre.

Throughout her career, Ria had been confronted by the implacable hostility between Irish playwrights seeking an audience in their native land, and those who maintained that local endeavors appeared mere homespun fashions when placed beside the international artistic creations of the cosmopolitan world. During the sustained struggle for control of the Abbey by these two forces, Ria resolutely remained on the fence, praising the avant-garde *The Old Lady Says, "No!"* while at the same time registering success after success in popular plays such as *Lady Precious Stream, The Rugged Path,* and in her own adaptation of *Wuthering Heights.* Perhaps posterity would have treated her more fairly had she taken sides during the long battle. Perhaps it would have made little difference in the end.

Ironically, most of Ria's problems might be summed up in the person of Ernest Blythe. He incorporated two elements of Irish national life which created most of the controversy that bedeviled the Abbey Theatre.

Blythe's patriotic insistence on the use the Irish language in the National Theatre was a direct attack on the Anglo-Irish contribution to the history of Ireland, and it was deeply resented by that cultured and educated class. They never forgave him for it. Ria admired the ascendancy class and wanted to be accepted among its members. She had no Irish, and she thought the manager's language policy would only serve to alienate those like her, the largest segment of the theatregoing public.

At the same time, Blythe's securing a government subsidy for the Abbey was the Trojan horse that, once inside the walls of the theatrical city, defeated the playhouse population, handing the reins of management over to nontheatrical people. Holloway reported in his journal that, in August 1925, W. B. Yeats addressed the Dail, telling them that, in effect, "the Abbey was always endowed one way or another since its inception: the actors and dramatists almost accepting nothing for their services at times..."[1] With Yeats and Lady Gregory at the head of the playhouse operation, no one could have foreseen that once the playwrights and performers surrendered their subsidy to the state, they eventually would lose control of playhouse policy.

Actors and playwrights constantly dispute playhouse policy with those who supply production money. The Boys resented their dependence upon Lord Longford's money, until they finally found themselves forced to bite the hand that fed them. On their own, MacLiammóir and Edwards became commercially conscious in their choice of plays for production. Their notoriety helped them to financial independence, and then they turned to the commercially lucrative world of motion pictures, television, and one-man shows.

As a national institution, the Abbey did not have the options which were open to the privately run Gate Theatre. One unforeseen result of the government subsidy was the ascendancy of Ernest Blythe to the manager's position. It also created unanticipated animosity among the performers and writers excluded by Blythe for language reasons, rather than acting talent, from its economic protection. While Ria was artistic director, the government contribution to Abbey expenses represented only a guarantee against foreclosure; it never gave the operation enough to make it independent of the box-office receipts. Nonetheless, it compelled the actors to accept the imposition of Blythe's linguistic policy.

After the disastrous Abbey fire, the government subsidy hardly covered the rent for the Queen's playhouse, making box-office support even more important. For Ria, this represented an opportunity rather than a hardship. She was first and foremost an actress and a complete woman of the theatre. She had the actor's instinct — nay, need — to please and be applauded by the playgoing public. She was willing to foster poetic theatre on a volunteer basis, but she would never have been content to play to the small audiences such work attracted. Furthermore, she knew that the literary public was by itself too small to support a professional repertory company. So Ria was forced by circumstances to reconcile the popular with the artistic, and these economic restrictions also created the theatrical conditions that required the assembling of a repertory company that acted as part-time stage managers, prompters, costumers, and property masters. Actors were thus involved in almost all production decisions. Finally, revivals replaced new plays that failed to attract enough paying customers to economically maintain playhouse viability. The emphasis was on popular, as well as poetic, plays performed by an effective acting ensemble. This financial situation enabled, almost forced, the Abbey to produce 75 new plays in Ria's 15 years as artistic director, providing opportunities for a host of developing playwrights.

In spite of her heroic efforts, the Anglo-Irish hostility toward Blythe, and the hiring practices required by his Irish policy, undermined the Abbey's theatrical reputation. The Anglo-Irish maintained they, and they alone, were the judges of artistic excellence. Their fashionable status in Dublin, their economic and educational position in local society, made them a force to be reckoned with, and Ria courted their approval and defended their opinions.

Ria's attempt to serve both the popular and the poetic on the Abbey stage, while distancing herself socially from the acting company, and personally from Blythe's language position, seemed to preserve her position at the theatre. At least her work was never openly attacked by the theatre's critics. They reserved their censorious criticism for Ernest Blythe. By the late fifties, however, Ria's deteriorating physical condition helped loosen her grasp of both policy strands and she quickly lost her grip on Abbey production conditions. In the end, she had failed to create supporters on either side of the argument. Her high theatrical standards, and her rigidly preserved distance from the society of the performers, created resentment among her troupe, while her success in shoring up the Abbey's tenuous economic position delayed Blythe's defeat, frustrating his critics' attempts to replace him as manager of the theatre. Within three years of Ria's resignation from the Abbey, Blythe and his Irish policy were both routed from the playhouse. After that, it was only a matter of time before the National Theatre would turn its back on its paying audience. At the time of this writing, the playhouse is so unpopular that it is currently demanding a two-thirds state subsidy of its operational costs.

Since Ria Mooney's accomplishments contradict the basic assumptions of the current Abbey policy, her memory has been scorned or neglected by the Dublin critical community. The plays that received so much press and popular approval during her tenure as artistic director have been almost completely ignored. Playwrights as successful and as distinguished as Shiels, Macken, Molloy, D'Alton, MacMahon, Tomelty, O'Donovan, McCann, Byrne, and Robinson, and their plays, have also been largely ignored by the cognoscenti and have received but few Abbey revivals. The quality of her acting troupe, though it has received international acclaim in the cinema and television world, has never been given a fair critical appraisal. Ray MacAnally, Marie Kean, T. P. McKenna, and Vincent Dowling, among others, have achieved international success as performers, while the memory of M. J. Dolan and Harry Brogan, Eileen Crowe and Angela Newman, Philip O'Flynn, Joe Lynch, Derry Power, Eddie and Geof Golden, Kathleen Barrington, Ronnie Masterson, Aideen O'Kelley, Brid Lynch, Joan O'Hara, and May Craig all remained green for those Irish audiences who witnessed their performances.

All that still exists of those splendid years of play production are scripts, newspaper clippings, and photographs of Ria's troupe and their productions. These give ample evidence of her extraordinary theatrical achievement in assembling, training, and directing a remarkably gifted group of actors. Reading the scripts (most of them are hard to find and out of print), one is struck by their craftsmanship, involved plots, complex characters, the contemporary conflicts that inspired them, and the poetic power of the dialogue that challenged the vocal abilities of the performers. The powerful confrontations in Macken's *Home Is the Hero*, the romantic gallantry and musical lyricism of Molloy's *The King of Friday's Men*, and Tomelty's atmospheric evocation of the roaring threat of the sea in *All Soul's Night*, offered an enormous challenge to the production capabilities of the Abbey, and contemporary press reviews provide ample evidence that Ria and her company gave a good account of themselves.

The National Theatre has honored those who created and sustained its presence in Ireland by decorating its lobby walls with portraits of Yeats, Lady Gregory, the Fays, Lennox Robinson, and John Millington Synge. Ria Mooney bore the burden of the heat of day throughout the Abbey's long exile at the Queen's, preserving its presence, in spite of attacks made upon the theatre from all sides. She directed an impressive list of fine plays while developing a generation of gifted Irish actors. It is time her portrait was placed alongside those worthies who remind modern Ireland that she has a duty to keep faith with her cultural heritage.

Plays Debuted at the Abbey Theatre, January 1948 to November 1963

List of plays given their first production at the Abbey Theatre during Ria Mooney's tenure as artistic director from January 1948 to November 1963.

1948

1. George Shiels, *The Caretakers*. February 16, 1948.
2. John Coulter, *The Drums Are Out*. July 12, 1948.
3. Lennox Robinson, *The Lucky Finger*. August 23, 1948.
4. M. J. Molloy, *The King of Friday's Men*. October 18, 1948.

1949

1. Bryan MacMahon, *The Bugle in the Blood*. March 14, 1949.
2. Joseph Tomelty, *All Soul's Night*. April 16, 1949.
3. Ralph Kennedy, *Ask for Me Tomorrow*. October 3, 1949.

1950

1. Seamus Byrne, *Design for a Headstone*. April 8, 1950.
2. Jack P. Cunningham, *Mountain Flood*, August 10, 1950.
3. Donal Giltinan, *The Goldfish in the Sun*. October 2, 1950.

1951

1. Maurice G. Meldon, *House Under Green Shadows*. Feb. 5, 1951.
2. Louis D'Alton, *The Devil a Saint Would Be*. Sept. 10, 1951.
3. Ann Daly, *Window on the Square*. October 22, 1951.
4. Seamus Byrne, *Innocent Bystander*. November 19, 1951.

1952

1. Walter Macken, *Home Is the Hero*. July 28, 1952.

1953

1. M. J. Molloy, *The Wood of the Whispering*. Jan. 26, 1953.
2. Louis D'Alton, *This Other Eden*. June 1, 1953.
3. M. J. Molloy, *The Paddy Pedlar*. Sept. 5, 1953.

1954

1. John O'Donovan, *The Half Millionaire*. Jan. 25, 1954.
2. John Malone, *John Courtney*. Feb. 22, 1954.
3. John McCann, *Twenty Years a-Wooing*. March 29, 1954.
4. J. M. Doody, *Knocknavain*. July 19, 1954.
5. Bryan Guiness, *A Riverside Charade*. July 26, 1954.
6. Joseph Tomelty, *Is the Priest at Home?* Nov. 8, 1954.

1955

1. John McCann, *Blood Is Thicker Than Water*. July 25, 1955.
2. M. J. Molloy, *The Will and the Way*. Sept. 5, 1955.
3. Pauline Maguire, *The Last Move*. October 24, 1955.
4. Walter Macken, *Twilight of a Warrior*. Nov. 21, 1955.

1956

1. Hugh Leonard, *The Big Birthday*. Jan. 23, 1956.
2. Francis MacManus, *Judgement of James O'Neill*. Feb. 20, 1956.
3. John McCann, *Early and Often*. July 16, 1956.
4. Denis Johnston, *Strange Occurrence on Ireland's Eye*. Aug. 20, 1956.
5. Brendan Behan, *The Quare Fella*. Oct. 8, 1956.
6. Tomás MacAnna, *Winter Wedding*. Nov. 26 1956.

1957

1. Hugh Leonard, *A Leap in the Dark*. Jan 21, 1957.
2. P. S. Laughlin, *Waiting Night*. Feb. 25, 1957.
3. Donal Giltinan, *The Flying Wheel*. April 22, 1957.
4. John O'Donovan, *The Less We Are Together*. July 22, 1957.
5. Niall Carroll, *The Wanton Tide*. Oct. 21, 1957.
6. John McCann, *Give Me a Bed of Roses*. Nov. 25, 1957.

1958

1. Walter Macken, *Look in the Looking Glass*. March 10, 1958.
2. Louis D'Alton, *Cafflin Johnny*. April 14, 1958.
3. Niall Sheridan, *Seven Men and a Dog*. April 28, 1958.
4. Denis Johnston, *The Scythe and the Sunset*. May 19, 1958.
5. John O'Donovan, *A Change of Mind*. Aug. 4, 1958.
6. James Plunkett, *The Risen People*. Sept. 23, 1958.
7. M. J. Molloy, *The Right Rose Tree*. Oct. 27, 1958.

1959

1. John McCann, *I Know Where I'm Going*. Jan. 26, 1959.
2. Eugene O'Neill, *Long Day's Journey into Night*. April 28, 1959.
3. John Murphy, *The Country Boy*. May 11, 1959.
4. Tomas Coffey, *Stranger Beware*. Aug. 17, 1959.
5. Anne Daly, *Leave It to the Doctor*. Sept. 14, 1959.
6. John D. Stewart, *Danger, Men Working*. Oct. 19, 1959.
7. Peter Hutchinson, *No Man Is an Island*. Nov. 9. 1959.
8. Criostoir O'Floinn, *In Dublin's Fair City*. Nov. 30, 1959.

1960

1. John McCann, *It Can't Go on Forever*. Jan. 31, 1960.
2. Sean Dowling, *The Bird in the Net*. March 28, 1960.
3. John O'Donovan, *The Shaws of Synge Street*. April 25, 1960.
4. Tomas Coffey, *Anyone Can Rob a Bank*. Aug. 1, 1960.
5. Bryan MacMahon, *The Song of the Anvil*. Sept. 12, 1960.
6. St. John Ervine, *The Lady of Belmont*. Oct. 31, 1960.
7. Anthony Butler, *The Deputy's Daughter*. Nov. 14, 1960.

1961

1. Richard Johnson, *The Evidence I Shall Give*. Jan. 10, 1961.
2. John McDonnell, *All the King's Horses*. March 20, 1961.
3. John McCann, *Put a Beggar on Horseback*. April 10, 1961.
4. Bryan MacMahon, *The Honey Spike*. May 22, 1961.
5. Tomas Coffey, *The Long Sorrow*. Sept. 19, 1961.
6. Eamon Cassidy, *Brave Banner*. Dec. 4, 1961.

1962

1. Donal Giltinan, *A Light in the Sky*. Feb. 27, 1962.
2. Kevin Casey, *The Living and the Lost*. March 19, 1962.
3. Brian Friel, *The Enemy Within*. Aug. 6, 1962.
4. John McCann, *A Jew Called Sammy*. Aug. 27, 1962.
5. John B. Keane, *Hut 42*. Nov. 12, 1962.
6. Eugene O'Neill, *Ah, Wilderness!* Dec. 12, 1962.

1963

1. John O'Donovan, *Copperfaced Jack*. Feb. 25, 1963.
2. John B. Keane, *The Man from Clare*. Aug. 5, 1963.
3. Reinhardt Raffalt-Steven Vas, *The Successor*. Sept. 30,1963.
4. Michael Mulvihill, *A Sunset Touch*. Nov. 11, 1963.

Notes

Chapter One

1. The entire episode is covered in footnote #4 of Tomás MacAnna, "Ernest Blythe and the Abbey," in the excellent collection entitled *The Abbey Theatre—Interviews and Recollection*, edited by E. H. Mikhail (Totowa, New Jersey: Barnes and Noble Books, 1988), pp. 167–72.

2. For a thorough study of Lennox Robinson see Michael J. O'Neill, *Lennox Robinson* (New York: Grosset and Dunlap, 1964) and for the final years, pp. 157–61.

3. Ernest Blythe provoked criticism from many sources. Among the most entertaining is *Meet Mr. Blythe* in Mikhail's collection *The Abbey Theatre*, pp. 161–66, presumed to be the work of Sean O'Faolain.

4. MacAnna, "Ernest Blythe and the Abbey Theatre," in *The Abbey Theatre*, pp. 167–72.

5. P. S. O'Hegarty gave a spirited reply to the degenerate state of the Abbey in *Irish Times*, Sept. 6, 1944.

6. Des Hickey and Gus Smith, *A Paler Shade of Green* (London: Leslie Frewin, 1972), p. 55. For Abbey rates in 1944, see p. 50. For a more complete portrait of McKenna see Micheál Ó hAodha, *Siobhan, a Memoir of an Actress* (Dingle, Co. Kerry: Brandon Book Publishers Ltd., 1994).

7. This memory is from his introduction to "Players and the Painted Stage, the Autobiography of Ria Mooney," edited by Val Mulkerns for *George Spelvin's Theatre Book*, Vol. I, Numbers 2 and 3, Summer and Fall, 1978, p. 4.

8. This and all Ria Mooney's childhood memories are from her "Autobiography."

9. From "RTE Guide, Aug. 19, 1966." Reprinted in Mikhail's *The Abbey Theatre*, p. 158.

10. This and all of the references to that mine of accurate Abbey information are taken from *Joseph Holloway's Abbey Theatre*, a selection from his unpublished journal "Impressions of a Dublin Playgoer" (Carbondale and Edwardsville: Southern Illinois University Press, 1967), p. 231.

11. Holloway, journal, pp. 212–13.

12. Holloway, journal, p. 216

13. Holloway, journal, pp. 217–18.

14. For an interesting discussion of the incident and the play itself see Joseph T. Shipley, *Guide to Great Plays* (Washington, D.C.: Public affairs Press, 1956), pp. 463–65.

15. Holloway, journal, p. 251.

16. Mooney, "Autobiography," p. 42.

17. Mooney, "Autobiography," p. 45.

18. Holloway, journal, p. 252.

19. Holloway, journal, p. 254.

20. Both Sheehy-Skeffington's protest in the *Independent* and O'Casey's reply in the *Irish Times* are reprinted in full in Holloway, journal, pp. 255–60.

21. Holloway reports the occasion in full, including the fete for Mr. and Mrs. Ernest Blythe on the Abbey stage that evening in Holloway, journal, pp. 243–44.

Chapter Two

1. Holloway, journal, p. 248.

2. Mooney, "Autobiography," p. 56.

3. *Joseph Holloway's Irish Theatre, Vol. I — 1926–31,* edited by Robert Hogan and Michael J. O'Neill (Dixon, California: Proscenium Press, 1968), pp. 11–12.

4. *Holloway's Irish Theatre,* vol. I, p. 15.

5. Holloway, journal, p. 271.

6. Mooney, "Autobiography," p. 54.

7. Mooney, "Autobiography," p.55.

8. Mooney, "Autobiography," p. 56.

9. The account of this tour appears in Mooney, "Autobiography," pp. 57–61.

10. From an interview of Mary Manning Adams conducted by the author in her Cambridge, Mass., apartment on Tuesday, April 30, 1996.

11. From Mary Manning Adams interview.

12. From Mary Manning Adams interview.

13. Mooney, "Autobiography," p. 61.

14. *The Best Plays of 1927–28 and the Year Book of the Drama in America,* edited by Burns Mantle (New York: Dodd, Mead and Company, 1928), p. 350.

15. Mantle, *Year Book, 1927–28,* pp. 459, 469.

16. *The Oxford Companion to the Theatre,* edited by Phyllis Hartnoll, second edition (London: Oxford University Press, 1957), p. 565.

17. Mooney, "Autobiography," p 72.

18. Burgess Meredith, *So Far, So Good: A Memoir* (Boston: Little, Brown and Company, 1994), p. 39.

19. Robert A. Schanke, *Shattered Applause: The Lives of Eva Le Gallienne* (Carbondale and Edwardsville: Southern Illinois University Press, 1992), p. 71.

20. Quoted in Schanke, p.69.

21. Schanke, p. 67.

22. Schanke, p. 67.

23. Mantle, *Year Book, 1928–29,* p. 383.

24. Schanke, p. 81.

25. Schanke, p. 82.

26. Mantle, *Year Book, 1928–29,* pp. 473–74.

27. The complete story is wonderfully told in Christopher Fitz-Simon, *The Boys* (London: Nick Hern Books, 1994), pp. 55–60.

28. For an extended discussion of the effects of partition and the position of the Irish language in the Free State see Terence Brown, *Ireland: A Social and Cultural History, 1922–85* (London: Fontana Press, 1985) Part I, 1922–32.

29. See *A Biographical Dictionary of Irish Writers,* edited by Anne M. Brady and Brian Cleeve (Mullingar, Ireland: The Lilliput Press Ltd., 1985), p. 113.

30. Fitz-Simon, p. 58.

31. Hickey and Smith, p. 63.

32. Mary Manning, "Youth's the Season…?" in *Plays of Changing Ireland,* edited by Curtis Canfield (New York: The Macmillan Company, 1936), p. 324.

33. This story is an amalgam of the report given by both parties in Mooney, "Autobiography," p. 79, and in *Holloway's Irish Theatre,* vol. I, p. 49.

34. Mooney, "Autobiography," p. 80.

35. *Holloway's Irish Theatre,* vol. I, p. 49–50.

Chapter Three

1. Mantle, *Year Book, 1929-30,* pp. 393, 402–3, 458–59.

2. Mooney, "Autobiography," p. 90.

3. Meredith, *So Far, So Good,* p. 32.

4. This Frenchman's romantic play is about the ill-fated son of Napoleon and was first played by Sarah Bernhardt. For an extended discussion see Shipley, *Guide to Great Plays,* pp. 59–60.

5. Schanke, p. 84.

6. Mantle, *Year Book, 1929–30,* p. 458.

7. Mooney, "Autobiography," p. 95.

8. Schanke, p. 89.

9. Schanke, p. 89.

10. Schanke, p. 90.

11. Mantle, *Year Book, 1930–31,* p. 250.

12. Mantle, *Year Book, 1930–31,* p. 223.

13. Mooney, "Autobiography," p. 90.

14. Mooney, "Autobiography," p. 98.

15. For a description of her final days see Elizabeth Coxhead, *Lady Gregory: A Literary Portrait* (New York: Harcourt, Brace and World, 1961), pp. 207–14.

16. *Holloway's Irish Theatre, Vol. II — 1932–37,* pp. 32–33.

17. This entire story is engagingly told in John Cowell, *No Profit but the Name: The Longfords and the Gate Theatre* (Dublin: The O'Brien Press, 1988), pp. 8–11.

18. Holloway, journal, p. 270.

19. For an extended portrait see Micheál MacLiammóir, *All for Hecuba* (Dublin, Progress House, 1961), pp. 120–23.

20. These lists and tour arrangements, as well as the Yeats argument with the government, can be found in Hugh Hunt, *The Abbey* (New York: Columbia University Press, 1979), pp. 145–47.

21. Mantle, *Year Book, 1932–33,* p. 407.

22. For the circumstances of this production and critics John Mason Brown's and Richard Lockridge's comments see Schanke, pp. 102–3.

23. These comments can be found in Hickey and Smith, p. 63.

24. Ria's tour experiences can be found in her "Autobiography," pp. 102–4.

25. MacLiammóir adds to this picture that "she was a serious person and the national passion for malicious commentary that adds such zest to Irish life, as a burning sauce to a tepid dish, had no more attractions for her than for Coralie" (Carmichael, a leading actress in the Gate Theatre). In MacLiammóir, *All for Hecuba*, p. 167.

26. MacLiammóir quotes his colleague, Hilton Edwards, describing the differences as follows: "The Abbey set out to show Ireland to herself and then to the world,… we in the Gate began by attempting to show the world to Ireland." In MacLiammóir, *All for Hecuba*, p. 355.

Chapter Four

1. This entire confrontation is charmingly related in MacLiammóir, *All for Hecuba*, pp. 164–67.

2. Mooney, "Autobiography," p. 104.

3. See *Joseph Holloway's Irish Theatre, Vol. II — 1932–37*, p. 30.

4. Mooney, "Autobiography," p. 105.

5. See MacLiammóir, *All For Hecuba*, p. 167.

6. See *Holloway Irish Theatre*, vol. II, p. 30.

7. For Holloway's report on the entire season, see his journal for the year 1934, vol. II, pp. 30–39.

8. Holloway, journal, p. 36.

9. This wonderful story is related in Cowell's *No Profit but the Name*, p. 85.

10. The appointment of Blado Peake and subsequent critical reaction is related in Hunt, pp. 148–49.

11. Frank O'Connor, *My Father's Son* (Boston: G. K. Hall, 1985), p. 178.

12. Fitz-Simon, *The Boys*, p. 86.; and Holloway, journal, p. 37.

13. Quoted in Fitz-Simon, p. 86.

14. Fitz-Simon, p. 86.

15. Mooney, "Autobiography," p. 104.

16. Holloway, journal, p. 39.

17. Mooney, "Autobiography," p. 106.

18. Hunt, p. 150.

19. O'Connor, p. 181.

20. Holloway, journal, p. 56.

21. Mooney, "Autobiography," pp. 118–20.

22. From an interview with Val Mulkerns Kennedy, conducted by the author at her Dublin home on March 12, 1996.

23. Holloway, journal, p. 42.

24. Mooney, "Autobiography," p. 109.

25. Mooney, "Autobiography," p. 111.

26. Holloway, journal, p. 48.

27. Cowell, p. 86.
28. Hunt, p. 153.
29. Holloway, journal, p. 52.
30. Fitz-Simon, p. 91.
31. This backstage strife is recounted colorfully in the following: Hunt, pp. 154–56; Holloway, journal, 1932–37, pp. 58–59; and O'Connor, pp. 183–86.
32. Holloway, journal, p. 58.
33. Holloway, journal, p. 59.
34. Hunt, pp. 155–56.
35. For a full and exciting account of this significant Abbey opening, see Phyllis Ryan's *The Company I Kept* (Dublin: Town House and Country House Publishers, 1996), pp. 57–63.
36. Holloway, journal, p. 69.
37. Mooney, "Autobiography," p. 113.
38. For a complete listing of the Abbey Theatre Players in New York see Mantle, *Year Book, 1937–38*, pp. 374–78.
39. For Ria's remembrance of that tour, see her "Autobiography," pp. 114–17.
40. O'Connor, p. 203.
41. For this story, see Hunt, p. 160; and O'Connor, pp. 219–20.
42. Hunt, p. 163.
43. Holloway, journal, vol. III, 1938–44, p. 14.
44. Hunt, p. 161.
45. O'Connor, p. 231.
46. Holloway, journal, p. 24.
47. Holloway, journal, p. 43.
48. Holloway, journal, pp. 45–47.
49. Holloway, journal, pp. 52–53.
50. Holloway, journal, p. 54.

Chapter Five

1. Brinsley Macnamara's appreciation of F. R. Higgins was printed as broadcast on Radio Eireann on Wenesday night, January 8, 1941, in the *Irish Times*, Thursday, January 9, 1941, p. 4.
2. This information and the poem entitled "Auction" are from the *Irish Times* obituary of January 9, 1941, p. 6.
3. This and an extended list of notables printed on Friday in the *Irish Times*, January 10, 1941, p. 6.
4. From Macnamara broadcast, the *Irish Times*, January 9, 1941, p. 4.
5. This and the following story of F. J. McCormick are from Mooney, "Autobiography," in Spelvin, vol. I, no. 3, pp. 67–68.
6. O'Connor, p.184.
7. Quoted in Fitz-Simon, p. 138.
8. Quoted in Brown, *Part II, 1932–1958*, p. 176.
9. Quoted in Brown, p. 177.
10. Quoted in Brown, pp. 176–77.
11. Quoted in Fitz-Simon, p. 138.

12. For an extended discussion of the Gate productions at the Gaiety Theatre during the war years, see Fitz-Simon, pp. 128–42.

13. Mooney's work as a director at the Abbey is summarized in her "Autobiography," pp. 70–71.

14. Mooney's attitude toward the Dublin Verse-Speaking Society can be found in her "Autobiography," pp. 72–73.

15. Fitz-Simon, p. 128.

16. Mooney, "Autobiography," p 69.

17. For this and the story of the English production of *Red Roses for Me*, see Mooney "Autobiography," pp. 74–81.

18. Mooney, "Autobiography," p. 83.

19. For conditions at the Abbey at that time, see Hunt, pp. 169–75.

20. From an interview with Aideen O'Kelley, conducted by the author in New York City on Friday afternoon, April 26, 1996.

21. For the sequence of offers by Embassy Theatre and Meredith, see Mooney, "Autobiography," p. 85.

22. Mooney, "Autobiography," p. 85.

Chapter Six

1. W. B. Yeats quoted in Gabriel Fallon, *The Abbey and the Actor* (Published by The National Theater Society Ltd., 1969), p. 39.

2. Fitzgerald quoted in Fallon, p. 31.

3. Lane's *The Psychology of the Actor,* quoted in Fallon, p. 35.

4. The story of Ria's visit with George Shiels is found in her "Autobiography," pp. 88–89.

5. Robert Hogan, *After The Irish Renaissance* (Minneapolis: The University of Minnesota Press, 1967), p. 39.

6. Phyllis Ryan, *The Company I Kept* (Dublin: Town House, 1996), p. 112.

7. From an interview of Ronnie Masterson conducted by the author in Ireland on March 13, 1996. All of the following quotes and stories attributed to Masterson are from that interview.

8. Mooney, "Autobiography," p. 89.

9. The *Irish Times*, August 16, 1948.

10. Mooney, "Autobiography," pp. 89–90.

11. From an interview conducted by the author with Mrs. Kennedy in Dublin on March 12, 1996.

12. From Molloy's preface to *The King of Friday's Men* in *Three Plays by M. J. Molloy* (Newark, Delaware: Proscenium Press, 1975), p. 9.

13. All the quotes from the play are from *Three Plays by M. J. Molloy.*

14. Hunt, p. 174.

15. MacAnna, pp. 168–70.

16. The *Irish Times,* February 1, 1949.

17. The *Irish Times,* March 2, 1949.

Chapter Seven

1. The following discussion of the language question appears in Brown, pp. 190–200.

2. The conditions of Irish rural life and the statistics of immigration can be found in Brown, pp. 184–89.

3. Myles na gCopaleen quoted in Brown, p. 193.

4. Quoted in Brown, p. 201.

5. Ulster poet John Montague quoted in Brown, p. 213.

6. From an interview conducted by the author at the home of Val Mulkerns Kennedy on March 12, 1996.

7. From Hunt. The author's description of the fire is on pp. 174–75.

8. Hogan, p. 74.

9. Hogan. The author's discussion of *Design for a Headstone* can be found on pp. 74–75.

10. All the newspaper reviews appeared in the papers cited on the day after the opening, unless otherwise noted.

11. Mooney, "Autobiography," pp. 90–91.

12. Hunt, p. 175.

13. Quote from the *Irish Press*, Aug. 11, 1950.

14. The *Irish Press*, Aug. 11, 1950.

15. Mooney, "Autobiography," p. 91.

16. The Dublin pantomimes are all mentioned in the *Irish Press*, Feb. 6, 1951.

17. Val Mulkerns Kennedy mentioned Mooney's high expectations for Maurice Meldon, who died at 32, following a fall from his bicycle. Hogan's reference to him as the "most exciting new voice" appears on p. 226.

18. This neat summary is a quote from the review in the *Irish Times*, Feb. 6, 1951.

19. Mooney, "Autobiography," pp. 94–95.

20. Mooney, "Autobiography," pp. 101–102.

21. Hunt, p. 176.

22. Mooney, "Autobiography," p. 102.

23. Ria tells the story in her "Autobiography" on pp. 103–104, as well as to the camera. The film is included in the RTE special, *Between the Canals*, 1981.

24. Mooney, "Autobiography," p. 104.

25. Mooney, "Autobiography," p. 93.

26. The *Irish Press*, Sept. 11, 1951.

27. The *Irish Press*, Sept. 11, 1951.

28. Hunt, p. 177.

29. From an article in the *Irish Times* of July 19, 1951, entitled "Abbey burning did not stop play."

30. Fitz-Simon, pp. 145–146.

31. Hunt, p. 177.

32. From an interview by the author with Kathleen Barrington in the Abbey cafe on March 12, 1996.

33. Mooney, "Autobiography," p. 105.

34. Mooney, "Autobiography," p. 113.

Chapter Eight

1. Reviews appeared in both the *Irish Press* and *Irish Independent* on Tuesday, October 23, 1951, but the *Irish Times* never even bothered to cover the production.
2. Brown, p. 236.
3. This information and the quote from Brendan Kennelly's *Westland Row* can be found in Brown, p. 237.
4. All the newspaper reviews appeared in the papers cited on the day after the opening, unless otherwise noted.
5. *Irish Independent,* Tuesday, November 20, 1951.
6. From "Other Theatres," *Irish Independent,* November 20, 1951.
7. *Irish Times,* February 12, 1952.
8. This summary of and all the quotes from the play are from Walter Macken, *Home Is the Hero* (New York: The Macmillan Company, 1953).
9. Hogan's review of the play is in *After the Irish Renaissance,* p. 68.
10. This and the following quote from Hogan are in his *After the Irish Renaissance,* p. 65.
11. Hunt, p. 181. "Press criticism of the theatre's policy was mounting; a leading article in the Irish Times declared the Abbey was no longer entitled to the name of the National Theatre."
12. This plot summary is from the printed version of the play to be found in M. J. Molloy, *Three Plays,* p. 123.
13. Molloy, pp. 125–26.
14. *Irish Press,* Tuesday, January 27, 1953.
15. *Irish Independent,* Tuesday, January 27, 1953.
16. *Irish Times,* Tuesday, January 27, 1953.
17. *Irish Press,* Monday, September 7, 1953.
18. *Irish Times,* Monday, September 7, 1953.
19. Molloy, p. 98.
20. *Irish Press,* Monday, September 7, 1953.
21. From an interview with Dublin actor, Derry Powers, conducted by the author in the lounge of the Montrose Hotel on Tuesday, March 12, 1996.
22. A more complete discussion of the Abbey's frustrating design plans is covered in Hunt, pp. 19–81.
23. Quoted in Hunt, p. 183.
24. Hunt, p. 185.
25. Hunt, p. 185.
26. Mooney, "Autobiography," p. 113.
27. From Molloy's play included in *Three Plays,* Act III, the living room of French Hall — nightfall of St. Brigid's Day, p. 95.

Chapter Nine

1. Mooney, "Autobiography," pp. 98–100.
2. From an interview conducted by the author with Val Mulkerns Kennedy on March 12, 1996.

3. From an interview conducted by the author with Ronnie Masterson on March 13, 1996.

4. From an interview with Aideen O'Kelley conducted by the author on April 26, 1996.

5. Alan Simpson in "Behan: The Last Laugh," in *A Paler Shade of Green*, edited by Des Hickey and Gus Smith (London: Leslie Frewin Publishers Ltd., 1972), p. 210.

6. Quoted in Hickey and Smith, p 170.

7. Quoted in Hickey and Smith, p. 170.

8. Quoted in Hickey and Smith, p. 188.

9. Quoted in Hickey and Smith, pp. 180–81.

10. *Irish Press*, January 26, 1954.

11. *Irish Press*, February 23, 1954.

12. *Irish Press*, February 23, 1954.

13. *Irish Independent*, March 30, 1954.

14. *Irish Independent*, March 30, 1954.

15. *Irish Press*, March 30, 1954.

16. Hunt, p. 182.

17. Hogan, p. 9.

18. Quoted in Hogan, pp. 9–10. This article was published in *Theatre Arts*, XVIII (February 1934), pp. 126–27.

19. From an interview conducted by the author on July 22, 1997.

20. Quoted in Hickey and Smith, pp. 24–28.

21. Hogan, p. 11.

22. Mooney, "Autobiography," p. 114.

23. Mooney, "Autobiography," p. 114.

24. Hogan, p. 19.

25. From an interview conducted by the author with Val Mulkerns Kennedy, March 12, 1996.

26. From an interview conducted by the author with Vincent Dowling conducted on July, 22, 1997.

27. This perception comes from many conversations the author had with Ray MacAnally in May-June 1981, during a production of George Shiels', *The Passing Day*, which the author directed, and in which Mr. MacAnally played the leading role.

28. From an interview with Derry Power conducted by the author on March 12, 1996.

29. From an interview with Masterson conducted by the author on March 13, 1996.

30. From an interview with Barrington conducted by the author on March 12, 1996.

31. From an interview with O'Kelley conducted by the author on April 26, 1996.

32. From an interview with Dowling conducted by the author on July 22, 1997.

33. From an interview with Barrington conducted by the author on March 12, 1996.

34. From an interview with Dowling conducted by the author on July 22, 1997.

35. From an interview with Dowling conducted by the author on July 22, 1997.

36. From an interview with Dowling conducted by the author on July 22, 1997.

37. From an interview with O'Kelley conducted by the author on July 22, 1997.

38. From an interview with Derry Power conducted by the author on March 12, 1996.

39. From an interview with Dowling conducted by the author on July 22, 1997.

40. From an interview with O'Kelley conducted by the author on April 26, 1996.

41. From Hickey and Smith, p. 213.

42. Hickey and Smith, p. 212.

43. This story is told by Alan Simpson in Hickey and Smith, pp. 212–16.

Chapter Ten

1. *Irish Independent*, November 9, 1954.

2. Joseph Tomelty, *Is the Priest at Home?* (Dublin, James Duffy and Co. Ltd., 1957), Act III, p. 70.

3. *Irish Independent*, November 9, 1954.

4. Mooney "Autobiography," p. 106.

5. Quoted in Deirdre Bair, *Samuel Beckett* (New York: Harcourt Brace Jovanovich, 1978), p. 453.

6. Quoted in Bair, pp. 453–54.

7. Hickey and Smith, p. 217.

8. Bair, pp. 203–4.

9. Mooney, "Autobiography," pp. 115–16.

10. *Irish Press*, November 25, 1955.

11. *Irish Independent*, November, 22, 1955.

12. *Irish Times*, February 14, 1956.

13. *Irish Independent*, February 24, 1956.

14. *Irish Press*, February 22, 1956.

15. *Irish Times*, December 1, 1956.

16. *Irish Press*, August 21, 1956.

17. *Irish Independent*, August 21, 1956.

18. *Irish Times*, September 8, 1956.

19. *Irish Press*, October 9, 1956.

20. *Irish Press*, January 22, 1957.

21. Fitz-Simon, p. 210.

22. Quoted in Fitz-Simon, p. 212.

23. Fitz-Simon, p. 212.

24. *Irish Times*, March 25, 1957.

25. From an interview conducted by the author with Vincent Dowling, July 22, 1997.

26. Hickey and Smith, p. 128.

27. Anna Manahan quoted in Hickey and Smith, pp. 130–31.
28. *Irish Press*, July, 23, 1957.
29. Hickey and Smith, p. 134.
30. Hilton Edwards quoted in Hickey and Smith, p. 135.
31. Hickey and Smith, p. 151.
32. The entire correspondence between Smith and O'Casey can be found in Hickey and Smith, pp. 139–49.

Chapter Eleven

1. *Irish Press*, March 11, 1958.
2. *Irish Press*, March 11, 1958.
3. From an interview conducted by the author with Vincent Dowling, July 22, 1997.
4. *Irish Independent*, April 8, 1958.
5. *Irish Press*, April 29, 1958.
6. *Irish Times*, May 20, 1958.
7. O'Connor, p. 17.
8. Mooney, "Autobiography," pp. 119–20.
9. *Irish Independent*, January 27, 1959.
10. This story of the rehearsals and performance of *Long Day's Journey* are from an interview with Vincent Dowling conducted by the author on July 22, 1997.
11. From and interview conducted by the author with Kathleen Barrington, March 12, 1996.
12. Mooney, "Autobiography," p. 115.
13. *Irish Independent*, April 19, 1959.
14. *Irish Press*, April 29, 1959.
15. This history of the first production of *Sive* is wonderfully told by Gus Smith and Des Hickey in their biography entitled *John B.: The Real Keane* (Cork, The Mercier Press, 1992), pp. 54–61.
16. From an interview conducted by the author with Vincent Dowling, July 22, 1997.
17. From an interview conducted by the author with Val Mulkerns Kennedy, March 12, 1996.
18. Tomás MacAnna, quoted in Mikhail, p. 170.
19. Tomás MacAnna, quoted in Mikhail, p. 170.
20. Tomás MacAnna, quoted in Mikhail, p. 170.
21. This information about the Dublin Theatre Festival is from the *Irish Independent*, September 15, 1959.
22. *Irish Independent*, October 11, 1959.
23. *Irish Independent*, November 1, 1960.
24. *Irish Independent*, November 15, 1960.
25. From an interview conducted by the author with Val Mulkerns Kennedy, March 12, 1996.

Chapter Twelve

1. Hunt, p. 185.
2. David Thornley quoted in Brown, pp. 243–44.
3. *Irish Press*, September 20, 1961.
4. Brady and Cleeve, *A Biographical Dictionary of Irish Writers*, p. 85.
5. *Irish Press*, August 7, 1962.
6. *Irish Independent*, August 7, 1962.
7. *Irish Press*, December 13, 1962.
8. *Irish Independent*, February 26, 1963.
9. *Irish Press*, February 26, 1963.
10. Hogan, p. 257.
11. Hogan, p. 79.
12. Hogan went so far as to suggest Charles Laughton for the Lord Chief Justice. Anyone reading the text would, I think, immediately nod their head in agreement with such casting. See Hogan, p. 79.
13. Mooney, "Autobiography," p. 116.
14. Hunt, p. 185.
15. From an interview conducted by the author with Val Mulkerns Kennedy, March 12, 1996.
16. Mooney, "Autobiography," p. 116.
17. Mooney, "Autobiography," p. 116.
18. Mooney, "Autobiography," p. 116.
19. Mooney, "Autobiography," p. 117.
20. Micheál Ó hAodha, *The Abbey — Then and Now* (Dublin, The Abbey Theatre, 1969), p. 84.
21. From a letter in the possession of Val Mulkerns Kennedy written to her after the first issue of Mooney, "Autobiography."
22. From an interview conducted by the author with Mary Manning Adams, April 30, 1996.
23. Mooney, "Autobiography," p. 12.
24. *Irish Times*, January 5, 1973.

Epilogue

1. Holloway, p. 243.

Bibliography

The Abbey Theatre — Interviews and Recollections, edited by E. H. Mikhail. Totowa, N. J.: Barnes and Noble Books, 1988.

Bair, Deirdre. *Samuel Beckett*. New York: Harcourt, Brace, Jovanovich, 1978.

The Best Plays of 1927–28, edited by Burns Mantle, New York: Dodd, Mead and Company, 1928.

The Best Plays of 1928–29. New York, 1929.

The Best Plays of 1929–30. New York, 1930.

The Best Plays of 1930–31. New York, 1931.

The Best Plays of 1932–33. New York, 1933.

The Best Plays of 1937–38. New York, 1938.

Biographical Dictionary of Irish Writers, edited by Anne M. Brady and Brian Cleeve. Mullingar, Ireland: The Lilliput Press, Ltd., 1985.

Brown, Terence. *Ireland: A Social and Cultural History, 1922–85*. London: Fontana Press, 1985.

Cowell, John. *No Profit but the Name: The Longfords and the Gate Theatre*. Dublin: The O'Brien Press, 1988.

Coxhead, Elizabeth. *Lady Gregory: A Literary Portrait*. New York: Harcourt, Brace and World, Inc., 1961.

Dowling, Vincent. *Astride the Moon — A Theatrical Life*. Dublin, Ireland: Wolfhound Press, 2000.

Fallon, Gabriel. *The Abbey and the Actor*. Dublin: Published by the National Theatre Society, Ltd., 1969.

Fitz-Simon, Christopher. *The Boys*. London: Nick Hern Books, 1994.

Hickey, Des, and Gus Smith. *A Paler Shade of Green*. London: Lesley Frewin, 1972.

Hickey, Des, and Gus Smith. *John B.: The Real Keane*. Cork: The Mercier Press, 1992.

Hogan, Robert. *After the Irish Renaissance*. Minneapolis: The University of Minnesota Press, 1967.

Hunt, Hugh. *The Abbey: Ireland's National Theatre, 1904–79*. New York: Columbia University Press, 1979.

Irish Drama 1900–1980, edited by Coilin D. Owens and Joan Radner. Washington, D.C.: The Catholic University of America Press, 1990.

223

Joseph Holloway's Abbey Theatre: A Selection from His Unpublished Journal, "Impressions of a Dublin Playgoer," 1899–1926, edited by Robert Hogan and Michael J. O'Neill. Carbondale and Edwardsville, Illinois: Southern Illinois University Press, 1967.

Joseph Holloway's Journal. 3 vols., 1926–31, 1932–37, 1938–44, edited by Robert Hogan and Michael O'Neill. Dixon, California: Proscenium Press, 1968–70.

Krause, David. *Sean O'Casey: The Man and His Work.* New York: The Macmillan Company, 1975.

Macken, Walter. *Home Is the Hero.* New York: The Macmillan Company, 1953.

MacLiammóir, Micheál, *All for Hecuba.* Dublin: Progress House, 1961.

Maxwell, D. E. S. *A Critical History of Modern Irish Drama 1891–1980.* Cambridge, England: Cambridge University Press, 1984.

Maxwell, D. E. S. *Brian Friel.* Lewisburg, Pennsylvania: Bucknell University Press, 1973.

Meredith, Burgess. *So Far, So Good: A Memoir.* Boston: Little, Brown, and Company, 1994.

Molloy, M. J. *Three Plays by M. J. Molloy.* Newark, Delaware: Proscenium Press, 1975.

Mooney, Ria. "Players and the Painted Stage," *The Autobiography of Ria Mooney,* edited by Val Mulkerns, in *George Spelvin's Theatre Book,* vol. 1, numbers 2 and 3, Summer and Fall, 1978.

O'Connor, Frank. *My Father's Son.* Boston: G. K. Hall, 1985.

O'Connor, Gary. *Sean O'Casey: A Life.* New York: Atheneum, 1988.

Ó hAodha, Micheal. *The Abbey— Then and Now.* Dublin: The Abbey Theatre, 1969.

Ó hAodha, Micheal. *Siobhan: A Memoir of an Actress.* Dingle, Co. Kerry: Brandon Book Publishers, Ltd., 1994.

O'Neill, Michael J. *The Abbey at the Queen's— The Interregnum Years, 1951–1966.* Nepean, Ontario, Canada: Borealis Press, Ltd., 1999.

O'Neill, Michael J. *Lennox Robinson.* New York: Grosset and Dunlop, 1964.

The Oxford Companion to the Theatre, edited by Phyllis Hartnoll, second edition. London: Oxford University Press, 1957.

Plays of Changing Ireland, edited by Curtis Canfield. New York: The Macmillan Company, 1936.

Ryan, Phyllis. *The Company I Kept.* Dublin: Town House and Country House Publishers, 1996.

Schanke, Robert A. *Shattered Applause: The Lives of Eva Le Gallienne.* Carbondale and Edwardsville: Southern Illinois University Press, 1992.

Shipley, Joseph T. *Guide to Great Plays.* Washington, D.C.: Public Affairs Press, 1956.

Tomelty, Joseph. *Is the Priest at Home?* Dublin: James Duffy and Company, Ltd., 1957.

Interviews

The following interviews were especially important to this study. They were conducted by Des Hickey and Gus Smith, and appeared in their volume, *A Paler Shade of Green,* London: Lesley Frewin, 1972.

"Cusack: Every week a different school."
"Siobhan McKenna: 'I modeled Joan on my mother.'"
"Johnston: 'Did you know Yeats? And did you lunch with Shaw?'"
"Edwards and MacLiammóir: We must be talking..."
"MacGowran: Waiting for Beckett."
"The Drums of Father Ned: O'Casey and the Archbishop."
"Rodway: Stephen D. and After."
"Leonard: Difficult to say 'No.'"

Sean O'Faolain's article in his periodical *Bell*, of October 1941, entitled "Meet Mr. Blythe," as well as Tomás MacAnna's "Ernest Blythe and the Abbey" in *Threshold*, no. 26, Autumn 1975, which are reprinted in Mikhail's *The Abbey Theatre*, Totowa, N. J.: Barnes and Noble Books, 1988, were personal or eyewitness accounts of the major figure in this study, and, as such, were central to the development of Ria Mooney's story.

The following interviews were conducted by the author of this study.

Mary Manning Adams, Cambridge, Massachusetts, April 30, 1996.
Kathleen Barrington, Dublin, Ireland, March 12, 1996.
Vincent Dowling, Lennox, Massachusetts, July 22, 1997.
Mrs. Val Mulkerns Kennedy, Dublin, Ireland, March 12, 1996.
Ronnie Masterson, Dublin, Ireland, March 13, 1996.
Aideen O'Kelley, New York City, April 26, 1996.
Derry Powers, Dublin, Ireland, March 12, 1996.

Newspaper Reviews

All the new play reviews of productions produced at the Abbey while Ria Mooney was artistic director from 1948 to 1963 which were published in Dublin's three leading daily papers, the *Irish Times*, the *Irish Press*, and the *Irish Independent*, were consulted.

Index

Boldfaced numbers indicate photographs.

227